Darla: It was my pleasure to be your
"Acting" ARO during the first ever National
AHRO Intern training conference held in VISN8
St. Pete, FL (May 14-18, 2012). I wish you the
best in your leadership journey in the VA.
This book is written by a VA Accountant who
became a Director. And some lessons he
learned along the way — *[signature]* Neal Hamilton
HRO Tampa, FL

My Life in the VA: Lessons in Leadership

iUniverse, Inc.
New York   Bloomington

My Life in the VA: Lessons in Leadership

iUniverse books may be ordered through booksellers or by contacting:

iUniverse
1663 Liberty Drive
Bloomington, IN 47403
www.iuniverse.com
1-800-Authors (1-800-288-4677)

Because of the dynamic nature of the Internet, any Web addresses or links contained in this book may have changed since publication and may no longer be valid. The views expressed in this work are solely those of the author and do not necessarily reflect the views of the publisher, and the publisher hereby disclaims any responsibility for them.

ISBN: 978-0-595-52512-6 (pbk)
ISBN: 978-0-595-51258-4 (cloth)
ISBN: 978-0-595-62565-9 (ebk)

Library of Congress Control Number: 2009931968

Printed in the United States of America

iUniverse rev. date: 8/24/2009

My Life in the VA: Lessons in Leadership

by Frederick Malphurs

Contents

Introduction

After graduating from the University of Florida and working briefly in public accounting, I accepted a job offer from the Veteran's Administration (VA). I went to visit my grandmother and dad in West Palm Beach early in 1969. When I got to my grandmother's house, which backed up to the West Palm Beach Canal, I told my dad that I accepted a job offer from the VA. I was going to be an accounting trainee at the new VA medical center in Gainesville, Florida. He frowned and looked away. He had wanted me to be a pharmacist. He was a teacher. I permanently ruled out his occupational suggestion and his profession. He said to me, "Freddy, you're going to have to get a new job in five years." He wasn't the only one who felt this way. Many felt that the WWII and Korean veterans' issues would be transitory and that community hospitals could assume their care after a few years. Later on, he used the VA off and on for his health care. In fact, he died in the Miami VA Medical Center in December 1974. The care and caring that he received there reaffirmed in me once again that the VA delivers quality health care.

So what exactly had I gotten myself into? For thirty-seven years, I had the privilege of serving America's veterans as an employee of the Veterans Health Administration (VHA), which is part of the cabinet-level Department of Veterans Affairs, commonly referred to as the Veterans Administration (VA). The VHA is a tremendous organization. It manages both the exciting and the mundane tasks of providing health care and certain benefits to over 5 million American veterans annually—a gigantic task indeed. There are no published accounts about VA management experiences, so I decided to write an account of my own career. My account will provide actual cases with leadership and management commentary. I will also share the devotion to duty and mission that I so often witnessed in the actions of my fellow VA employees. The challenges the VA has met and those the VA is still striving to overcome are also discussed.

Leaving a record for my own descendents is also part of the plan. Perhaps it will help them figure their old poppy out, reform their opinions of the choices he made, and leave them with a written legacy to support a better understanding of the unique sacrifices and contributions a career civil servant must make.

The book will be helpful to all who are considering a federal career or for those who want an insider's account of health-care delivery in a system increasingly being cited as a good example to build on for health-care reform. I have tutored many who desired a career in health-care management; this book is intended to codify some of the lessons that I proffered them. In addition, I have often heard mid-level managers say that management books offer little for them. Most management books do have something to offer, but the reader does have to extrapolate. The cases that I describe are written from my perspective as a mid-level manager and should provide actual examples closer to their reality that mid-levels can better appreciate.

The world that I inhabited for thirty-seven years provides historical perspective and political science insights. Certainly, a career federal executive is a rarely heard perspective on the issues and operations of federal government. I refer to my experience of working for eight years in VA Central Office as having been in the bowels of the bureaucracy. I wish to shed light on the political processes, the uncoordinated public policies, the failure to develop and report real information, and the politics of doing or not doing the right thing.

What I am really trying to accomplish by writing this book is to enhance learning for all of those who choose a career in health-care management and to make this great nation even better. Our government has plenty of room for improvement. At the time this book was written, the news reported the firing of seven U.S. attorneys and the loss of e-mails of those in the White House who were involved in this unfortunate situation. This is another example of human resources management that wouldn't be tolerated of a career official. Also in the news these last few months has been the significant, justifiable criticism of the VA response to returning Iraq and Afghanistan veterans. These news stories simply support my belief that there is much to improve.

Having spent three decades and parts of two other decades in the employ of the Veterans Health Administration, I write this book with a passion to improve this great system. My experience in the VA reflects an underfunded and underanalyzed health-care delivery system of immense national import and responsibility. The VA health-care system is in many ways like a stealth bomber: it works along quietly and expertly without drawing much attention until something bad happens. The negative event is captured in the media and popularized by congressional committees and individual congressmen. I write to reflect these experiences from someone who was a health system executive and an executive in the VA headquarters in Washington.

To maintain the readers' interest and to pace the flow of actions, activities, and significant events, I am condensing my career experiences quite a bit. As for the innumerable meetings I attended on budget, personnel decisions, quality, and the like, I am only relating the ones that highlight an entertaining or educational aspect. Having transferred within the VA thirteen times and been assigned to three long-term details, the minutiae piles up. Therefore, I have aimed for the high points and those that have some educational or humorous interest.

During my career, the many friends, stalwart performers, cagy veteran managers, dedicated physicians, nurses, pharmacists, dentists, and other professionals far, far outnumber those villains who appear in some of the anecdotes. Because almost all of these people are still alive (and indeed most of them still employed by the VA or in the health-care field), I have chosen to use fictitious names for the villains and some notables while describing to the best of my ability the actual events. Where the event may have gathered some notoriety within the VA, I have carefully shaded the description so that the locale and the concerned parties may continue to enjoy their relative anonymity. I have also deliberately not used patients' names where the disclosure might cause them discomfort so that I can maintain my professional confidentiality. Where the name of a patient, employee, or veteran is given, it is because the information was obtained outside of the clinical or administrative arena, or the patient/employee/veteran has expired.

Some career executives don't move much, but I did. I was assigned to nine different VA medical centers and was assigned to the central office in Washington DC three different times. Therefore, I have described events that happened in several different locations. As much as possible, I have kept time and place relatively intact.

I am a proponent of case studies. The VA is a large organization and it does not do nearly enough to prepare its employees to deal with the complex and sometimes acrimonious situations with which they will be confronted, and case studies would help. My hope is that this book will serve as an introduction to pertinent management issues for recent arrivals to the federal executive ranks. Readers should note that the cases provided are not examples of the multitudes of fine, dedicated personnel of the VA. These cases are exceptions to the rule, but the executives' attention and focus is often on the exceptions, not the exemplary, hard working people who make the VA health system the outstanding care delivery system it is. Congress and the media force executives to focus on the exceptions.

At times, I will be talking about the various interacting participants during my career. I have profound respect for them and do not intend for my perspective on the described events to cause them any concern. I consider many of them to be part of my extended family. I apologize now for any offense that I may have unknowingly created. Send me an e-mail, and I will buy you lunch to make it up to you when the opportunity presents.

My own family sacrificed a lot. To them, I owe so much and love so dearly that I can't imagine my life or career without them.

Management consultants are an often used utility for health-care executives. I would be remiss to not mention the greatest of them all, the late Peter Drucker. Having read Drucker extensively throughout my career, I have a debt to him for all of his sage advice and guidance. I often talked about Drucker to my staff and tried to apply that learning to my own endeavors. Throughout my career, I often consulted with his various writings as well as other writers on management and leadership. I learned from them and from my many colleagues.

Finally, in the appendices, I have listed my recommendations for health-care reform and for improved government. These lists are not intended to be all-inclusive, but rather to highlight some specifics too often ignored in the debates. I also include a list of the indicators that a government official does not want to do the right thing. Appendix D is an ethics constitution and guide for Veterans Health Administration leaders, which I helped to develop.

I intend the health-care and governmental reform appendices to further the societal debate on the need to reform health-care financing and delivery in particular. I believe the VA could be a model for this effort. Others have said the VA could be a national laboratory to study innovations in a controlled environment and used to hasten the adoption of technology proven to benefit patient care and improve patient safety. The VA has already been a model for health-care cost containment, probably too much so. I aspire to improve our entire health-care system. We should all desire to leave the next generation better health and a better, cheaper delivery system.

Chapter 1: Lessons Learned

Some of my colleagues and I discussed and ultimately formulated ten leadership concepts by which we would gauge our performance as leaders. Leadership has many parameters. My colleagues and I settled on ten which we felt were the most important. Of these, two were included based on our own organizational assessment. These ten leadership concepts are as follows: (1) engage in critical thinking, (2) accept challenges, (3) improve human resources management, (4) master the management of conflict, (5) constantly improve customer service, (6) accept full responsibility, (7) maintain the highest ethical standards, (8) constantly improve communications, (9) improve data management, and (10) sustain a culture of high performance. These ten leadership concepts are important to anyone who is starting a career in health care or entering the ranks of federal senior management.

Seeking knowledge and improving in any career should be lifelong goals. Gaining the perspective and the balance required is critical to developing the judgment to make better decisions. These three lifelong goals to succeed in your job are part of the support structure for the leadership qualities that we decided upon. Understanding yourself (your education, culture, and character) and your reactions is necessary to achieving success. Putting all of this together will require effort.

As American citizens, we are expected to vote in elections. We vote for the leaders of groups, employee associations, civic clubs, unions, and the like. Yet for federal executives, there is no clear vote. We don't know whether we are wildly successful or simply scrapping by; therefore, a strong leader must be aware of the total environment surrounding him or her. Without this reaffirmation periodically, the federal executive must seek continual feedback, not only from his or her supervisor, but from colleagues and direct reports as well. Getting continuous feedback and accepting responsibility are the basics of leadership. Federal executives are simply those who have made themselves attractive candidates to be selected. Someone once told me that the folks in the senior executive ranks were the ones who figured out how to game the system the best. This does not mean that they had the largest egos, performed the dirtiest tricks to eliminate the competition, or resorted to illegalities to get where they wanted to go. Rather, the vast majority of career executives got where they wanted to go in their career because they figured out what the bosses were looking for. They rose to the top in any pool of possible contenders. They did this by not overpromising or pretending to be something they weren't. They had the credentials of education, proven performance, the ability to get along well with others, and they didn't rock the boat. In other words, they sought knowledge and improvement, gained perspective and balance, and understood themselves. For me, these ten leadership requirements supply the framework by which I could measure my own performance as a leader.

In any job, it is important to first accept responsibility, a most visible leadership element. It is easy to rationalize away your failures and to assign blame to your co-workers or to the tools and resources that you were given to complete the task. Analyze the reasons for any failures. Failures are prime learning opportunities.

Having read many self-appraisals, I know there is a huge gap between how most folks think they are doing in their job and the reality. Far too many of us are prone to delusional ideas about how good we are. Knowing what you are thinking, even if that thinking is unconventional, is an important quality. If your assessment differs from that of your supervisor, you should discuss the variance with your supervisor. If the decision is firm regarding your performance evaluation, then, as an aspiring high performer, you must give yourself the task of improving the supervisor's impression, even if it means taking on unpleasant or undesirable tasks. You had the opportunity to convince your supervisor of what you consider the truth to be. You had your say. You have acted responsibly. Write up your thoughts in some detail and file them away. If you decide to write your memoirs, this record will be useful. If it turns out you were wrong, this too will be a useful reminder in humility.

In any managerial or leadership position, you must accept challenges, which may even come from your direct reports. Accepting and meeting challenges hones leadership skills. And, this is usually not possible through performing in your customary role. Your direct reports may question one or more of your decisions. If you cannot adequately explain your decision to them or to your supervisor or your community of interest, then perhaps you should reconsider. Sometimes, someone higher in the executive ranks is looking for someone to head up a team or to perform a detail or significant task that might depend on how well you perform a job. And once an executive asks you to perform a special task, do your best to comply. I accepted almost all of these opportunities to be challenged through special assignments, and those that I didn't accept were related to family reasons, not the difficulty of the assignment. Plan to succeed. Put in the sweat equity required to be successful. Make an operating plan. Update the plan every day. Communicate to the person who chartered your detail or temporary assignment at least weekly, and copy your supervisor. Nobody likes surprises.

Human resources will be a challenge for any federal executive. It seems inherent that someone (or many someones) will object to even the most rational of human resources actions. The executive branch of human resources (HR) leadership of the VA has been extremely limited in the development of systems and sometimes politicized. The VA's human resources management has been in need of improvement for a long time. Of course, there are some genuinely excellent HR advisors. In the VA, HR seems unable to reengineer, indifferent to developing analyses or intelligence. Faced with these apparent circumstances, HR top leadership in the VA seems to have settled into a comfortable rut of minimal management, maintaining the status quo, not recognizing their own improvement potential, and passive resistance to change. There are pockets of excellence. But even these pockets of excellence are symbolic of the failure to apply systems thinking, to find out what really works and expand on it.

So how does this problem relate to you? Each executive and his/her HR support essentially have to figure out each HR problem as if for the very first time—unless there is compelling case law and somebody remembers it. Each labor relations expert and labor relations lawyer has his/her own opinions. These opinions are intended to influence, even compel the executive's decision making. In the event of a negative outcome, their guidance, to paraphrase John Nance Garner, is not worth a bucket of warm spit. For instance, on one occasion I was told by

HR and counsel that I had an absolute ability to terminate a part-time physician. This proved not to be the case. The executive is out there on a limb, with HR and legal support happily sawing off the limb at the first sign of trouble.

Evaluating your employees will be even more of a challenge. Individual managers must learn to have an authentic evaluation system, and in most cases with little reason to thank HR. HR seemingly stays behind the curve on professional expertise, analysis, and intelligence about evaluations. This sad circumstance has arisen over the years and would defeat even the happy warriors of Lake Wobegon, where all the children are reputedly above average.

I have learned that managers desire to be considered wonderful in their own appraisal. I have often described these degrees of wonderfulness: An Inspiration to Us All, Unbelievably Wonderful and Godlike in Every Way, and so on. But in truth, I wanted to be at the highest level of performance, and I am quite sure that nearly every manager and leader wants to be outstanding as well. Without HR authorization, I developed a set of rules to guide me through this difficult, annual occurrence:

Rule 1. If an employee is within the first year of a new job with a promotion, he or she will receive a fully satisfactory rating. This comes with the following caveat: if the manager or leader can convince me that this is as good as it is going to get and he or she therefore deserves a higher rating, then I will know for sure that I have hired the wrong person.

Rule 2. If an employee accomplishes the job at an outstanding level, causes no serious disruption in the organization by being difficult to work with, and so forth, then he or she will be meeting the requirements of the job but not exceeding them; therefore, he or she will receive a fully satisfactory rating.

Rule 3. If an employee accomplishes the requirements of his or her job, meets or exceeds all assigned performance measures, *and* takes on broader leadership responsibilities, such as successfully chairing the resource management committee or take on a difficult acting assignment, then he or she will *probably* receive an outstanding rating.

Rule 4. If an employee meets all the requirements in Rule 3, and he or she plays a prominent role in improving performance through leading a quality improvement team, he or she will receive an outstanding rating.

Rule 5. If an employee proves to me that he or she cannot or will not manage the resources assigned to him or her, I will reassign those responsibilities to those who have proven that they can manage and lead. Exception: If there is more than one underperforming employee, I will take action against the worst first. This is because taking adverse actions against managers can be incredibly time-consuming for the leader.

In the event of a formal reaction by an employee, such as the employee filing a formal complaint, your HR representative or their supervisors will look carefully at the actions you have taken and probably find something to criticize—even when you have followed their advice. This is second-guessing, hindsight when more facts are clearly known, or Monday morning quarterbacking. You must act to address the issue of the underperformers, however, because others will be gauging your performance by your willingness to take on the nonperformers. There are no perfect cases; you must see your duty, no matter how potentially disagreeable, and do it.

Managing conflict is something that you will have to do. It is unavoidable. To do nothing when faced with conflict is not an option. My worst forced choice came when I was the VA's network director in upstate New York. Faced with a decreased budget, among the many tough decisions that were made was a decision to close two in-house renal dialysis units. I chose this option because the patients receiving dialysis were all eligible for Medicare. So we shifted the workload from the VA to Medicare. This is against public policy, we knew. By carefully working the communities of interest, we succeeded. Of course, there was a VA dialysis committee who was righteously upset with us for closing two of the best VA dialysis units in the nation. The VA dialysis committee was effectively representing its internal customers: patients and providers. They complained to Dr. Kizer, the VA's undersecretary for health, who questioned me exhaustively. I prevailed in the end, not proud of the decision I was forced to make, but meeting the bottom line is essential. The VA dialysis committee was effectively representing its internal customers: patients and providers. Do not be a budget buster, but also understand that decisions will often be seen in terms of winning (not so often) and losing (much more frequently).

A strong customer service orientation is a must. Top-down management cannot be effective leadership. In the federal government, customer service is directed toward those customers of a federal activity or function. I will not be talking about those public customers, in the case of the VA, veterans, which is, of course, critically important. As with the Social Security Administration, the Veterans Health Administration carefully and continuously measures the reactions of its customers to the services provided. Rather, I will be talking about internal customers. Every business and organization has internal customers, if none other than its own employees. For example, a budget office must identify its customers, talk to them periodically, and have a safe means of getting feedback. Customers include the appropriate committees and their staffs from the Hill and other federal offices, such as OPM, OMB, DOD, and so forth. Tracking official correspondence, e-mails, and telephones calls will provide valuable intelligence over time. This intelligence will help a leader evaluate staff, develop better educational materials, and provide a means of improving service for those customers whose opinions are critically important in developing your career and getting your mission accomplished.

Being a federal senior executive requires ethical standards, a vital but frequently neglected area of leadership. The Veterans Health Administration (VHA), under Dr. Kizer's leadership, once published a code of ethics for its senior executives. In fact, I chaired the subcommittee that developed it. It was very much like you'd expect it to be. The VHA's network directors and chief officers were put on closed circuit TV, and we signed the code in front of our employees (if any of them bothered to go to the library and watch the video) and Dr. Kizer. That was the last significant involvement that any of us had with the code. The actual ethics code is found in appendix D.

The one element of the code that I couldn't persuade my colleagues to include in the final version presented to Dr. Kizer was one that required an executive to inform on his or her fellow executive if he or she suspected a code violation or significant malfeasance. I suppose that they were afraid of repercussions. I did reference the West Point Honor Code: Do not lie, cheat, or tolerate those who do.

I once told my supervisor, a regional director, of what I believed was significant misconduct at a neighboring VA medical center. I reported it on three separate occasions. The last time I brought up the issue, I presented my regional director with a letter from a young lady in management at that facility who was angry at the management and leadership issues there. After my regional director read the letter, she frowned and said, "She's immature and overreacting." After this third time and after I subsequently was accused of a vendetta against my colleague, I quit reporting examples of his poor leadership. Three months after the letter incident, I found a headline in my local newspaper proclaiming a disastrous management situation at that same medical center. My colleague, the director, went on sick leave and eventually retired. Various teams investigated the situation for months. Their findings were much, much worse than anything I had imagined. My supervisor, the regional director, was a pioneering woman executive in the VA. Though I didn't agree with her on this issue, I respected her and still do.

There is a real limit to how many times, anyone can try to personally intervene in situations that only indirectly affect them. I am arguing for updated standards, signed by each executive, both political appointees and career, as a very good starting point for setting expectations with federal management.

In Washington DC, however, a more adverse ethics situation exists: Potomac Fever. Potomac Fever has many facets: egotism, perception management through spin control—which is issuing only the most positive aspects of an issue and repeating them frequently—and lack of attention to detail (because what might get in the paper in Albany, New York, for example, is unlikely to make the newspapers in DC). Lily Tomlin once said, "Just when I think that I have become too cynical, something else happens, and I find out that it wasn't enough." That sums up my experience in over eight years working in Washington DC. Therefore, I am convinced that cynicism is a fundamental symptom of Potomac Fever. The DC career federal executive desires to reach retirement eligibility without a preliminary career-ending problem.

Going along to get along leads to a slippery slope. The executive does as directed by superiors but knows that if embarrassment results for the agency or the political head of the agency, then career-ending problems will almost certainly result in a kind of musical chairs. When the music stops, someone will not have a chair. Internally, career executives are told to uphold lofty standards, and there is the public pronouncement of these standards in newsletters and the like. The political executive (an executive appointed by the president and usually without career status) stakes out a position of high ground, much like Fort Apache. If only he or she could get those pesky Indians (career executives and their employees) to avoid mistakes, errors, flaws, and so on, the federal government would be a far more cost-efficient and admired system. Only the federal Fort Apache is also under attack from contractors, Congress, the media, the OMB, and the GAO, among others. There are always others with an axe to grind. In addition, there are numerous conduits to get an issue addressed. Unable to secure a government contract? Write your congressman, visit with the secretary, take your case to court, or attack the fairness of the process or the managers engaged in the process. However, in contracting, for example, there are invisible conduits to the cabinet secretary from consultants.

It seemed to me that various decision makers who report to the secretary read the tea leaves, or rather the wink and nod of someone who knows the secretary's desires, and a contract gets awarded. Without a strong ethical stance, these executives will not risk their career by ignoring the secretary's signals. Sometimes, it is the consultant called in by the secretary to review the situation who sends the signals or finds the flaw that permits awarding the contract to the secretary's preferred contractor. By awarding contracts in this way, the secretary may have feathered his future nest out of government or merely responded to political pressure. The career employees along the chain of bidding (if there were any) know that they did what they had to do. None of them want to end their careers over a contract that in all likelihood will be but one tree in forest of many thousands that never see the light of day.

Communication within the bureaucracy is a vital aspect of leadership and seems always to be in need of improvement. Communication is far too important to leave in the hands of the communications professionals. Lateral communication is critically neglected. Dr. Kizer created an intermediate organization of networks that managed groups of hospitals, nursing homes, outpatient clinics, and domiciliaries. Network 2, which I headed for six and half years, implemented an end-of-week reporting system called Items of Interest, or IOIs. Having a weekly method of communication upward and to your direct reports is critical. If your direct reports share it further, so much the better. Sending your IOIs to those at the same level of the organization that you are located in is also a great idea. Thinking critically about what your organization accomplished during the week is a fabulous way to measure progress toward the next deadline. Furnishing key offices such as HR, budget, engineering, or acquisition with the opportunity to provide feedback is also important.

Nothing illustrates accountability more than having a written record that shows your organization's focus, effort, ingenuity, and passion for accomplishment. Having been to the secretary's staff meetings on several occasions and having been in attendance at other high-level executive staff meetings, I am convinced that nothing gets accomplished in such meetings except for learning the attitudes and concerns of the leader of the meeting. Certainly, high-profile items, accomplishments (usually individual), and amusing anecdotes are reported, but minutes are seldom kept and, if they are, they aren't circulated for veracity or completeness. Staff meetings for the purpose of communication are nearly a complete waste of time. I say nearly only because there is some networking that goes on before, after, and during the meeting.

Another aspect of communication is presentations. I once saw a surgeon general report to the VA on the army's anthrax inoculation program. He brought twelve support staff with him, including a staff sergeant to manage the slide show! In the group he brought with him were physicians, nurses, pharmacists, the contracting officer, and several others whose purpose I never figured out. This was a very important issue at the time and worthy of VHA executives' attention. But the approach was overkill. I don't know if that was the surgeon general's typical approach to presenting but simply introducing all the folks was tedious.

The successful senior executive must be able to present. He or she has PowerPoint slides to be sure. He or she must be totally familiar with them and able to respond to questions. Having a handout of all the slides is also a good idea. Having set through innumerable presentations, I have become a critic of the state of the art. Truly successful presentations occur about 15 per cent of the time. Let me also mention town meetings, which generally do not have a slide show. The executive should be prepared to give five to ten minutes of an overview of the issues and then take questions. That's right: take questions directly from the audience. Having the crowd submit questions in advance in writing is often seen as an evasion from potentially tough questions and a control mechanism to avoid embarrassment.

Executives must be knowledgeable about their own data and the data from the organization for which they are responsible. If adequate data does not exist, the executive should create it, preferably through programmed mining of the database, but at least self-reporting through some manual means if nothing else is possible. As soon as you begin using the data, the data will start to get better. For example, if your office manages intake of applications, consider counting the number of complete, incomplete, and what areas on the form are most often misunderstood. This will work with not just budget data, but HR, performance, workload, and so forth, allowing you to keep your direct reports and your supervisor informed. Develop factoids. Have graphs on key data on display in your office or the conference room. Discuss the trends and what those trends mean. By doing so, the manager builds the knowledge of the entire office.

Computer project management is often a critical failure in the federal government and in health care in general. Computers are vital to effective communication. Users must be involved in an ongoing and meaningful way. Contracts should be compact and kept integrated to the whole. Large, multifunctional programming contracts should be avoided. Accomplishing valid reengineering along with programming and software is highly desirable. Communicating the accomplishments and the ongoing inquiries to the chief operating officer on a weekly basis is critical. He or she can stay up-to-date much more quickly compared to establishing regular meetings. The key stakeholders should be briefed continuously. Creating a forum for new ideas like NASA has done where anybody can submit proposals for needed redesigns is a great way to tap into the vast pool of Yankee ingenuity that lies outside the walls of Fort Apache. The word *robust* should be banned as a descriptor for the desired software. The objective should be: does it work? When it does work, then success should be declared.

The project should not end there, of course. It is a platform that must be continuously built upon. The federal government has such a success story. It is the VA's VistA health-care medical record. Despite numerous setbacks in recent years and attacks from vendors, it is still the best example of large-scale software development in the federal government.

Sustained high performance should be the ultimate goal of the executive. Too often, the real goal is survival, and that's understandable. But there is nothing better than sustained high performance. To achieve this, one has to take risks. In reading the cases in this book, the reader will see that in my own career I have taken risks. In a few instances, I lost the bet. But I still feel that I did the right thing, and I would make each and every decision again. A high-performing executive also needs a high-performing team. The team must have a passion to get to the next level of high performance. That requires systems thinking, critical thinking, analytical ability, a high level of effective communication, and risk taking. Meeting changing demands and constant challenges is part of the executive package required to sustain high performance.

The nation and its elected political leadership can be proud of its federal career executives. I also believe that there is plenty of room for improvement. Each of us can always do a better job. That's why we need improvement in the acceptance of responsibility, in applying critical thinking, in accepting challenges, in improving human resources management, in making personnel evaluations meaningful and accountable, in managing conflict, in improving customer service, in maintaining a high standard of personal and professional ethics, in improving communications, in managing data and information, in computer project management, and in creating a culture of sustained high performance.

Chapter 2: You Must Have a Code That You Lead By

Setting expectations is a critical aspect of a leader's work. They allow for a high level of internal consistency. In fact, the actions of the leadership team should be consistent with the leader's ethics, style, positions, and strategies. Neither managers nor employees should have to guess about their supervisor's reaction to events in the workplace. Developing a code that covers and defines these important expectations is far more critical than selecting the group's values or reshaping the mission statement. The code will shape the values, strategies, objectives, and mission in ways that merely stating those words would never do. Annette Simmons in her book *A Safe Place for Dangerous Truths* states, "When norms develop by default rather than by design, they focus either on eliminating conflict or diverting energy in a blame routine, thereby missing the opportunity to learn." Annette's book was published by AMACOM in 1999.

The purpose of the leadership code is to establish expectations for all the managers in the organizational unit. It should be a living, breathing, debatable document that is discussed in e-mails and meetings, particularly when there is a situation that has created dissonance in the organization. The goal is to maintain the highest level of achievement and performance, individually and collectively. I have often used the analogy of the wolf pack: collective goals and individual action. Each member of the pack seems to know what is expected of them and acts accordingly for the benefit of all.

In VHA's Network 2, we developed a reasonable and prudent index. This index describes those situations in which wider involvement is necessary. Situations may include those tough budget, management, or human resource decisions that require consultation with others who have a stake in the outcome. Very often, such decisions are made in private, and those who had a stake in the outcome—but didn't have a voice—are left to sulk and/or simply get over it. There is a better way. A reasonable and prudent leadership index includes the following:

1. The individual—with the participation of the team members who are able to participate in the discussion and development

of a solution—will involve potential stakeholders.

2. The inclusion of those involved will not slow down the discussion. The stakeholders will be given an opportunity to provide input and dialogue. The decision stays on its timeline.

3. The discussion can occur face-to-face or via e-mail. Those conversations will always reflect kindness and dignity by using the following basic rules of trust: don't demean others; don't talk over them; don't intimidate, yell, and so forth; and don't be judgmental.

4. The team will be purposeful, persistent, resilient, relentless, data-based, and prepared.

5. The team will maintain momentum, meet all known deadlines, and always be optimistic.

6. Notes will be taken and retained, preferably electronically. The notes will be one source for the weekly reporting of items of interest.

7. Learning will occur intentionally throughout the organization by collaborating lessons learned.

8. FRED is the acronym for how all employees in the organization should behave: Friendly, Receptive, Effective/Efficient/ Energetic, and Dedicated. OK, maybe it should be FREEED.

9. The best decisions come from proposed solutions developed from diverse sources, relentless exposure to reality, constant internal critique, and a constantly improving learning base.

10. The focus for individuals and the team should be on success, results, creating value, and the future.

11. The team should maintain agility: how fast can the individual, its nominal leader, and the organization meet challenges and adapt to change.

The Network 2 code included other parts as well. The network had a code for demonstrating leadership in the managing of customer service, performance, strategy, knowledge, change, and challenge. I will cover these particular codes in various cases where they best apply.

Chapter 3
1947–1968: Freddy Lee

From childhood to college, there were some extraordinarily painful times for me. There were some high points, but mostly it was a drag. Throughout my writing, I will summarize certain experiences and memories that are funny, revealing, and perhaps illustrative of my adult character and personality. I offer my childhood and early career only as a guide to gaining a better perspective on the future leader and the decisions that he later made.

Strangely enough, one of my first memories was standing in the kitchen door, watching my father cook dinner and wondering, "I know who I am, but who are these people?" By these people, I meant my father, mother, and older brother. I didn't have the vocabulary necessary to really describe what was going on in my three- or four-year-old head. I had good reason to believe that I had been placed in a family of aliens. I didn't know that vocabulary word then either, of course. But that's the word that I use now to describe the interpersonal situations of my parents and brother, whereby their behaviors often seemed impossible to understand.

Dad was an alcoholic who disappeared for days at a time. Mom was from a rural Texas family and was ten years younger than Dad. She had difficulty contending with all the craziness that he threw her way. So Mom had trouble coping, but she tried very hard to make that marriage work. According to my immature mind, Mom loved my brother more than me. In fact, her entire family seemed to love my brother more. My dad and his family seemed to love me more. My brother was more needy or cuter, or something that made him attractive to my mother. Whatever it was, it never made a difference to me. I knew Mother loved me. Most of the time, I slept with Dad, and my brother slept with Mom. I thought my brother was just spoiled.

I withdrew. I mostly wanted to be left alone and escape by watching my favorite shows on TV. Western serials were my favorite. We lived in Edna, Texas, and later in Velasco, Texas, across the Brazos River from Freeport. I had fond memories of the big old house in which we lived in Edna. I learned in Edna that getting upset about my family situation was not worth it. One long afternoon when I was four years old, I turned over all the furniture in the living room. I had started taking apart those items that I could take apart when my mother discovered me. I didn't get punished, but it was then that I began to get the quizzical response from my parents for the things that I did. I loved going into the ditch in front of the house when it rained and playing with the crayfish. I understood the lectures I received about lightning and dirty water, but it never stopped me. Fortunately, it doesn't rain much in Texas. I also have memories of screams in the night and being handed over a barbed wire fence that I can't place in any larger explanation. I also have a couple of scars that no one seems to know about.

Sometimes, we would travel to my maternal grandmother's house near Teague, Texas. I wouldn't call these trips vacations, although I didn't mind going. It wasn't all that great, because my mother's family favored my brother like they did. Mom's father had died by then. These trips were hot and confining, and my parents were usually angry, alternately arguing or sulking. Once there, I was usually left in peace. I watched my grandmother and visitors play dominoes in the parlor. I came to understand that Grandmother was a dominoes expert in doing the math calculations required for the game. Most of the domino players chewed tobacco. There was a large can used for tobacco spit for every table. There was no TV, but there was a lot to see and many places to explore.

During one of these visits, I was left toddling around in the backyard. I remember smelling a beautiful yellow iris and watching a bumblebee making its way from flower to flower. When I woke up in the car, I immediately remembered the bumblebee and realized that I had been stung from the slight ache on the side of my head. As I lifted my head, my mom, grandmother, and uncle excitedly noted my return to the conscious world, just as we entered the physician's office parking lot. My uncle did a U-turn, and we returned to Grandma's house out in the sticks. It was thirty years before I learned that I was allergic to bee stings. None of the family really seemed to believe in doctor's visits, or maybe it was just that they didn't want to pay for the doctor's visit.

I was left alone a lot. I certainly had the freedom to explore and imagine. Mom and Dad seemed to argue and shout at each other often.

Sometimes my brother and I would be left with relatives for days, some-times weeks at a time. At other times, Dad would go off for days at a time. He would disappear without notice and return unannounced. I knew my family unit was different. I began a long period of withdrawal whenever possible, usually through reading.

I really looked up to my older brother, but as time went on, I learned to avoid him as well. Something wasn't quite right with him. It was a lot more than using his younger brother as an experiment for the effects of tarantulas and other kinds of spiders, and centipedes on the human body. Sometimes it seemed he laughed at the wrong things, like people getting hurt.

On one occasion when I was about five years old, I was sitting in the outhouse—often referred to as the "Federal Building"—in back of Grandmother's little sharecropper home. They didn't have running water. A cistern captured rainfall, and a hand pump provided water for cooking and cleaning. I was sitting there in the outhouse, looking at the flies and bugs crawling around the mound of feces below. I was startled when my aunt Arlene opened the door and proceeded to sit down on the other hole. I looked away quickly, and I didn't see any-thing. I was flustered, mortified, and embarrassed. Why would anyone build a two-seater outhouse?

One day at our house in Velasco, Texas, I was perfecting my rear mount of a horse by practicing on the arm and back of an overstuffed chair. I watched a lot of Western serials and movies. I think it was Hopalong Cassidy who, in thrilling moments of escape or chase, would run for his horse, hit the horse on top of the rear end with his hands, and vaulted into the saddle. My interpretation didn't work quite that well, but I practiced until I vaulted into the back of the chair, hitting the lower part of my stomach and sliding down the back of the chair, where I lay on my back, gasping for air and feeling a lot of pain. I was never going to be able to perfect this cowboy technique without a pony to practice on. That, I thought, was the problem. I had rabbits and a dog. Once, my dad kept a calf for a month, but it was gone now. I was still lying there, contemplating, when my mother passed by on her way to the kitchen.

"Freddy Lee," she asked, "what are you doing?"

"I am laying down because I'm tired," I answered, hoping that was convincing. I really didn't like explaining myself. I had already learned that being tired or hurt were good cover answers.

"So you just quit going right there behind the chair? You couldn't get any further?" She seemed worried.

"Yes," I replied. I had also learned that brevity was good when interacting with the adults.

She helped me up and suggested that I lie down and take a nap. I went meekly, but I hated naps. This would prove to be a huge problem in kindergarten. I was figuring what I could do in bed.

Two days later, Mom saw me limping and asked me what was the matter.

"I'm sore. Nothing's the matter. I haven't done anything," I said, probably too quickly, thinking about being sent to bed again. I was getting close to perfecting the vault. I needed a slightly longer straightaway but was working around that. I was concerned about the creaking noise that the chair was making now every time someone sat in it. I was committed to not explaining.

Mother called the doctor. He examined me. Unbeknownst to me, there was an outbreak of polio on the coast of Texas, not too far from where we lived. The doctor said that it could be polio. I would have to be watched very carefully. I spent about three months of a long, hot Texas summer in bed being closely watched.

The next injury occurred during a rock fight that my brother and some of the neighborhood rowdies were in. I was not throwing rocks. I was enjoying the view from the down slope of a large pile of dirt. In fact, there were about twenty piles of dirt in the neighborhood. To this day, I cannot see a pile of dirt, sand, or any other natural material without feeling the youthful thrill that I got when I could play on one. While I was lying there on my back, enjoying the blue sky, I felt a sudden pain in my left eye. I ran as fast as I could to Mom. They took me to the emergency room. I had to wear a patch over my eye for about a month. From the beginning, there was little hope. The projectile that landed in my eye was a sandy rock. It caused nerve damage. I lost most of the vision in that eye.

I moved on, but Mom and Dad couldn't. I guess there was a certain amount of grief and guilt. Another day without adult supervision, and I had been hurt. I think that my dad and his side of the family thought that my brother had done it. He was on the next pile of dirt and was throwing rocks. I couldn't be seen by his adversaries, so for them to have done it would have been a long shot. But I don't know who did it. I do know that from then on, any rocks thrown anywhere in the general vicinity of the neighborhood resulted in me getting beat with a belt on my naked backside. This was even more encouragement for staying inside and entertaining my imagination with creative, indoor activities. One of my favorites was making cocktails from various types of soda.

One day, my dad just up and took my brother and me to Grandmother's house in Florida. After several days in the car, we arrived at her house in Miami. He was drunk most of that trip. I was happy to be out of the car. Eventually, my mother followed. Things never got any better between them, and the divorce proceedings started. Relatives picked up sides. My brother and I moved between them, mostly in Stuart, Florida, and Gainesville, Florida. The lawyers and the family fought until my mother quit trying, exhausted emotionally and financially. We were all ready for some quiet time.

I was in the second grade when we left Texas. I started third grade in Florida. I remember responding to a question from the teacher in Florida and the agonizing look on her face when she heard me talk. After that, I was in speech therapy for three years. My aunt Arlene and the other Texas relatives talked very slowly and through their nose. I later joked that my aunt Arlene in Texas was still saying good-bye to us because she talked so slowly. The high point during this time was when my Florida grandmother's fifth ex-husband came by to see my brother and me. He gave us both a silver dollar.

My great aunt Alice had married a lobster fisherman from Maine. My grandmother would go to see her, then my aunt Rosie went, and, soon enough, we were all going to Big Cranberry Island to visit during the summer. I enjoyed this, but before long my dad got a teaching job in Belfast, Maine, and we moved there full-time. Belfast was not a resort. Living there in the winter was a challenge. My new classmates complained that I didn't have a Southern accent. I blamed speech therapy. My dad was the principal of the junior high school I attended. Other than receiving some of the verbal abuse that they couldn't deliver to him, the time passed unremarkably, considering how attractive a target I was to my fellow students. Being the child of the principal is a lose-lose proposition. I recognized more weird things that my brother would do, like stealing money from me and cheating at board games. And I also learned not to confront him about it because he would get extremely angry with me. I did not want to have anything to do with him.

Probably because of school politics or his mental health, my dad was always on the losing side or he'd quit trying. We moved again after two years. This time we moved to Orono, Maine. He bought a little house way out of town without power or plumbing. I learned that it's a much more pleasant experience to use an outhouse in Texas than it is to use one in Maine. It was cold, but in the summer the mosquitoes and flies could probably kill you if stayed out long enough. I sensed in myself the disillusionment that many teenagers get when they finally realize that their parents—in this case, Dad—aren't quite what they ought to be. He slept an ungodly amount. He hadn't been drinking in six or seven years. I'll never know if he saw the disquieting changes in my brother, like his irrational anger at any academic or sports success that I had, but I sure did. I also began to realize that I was poor, very poor, and the main reason was all the craziness of sudden, multiple moves and poor money management that seemed to constantly surround us.

I enjoyed Orono High School, the first and best experience of my four high school career. I had fine classmates, and the teachers and administrators seemed to care and were competent. I had to walk over a mile to get to the school bus stop. I had good friends, but, in the middle of my sophomore year, Dad announced we were moving to Florida. I began a period of rebellion, quiet at first and then, more and more self destructive. I had my first two girlfriends—almost at the same time. Good things never seemed to last in my childhood. Leaving my friends in Orono was a terribly sad time.

I was sent to Miami to live with my grandmother. My brother moved in with a friend in Orono, so he stayed there. I went to Miami

Senior High School. I went from a small, collegial high school to the largest high school in Florida. We were on triple session, having slightly under five thousand students in just three grades. I lived with Grandmother until Dad got a job teaching in Boca Raton. We moved to Lake Worth, Florida. My dad had graduated from Palm Beach High School and had gone all the way through school there. Lake Worth High School was an improvement over Miami Senior—no cops patrolling the corridors for one thing. I made some friends. Even still, my personal revolt against Dad was beginning to take shape, adding fuel and just waiting to blowup.

After the first marking period of my junior year, I dutifully brought home my report card and showed it to Dad. He asked, "What happened to chemistry?"

I said, "Nothing." I walked away seething. I had seven college prep courses and had A's in six of them and one B in chemistry. I resolved then and there to fail chemistry. I also joined every beer party or recreational event I could find, and there were plenty. My chemistry teacher took my newfound lack of effort personally, and he tried many times to tease out from me what he was doing wrong. I did the man wrong, and I deeply regret that I never told him so. He wouldn't cooperate with my plan. He gave me enough D's so that I passed chemistry!

In the spring, I caught strep throat and missed three weeks of school. That was my diagnosis. My father wouldn't take me to see a doctor. I got into all kinds of trouble that year with the school and the law. I left the day after the school year was over without a word to my father and went to Miami to find Mother.

Fortunately, my mother let me stay with her. I stopped being a juvenile delinquent. I wanted to finish high school and go on to college as quickly as I could. After considering my options, I officially dropped out of high school, and the next day I enrolled in Lindsay Hopkins Vocational Technical High School. My mother taught there and got a very kind and decent guidance counselor to talk to me. It was his advice that I took. I only needed three courses to graduate and could get those done before Christmas. But there was an elevator fire that stopped school for three weeks, so I had to graduate in January. I was off to college and was mostly on my own. I consider myself to have been mostly self-raised. While I still have a lot of anger about it, I now know that it could have been worse. I survived. Many others have had worse upbringings.

As I attended college and worked at various part-time jobs, I settled down emotionally. I graduated from the University of Florida with a degree in accounting. I also got married just after college, and we soon had a beautiful daughter, Julie.

Chapter 4
1969–1970: Beginning a Career

In 1969, I began my career as a financial intern in the second largest hospital in Gainesville, Florida. I was glad the financial manager executives chose me but was uncertain this large, complex, and imposing hospital in the largest health-care system in the world was the place for me.

I was a graduate of the University of Florida and had majored in accounting. I was never totally convinced this was the right field for me, but I forged ahead. In what should have been my senior year of high school, I was at a loss for what to study in college. I reviewed the job listings in the *Miami Herald*. On that day, there were more jobs for accountants than any other profession. The die was cast. While in college, I had become very enamored with President John F. Kennedy and had decided to heed his advice to look for what I could do for my country, which I interpreted to mean going to work for the federal government. My new job was with the Veterans Administration's hospital in Gainesville, and so a federal job.

Soon I settled into doing reports, which required that I collect data from others in the hospital, crunch their numbers, and turn these numbers into reports that those executives accepted. The hard part for me initially was getting others in the hospital to do the work that was required to produce financial reports. My supervisors, of course, wanted to be seen by the high-level executives in the best possible light. Accordingly, I began to understand what the executives wanted to see, what they expected to see, what they should see, and most importantly, how we would respond to their probable and possible reactions to the various financial scenarios that we could foresee resulting from the findings.

This was what I definitely needed to learn, since the great university that had degreed me had not prepared me for the psychology of reporting the facts as represented by my individual opinion of the real data in the reports. Or perhaps the great university had offered this training and I had missed it. The latter is more likely. Those giving me the data were also opinionated. They often felt that no one needed to see their data. I found that leaders in the medical center had their own opinions, which weren't necessarily based on the facts.

I got to know many people throughout the organization and to learn more about the care and feeding of an information-lacking, but data-intensive, health-care beast. Most of the time, I was perplexed about the various events unfolding. I internalized these confusions, since my questions were not appreciated and were in fact often resented. The general attitude was that my questions took away from the real work. I tried talking to some of the junior staff from time to time but quickly realized that asking them raised suspicion of my motivations (including being some kind of anarchist, being plain stupid, or trying to make others look bad in some way). I was ambitious, and I really didn't mind paying my dues and formulating my own opinions. I cared very much about what others thought of me, but sometimes I was not considerate enough of their feelings and concerns.

I was young and fully capable of making mistakes and misstatements. I was too young and naïve to worry about what impact an ill-considered question or comment could have on my immediate career opportunities, and I certainly was not planning to overthrow the competition. My competition was with myself; I was trying to find my way. Had I known of the competition going on with my peers, I would not have changed my behavior or tried to intervene in theirs. I enjoyed the possibilities offered by new committee assignments and the requirements of the job. I was thrilled when I got to be in the center of activity and bored when I wasn't. Being in a large, dynamic environment was sometimes challenging, frequently dull, but never without opportunities to apply what little I had learned, to grow, and to continue to learn. I was far too occupied to worry about the light at the end of the tunnel.

The hospital I had chosen was only two years old. Many people from across the country had been brought in because of their expertise and experience. Along with their expertise and experience, they also brought their way of doing things, which included communications, management styles, and, most importantly, treatment of our patients. It was truly a hothouse of ideas, styles, and opinions.

A generational chasm existed in two ways. First, patients were coming to us who had been injured in the Vietnam War. Some were teenagers, most were in their twenties, and they were children of the sixties' experience. They felt slighted and resentful about their experiences while serving in the armed services and in coming home. Second, I learned that I was part of a small cadre of young people brought in to replace the so-called Class of Forty Eight. After World War II, this VA hospital system went on a vast expansion, as did the private health-care sector. The expansion was necessary to meet the demands of the huge numbers of returning WWII veterans.

In my hospital, the incoming patients from Vietnam clashed mightily with the senior managers and executives of the hospital. I witnessed some of these clashes between WWII administrators and their new, younger patients. The conflict transformed the VA's health system over the next decade, as it was forced to learn how to communicate with these newer veterans who challenged many of the beliefs and attitudes of the earlier veterans. All of us were affected, but some of those Vietnam veterans still hurt and carry their resentments to this day.

Smoking was permitted everywhere. The organization furnished ashtrays, and smoking occurred in every office and area of the hospital. I smoked as did many of my fellow employees, despite having the evidence published in scientific journals that smoking was harmful. At the close of the sixties, individual freedoms were in higher consciousness than the public's safety, health, or pocketbook. The VA canteen sold cigarettes without the federal or state taxes added, so it was a cheap source. The VA, despite its health-care mission, was reluctant to end the practice of smoking and feared the drastic reaction from veterans and their representatives, who clearly saw smoking as a right. One day I accidentally set a trashcan on fire in the office. My colleagues quickly poured their coffee on it to douse the fire. Each morning, I woke up coughing until I could clear my lungs. I would look at my fingers and see the nicotine stains. So, during the first year of my career, after four years of smoking, I decided to quit.

One day as I left the men's room closest to my work area, I passed a supervisor from another department. Two of my co-workers were out in the hall, laughing as he passed. They asked me if the supervisor had tried to kiss me. I said no. One of them said that I must not have been his type. I faked a slight laugh and went about my business. Later, I heard from one of my colleagues in accounting that top management was trying to fire the supervisor, who had recently been allegedly outed as a homosexual. The trumped-up charges are lost to history. The supervisor competently finished his career but most always seemed unhappy. I relate this anecdote to convey the tenor of the times, which allowed VA directors considerable autonomy. Women, minorities, and others worked in VA medical centers that were often dominated by one white man's views—the director's determination on what social conditions within that medical center should be.

I learned some new phrases: *doom and gloom, blood and guts,* and "If you've seen one VA, you've seen one VA." *Doom and gloom* essentially described the next year's expected budget. That budget was always anticipated to be bad, less than what would have allowed for full services, and the pessimists were usually right. *Blood and guts* was that part of a hospital's budget that concerned the direct delivery of care: the medications, the blood, the medical supplies, and so forth. Many thought that was the only critical part of the budget. It was wrong, of course, but the clarion call of "blood and guts" rang out in many budget meetings. Finally, "If you've seen one VA, you have seen one VA" was the supposed truism of the nation's largest integrated health-care system. The phrase attempted to justify differences in staffing or cost of operations as being essential because each medical center was unique.

Chapter 5
1970–1976: Learning the Ropes

As much as I learned, I slowly began to realize that it wasn't enough. As I moved up the ranks, particularly after I began to supervise forty people, I realized that I had to learn more. I began to read management literature consistently, which I continue to do to this day. Unlike now, where a list of pertinent management resources can easily be found, there were no suggestions from my supervisors about what to read or study.

This process of discovery led me to the works of Peter F. Drucker. Only Drucker, I was soon to learn, didn't provide to-do lists or even direct guidance about specific situations. He was a thinker who wrote cogently about management and organizations, but he was not going for the quick fix. I read and reread his books, but seeking answers somewhere in this great management thinker's work required thinking and extrapolation. His work affected me greatly, more so than I realized at the time. He was a futurist in the sense that he saw the future and articulated it clearly and cleverly. His work gave me a framework to address the issues that confronted me. It was not directly helpful, but it taught me to be thoughtful, to seek always to understand before reacting, and to use available information at all times.

At this time, I was not a health-care executive, nor did I aspire to be one. I simply wanted to be a better supervisor and manager. I searched for answers in management literature and sought advice from senior managers who seemed to be doing a good job. I wanted to learn and to be the best. I also wanted to stay out of trouble.

Health-care executives confront the same kind issues that are relevant for city managers, football coaches, principals, and managers of service organizations. In the federal sector, issues are confounded by the direct interface with the federal government and, to a lesser extent, government at all levels. Health-care organizations also reflect the values and culture of the communities in which they exist, just as they reflect the values and the culture of their parent organization.

One day our chief financial officer collapsed in the office. The ambulance carried him to the downtown trauma center. His employees cheerfully recounted how often he would say, "Well, they're going to have to carry me out of here." I learned that he was an unhappy worka-holic, a command and control adherent, who used all of this as an excuse not to effectively deal with his diabetic condition.

So what does this situation have to do with the writings of Drucker? As the chief financial officer situation unfolded, its tentacles held me firmly in their slimy grasp. The chief financial officer had completely ruined his health, would not be coming back, and had applied for retirement. The assistant chief financial officer was asked to draw up a report on the state of his office and of the hospital's finances, including a complete budget redo. Without a moment's hesitation, the assistant said, "I cannot do that."

Top management was perplexed because the assistant had been there for many years and seemed competent. Communication between the assistant and top management quickly ceased. I had just emerged into the outer fringes of middle management. Unknown to me, emer-gency discussions were held that came to the conclusion that I was the best person to insert into this vacuum as the chief financial officer. I was too dumb, too green, and too pathetically ambitious to even consider saying no.

Drucker's writings were important to my development in that they taught me that there was a better way, a higher calling for managers and leaders. The training available to me during those times was legalistic— what the regulations were and what would happen if I violated them. It was strict stuff and meant to set the limits and enforce the right and the wrong. Drucker taught me that management was to a great extent about the art of the possible. It was about what could and should be done, not just about what shouldn't be done.

The work was hard, and the long hours were difficult to man-age along with a personal life. During the next few months, our VA Central Office, which contained the political appointees and the usual headquarters staff of a large federal bureaucracy, decided that our liver transplant unit was not performing up to par. I checked into it.

I discovered to my horror that for the last two years we hadn't done a single transplant. I went to the chief executive officer and explained the situation. The surgery department had been funded the entire twenty-six positions, along with several million dollars. I was sent to see the chief of surgery. The chief of surgery patiently explained that he could not afford to give up a single position because of his workload. The liver transplant surgeons had transferred elsewhere, and there was simply no hope of reviving the program because the medical school had lost interest in recruiting for the VA program. In other words, they had their own liver transplant program. I went back to the director. I explained the situation. He agreed that we couldn't cut surgery and that we had to give the money back. It was up to me to finagle the budget. Cutting staff here and there, pruning already sparse budgets had to be done. I set about quietly to these tasks. Surgery was not cut. No one complained. The director was happy. It made me wonder what Drucker would say about this decidedly nonrational business development.

When I inherited my new office, it was filled with papers, reports, printouts, and an incredible assortment of reading material. I worked my way through it all, set up a filing system, and threw away years of antiquated material. One day, the door behind my desk opened, and an auditor nearing retirement age limped in, went to the stamp tree, pulled a stamp off, and limped back out. This transaction occurred without the employee saying a word to me. Rubber stamps were in minimal use, even when I entered the organization. But this tree, left to my supervision, had about a hundred different stamps. The stamps said among other things: lost discounts, no funds available, rejected, denied, no obligation (a government necessity), paid, and the like. I hadn't gotten around to the tree in terms of my priorities.

Since I didn't plan on using it, the next time the auditor limped in, I asked him to sit and explain to me the uses of all the stamps. I quickly stopped him during his recitation and asked him what would happen if I simply threw the tree and its stamps out. He looked perplexed; his visceral reaction showed that he was deeply offended. He said that it had been done that way for many years. I asked why the rubber stamps were in my office. He said the former CFO had wanted it that way and that he, the auditor, needed them to do his job properly. I gave him the stamp tree. He was confused but smiled broadly, satisfied that he had saved the tree. I asked about his personal life. He told me that he was married and had two kids, both in prep schools back east, and he spoke highly of the health care provided by Kaiser Permanente, which I had also signed up for. Because of his limp, I asked why he didn't park in the handicapped parking lot. He said he wasn't handicapped; that was for people who needed it. I told him that I admired his pluck.

During the same time, folks in the finance office were going through a spell of amazing bad luck. I was in the process of terminating the assistant who could but wouldn't do the budget. I had a secretary who could barely type but had acquired too many duties to have time to learn to type better. I also had several depressed staff with good reasons to be down. A payroll clerk had lost a young child to a rare disease. A supervisor's nephew and niece died in a car accident. An accounting technician lost her husband after a tragic illness. A single mom struggling to get off welfare lost her kids to the state social welfare agency. A young accountant who was desperately seeking a boyfriend made all the wrong decisions, resigned, and went back to Omaha and her parents. A new employee in payroll got arrested for kidnapping and rape. He came back a couple of days later, angry because the charges were filed by his father-in-law, and the couple had been married for a year.

While all this was happening, six months after I had moved into a duplex with three very young children, we got evicted by the new owner. The original owner hadn't informed us that the new duplex was for sale; he seemed more concerned with three additional months' rent than being honest. Still, we labored on, and I realized that it was my job to improve morale, at work and at home. My goal was to cheer up the office as much as possible. Morale was the responsibility of the person in charge. That was me.

One day a young veteran came into my office. He had applied for a junior-level accountant opening. His credentials were impeccable, the highest grades in accounting that I had ever seen. He wasn't sure about the job though; he was working as a food service worker and would have to take a pay cut to become an accountant. I finally convinced him that in the long run, he and his family would be much better off. He took the job but resented the government processes that required him to take a cut in pay. So I nurtured him and worked with him.

He stayed in the VA until he retired. But still, many employees would get angry, sad, and disappointed in the way the bureaucracy treated them. I decided that I would try to add humor to the workplace whenever possible and would work hard to change the organization. In the *Effective Executive*, Drucker wrote that effective executives know when a decision has to be based on principle and when it should be based on merit. I was successful in convincing this budding accountant that his best interests were represented in the long run. I began to believe that I had been successful in applying that. I kept reading and working, and slowly the depression in the finance office began to lift.

I was learning about top management. The previous CEO had retired. He liked me. I had listened with great interest about his rock-collecting hobby, and, as a result of his rock gifts to me, I had grown quite a collection of rocks myself. My wife didn't want a collection of rocks, and I found that they disappeared from the house about as fast as I could bring them home.

Anyway, the new CEO cleaned out his office, but not in the way that I had done, keeping that which was important. He cleared *everything* out of his office and ordered a lectern, a coffee table, an overstuffed sofa, and two matching chairs. To have a meeting, his secretary had to find the appropriate material and bring it to him. I learned quickly and always brought extra copies. I learned through the grapevine that he seemed to be happily married and had children.

Soon we had to go to budget hearings in San Francisco. We got there, but during an impromptu transit strike. The few cabs were taken, so I quickly rented a car. The CEO was concerned that the VA wouldn't reimburse him his share of the rental car. He should have understood that as the CFO, I would be the one authorizing the payment. I felt that we could stay at the airport for hours waiting for a cab or we could move on to the hotel and the meeting. The choice saved us hours and much frustration. Even still, he continued to ask about it throughout our journey.

At the hotel, we encountered more chaos. Many disenchanted customers were being sent to the bar while their rooms were presumably being cleaned. The clerk did not speak English, but she did have rooms for us. I was secretly elated. We took our keys and went to the elevator.

We found the rooms, which were side by side. I said goodnight and opened the door. Upon entering the room, I found myself looking at the surprised face of my director. The room had two doors opening to the hallway. We went back to the front desk. After much gesturing, we got different room keys. We went to the elevator and to a different floor. After opening the doors, we found two rooms connected by a wide opening. We gave up.

At about 8:00 pm, the director said he was going to a show. He clearly wanted me to go with him. I acquiesced. We got the rental car. I drove. I followed his directions, and we arrived at a warehouse area that seemed deserted except for a few cars. I immediately started worrying about having our rental car stolen.

Entering through a scuffed, scarred steel door, we slowly wandered through a musty, moldy hallway to a theater. The theater was quite large, but the only people were sitting in the first three rows. I was chilled and felt the dampness even with my jacket on. This rental arrangement must not have allowed for heat or much light, except for the stage. There were guys who had brought their wives or girlfriends. Guys were sitting in the darkest parts of the theater, seeking personal privacy. This made me feel intensely uncomfortable. We sat in the middle of the third row, with an excellent view of the stage. The various acts consisted of women doing things with various implements or other women. I was profoundly grateful when the show was over and the director got up to leave. After this experience, I learned to be quickly tactful in refusing any invitations that seemed remotely likely to lead to such sex shows. The memory is still painful for me to think about.

The rest of the trip was uneventful. The budget meetings were as anticipated. War stories were told. Some networking was accomplished. Very little data was used. All the involved medical facilities continued on in the same fashion that they had been for another year.

This director retired about a year later. I was relieved.

Drucker wrote about self-control and management by objectives. Management by objectives is a process by which agreed upon or assigned objectives are the primary goals of the organization. We were to perform management by objectives. I schemed to do as little as possible and essentially did management by my day-to-day thought process. That was all the changes and priorities required, and I found that the forces on me and finance service essentially mandated that I be flexible. I should have revisited my objectives from time to time and modified them. However, because I didn't, my ability and my organization's ability to meet its goals were lessened.

Chapter 6
1976–1980: The First Time in VA Central Office

As I grew in my career, I wanted more responsibility. I wanted to meet the next challenge. So when the opportunity came and I transferred to VA Central Office in Washington DC, I was excited, thrilled really, to be there. It was 1976, and the town was pumped with people, change, and excitement. It was our nation's two hundredth birthday. Washington was full of challenges, and all of government seemed charged with significance and opportunities. I was to be a systems accountant. Although I had relished my career in our health-care system, VA Central Office was where I thought the action was and where I felt that I could make a big difference—maybe even rise in the bureaucracy without having to make all the physical moves required of managers and executives in the field.

Having been greatly enamored with John F. Kennedy and with my limited understanding of Washington and the federal government of that era, I was bound to be disillusioned and disappointed by what I found at VA Central Office. Indeed, the way government worked seemed quite mysterious compared to what I remembered from civics class and U.S. history. Although I was just an observer to the larger affairs of the VA and government, I sensed both the hope and the despair that come with new initiatives and what seems like better ideas being buffeted, debated, criticized, and often defeated. I learned of reorganizations that seemed to come with annual regularity. The Veterans Health-Care System sure changed and reorganized with some frequency. It taught me that backsliding is easy and holding onto the status quo is often painless compared with trying to accomplish real, positive change.

At my first meeting, I ventured to make a comment about the possible implications of a proposed policy change on the medical facilities in the field. A senior executive quickly cut me off by saying, "The field thinks this change should be this way" and proceeded to outline a different policy that I felt would be much more work and would ultimately be overturned. I was struck by the irony of the situation. Just the past week, I had been in the field, and this senior executive hadn't been in the field in ten years. I also learned that I needed to take notes during the meetings. Most of the chairs of these groups or their nominal leaders appeared to recount previous work agreements in ways that I felt were ambiguous or deliberately slanted. Maybe they went to check with their bosses to find out what the right answers should be. That's the most optimistic spin that I can put on it.

The VA Central Office rumor mill was also a powerful phenomenon. A case in point concerned the senior executive who knew "what the field thought"—all 185,000 of them at that time. There were numerous versions of his story. He had been a director at a major facility in the Northeast. Whatever happened in the community resulted in his transfer to VA Central Office when someone complained about his efforts to their congressman. The congressman called the VA administrator, and, as was the custom at that time, the executive was brought into Washington to be recycled. Recycled meant that after two to three years the executive would be transferred to another medical facility. This would be after his "rehabilitation" was complete.

Of course, no true rehabilitation was ever begun, and, in the most desperate cases, such as the case of this senior executive, he was not talented nor connected enough to ever be rehabilitated. I cannot say if the rumor about his past was true. When confronted, this director agreed to a lateral reassignment. This is often the case, because it avoids formal complaints, possible due process, or other types of official confrontation. Sometimes, this is the quickest and best solution to a tangled web of difficulty.

Of course, there were very talented and dedicated people who worked in the VA Central Office. They worked hard, and, fortunately for our mission and the taxpayers, they got the work done. I estimated that I had about twenty hours of "real" work a week to do. The rest of the time I devoted to self-improvement through management readings and some analytical projects of my own design. After about six months as a systems accountant, I was fed up with my various assignments, none of which involved any systems accounting work, and had landed a job as a budget analyst, also in VA Central Office. I still only had about twenty hours of work to do, so I again set out to learn as much as I could about the organization and about management. I had always considered the library to be a fringe benefit of my job, so I visited the Central Office library as often as I could. And when I worked in the VA medical centers, I made extensive use of them as well. I also sought out extra assignments and details to other areas—anything that would expand my knowledge and skills.

Seeking out extracurricular assignments was how I ended up being sent to a very small facility in eastern Colorado. This facility had been a cavalry post and had historic significance, since Kit Carson's chapel was located on its grounds. The grounds of the facility could have been a setting for a Western movie. The reason for my visit was that the director of the facility had offended the congresswoman representing that part of eastern Colorado by responding to her inquiries—which were originally driven by complaints from employees about the director's decisions and actions—with sarcastic and challenging commentary. I was part of a team sent to ferret out the truth. Of course, my team's judgments about the allegations would determine the truth.

The director was cordial but bombastic in his ridicule of our mission. He defended himself, but we had to see the documents and check out the witnesses. One of the allegations was nepotism. His son did not work for the VA but as a lifeguard at the swimming pool run by the employee's association. Another accusation was that he allowed employees to watch the movies being shown to the patients. This was true, but hard to object to given the remoteness of the facility. We couldn't determine exactly how far the nearest movie theater was, but it was at least ninety miles. He had also allowed the local Future Farmers of America from the nearest high school, seventeen miles away, to board some of their animals, including horses, in the horse barns still on site. The barns were historic and had to be maintained by the VA. The Future Farmers kept the barns up–to-date and paid a minimal fee for the privilege. This was OK, too. The director readily admitted that he had built the largest barbecue that I have ever seen with his own hands. He said that the government paid for the materials, and he built it. It was in his backyard in his assigned government quarters. He said that anyone could use it; this seemed hardly likely. We were able to verify the government's purchase of the materials. And so it went.

The letters that he sent the congresswoman were not appropriate in tone, and the director did not seem to be accepting our recommendation that more respect should be shown her. We went back to Washington and submitted our report. The director was transferred elsewhere about six months later. This VA facility is now closed. This case taught me that leadership must communicate responsibly externally and internally. I learned that the communication should stick to the facts and avoid colorful opinion. Leadership should also be most focused on the mission: health-care delivery. This director's actions did not reflect that basic, essential of clear and direct internal and external communication.

Other duties included visiting most of the emerging medical schools. During this time, Congress had funded the VA for a medical school grant program. These schools were to be nurtured by the VA and funded for a three-year period until they had achieved independence and were self-sufficient. One of the objectives was to place medical schools in medically underserved areas. This was a fascinating task. It would be more than twenty years before additional medical schools were created in this country. Like the GI bill, this was congressional legislation at its finest.

During one of these visits, the chief of staff of the local VA and the team were at dinner with some community health-care leaders. The chief of staff was telling us how he had joined the Army Reserve Medical Corps. He had promised a local recruiter that he would find at least one of his physicians to join the army reserve. When that failed, he signed up himself. This chief of staff was a charming, articulate, and sophisticated Indian. I remember the CEO of the local academic health center saying, "Why did the army take a mongrel like you?"

The chief of staff laughed and said, "They just looked at my credentials."

While taking us around his medical center, I later saw this chief of staff stop a medical resident running down the hall. The medical resident said that he had been escorting a patient from admissions to his assigned bed in the hospital. The patient needed to use the bathroom on the way and had fallen off the toilet. The resident was running to get nursing help. The chief of staff went into the bathroom, cleaned the patient up, calmed him, and saw that the nurses got him to his bed expeditiously. I was proud of him as I am all of the caring superprofessionals in the VA.

Having heard from librarians of a book about the last half of the 1940s called *Ring the Night Bell,* written by Paul B. Magnuson, MD, I checked it out of the library and started reading it. This book was about the origins of VA affiliations that emerged after WWII. I found the book to be a tough read, and it was taking several weeks to get into it. I got an overdue notice, and I called and extended the loan. After a couple more weeks, I got a call from the librarian, who asked about the book. I told her that I was reading it but had gotten busy. She said they had another customer who wanted to read it. I said, "Could I have another week or two?" She said certainly. Another librarian called at the end of two weeks and asked about the book. I was finding it hard to believe that this book could possibly be in demand. I casually asked her who wanted the book. She said Max Cleland. I was stunned. Max Cleland was the administrator of the VA! I ran the book up the three flights of stairs to the library. I have never finished reading it.

Communication was all top-down and rumor mill. What anyone in the ranks heard and when they would hear it was haphazard. Often in VA Central Office (VACO), it seemed that people heard what they wanted to hear. Others in VACO seemed to work the system by starting rumors, such as so and so is getting promoted. They sent out trial balloons just to see what happened. Learning to listen well and hear what was being said became very important to me. I wanted my communication skills to be an acknowledged strength. I thought often about the various disparate pieces of information that I received.

The lack of lateral communication in formal organizations plagues the federal government to this day. The techno-specialists, the knowledge workers, tended to work and play together as a pack. These knowledge workers specialized in a multitude of data sets generated by the large, complex VA health system, for example, the social worker whose knowledge of the policy and the data generated from the VA's community nursing program. So organizational learning was difficult. The VA Central Office building does not even have an auditorium large enough to accommodate half of its employees. And this led to the inevitable mistake of the creation of programs and other organizational occurrences that started careers or ended them. One of the most notable was the leader who created a heart transplant program and funded it without the knowledge of anyone else. The budget office received the blame when it was discovered, on the grounds that they should have informed on the executive who created the program. The executive, however, was not punished. Of course, about every two years, there would be a reorganization of some significance, and every four years, a reorganization of most of the organization. Most of this was unnecessary, but, given the habitual problems with information and communication, probably inevitable. The reasons for all of this reorganizing and lack of communication are many, but increasing someone's power base, punishing the weak, discarding the nonperforming, and holding onto the knowledge within one's own power base are all likely to be in the mix.

Sometimes the rumor mill has it right first, but more often not. A case in point was the rumored departure of Rufus Wilson, the director of veterans' benefits. As is often the case, donations were sought, and a fancy dinner was held in his honor. Every leader has critics, and every organization has those who want to be seen in the best possible light. There are some whose ambitions and intellect lead them to stiff those who are no longer in power and to caress those gaining in power, prestige, and position. Anyway, within a week after Rufus's farewell dinner, it was announced that he was being nominated to be the deputy secretary. Those who had believed that they had seen the last of Rufus and chose not to honor his prior service were stunned, resentful, and remorseful that they had failed in this primal organization task: to be seen and to mingle with those achieving higher rungs of power.

About this same time, I came to know and respect the woman who was rumored to be Rufus's mistress. She was well-educated and intelligent. She had been Rufus's secretary once upon a time, and, when her marriage failed, the story I picked up in the halls was that she began the affair with him. She was naïve about the motivations of much of what went on around her but got her work done and was a good source of information and intelligence about what was going on in the organization and beyond. Most of my colleagues avoided her for fear that a misplaced statement would get to Rufus and their careers would be over before they knew it. But, from my own experience, the lady was trustworthy and meant to do only good for our organization. We would remain friends and associates until she retired.

Rufus was a fine leader and a humorist. He had lost an eye in the service and wore a black patch. His story, however, was that this came about when he had been invited to deliver the sermon one Sunday at his church. About halfway through what he thought was a highly motivating and moving sermon, the preacher's wife in the chorus up in the balcony was overcome with the vapors and fell over the railing. Her feet got entangled in the railing, and she dangled there upside down, her robes and dress cascading down over her head. The preacher leapt to his feet and screamed, "Whosoever looks upon my wife's naked body shall be smitten blind!" Rufus thought that he would risk one eye.

My work continued to be directly associated with budget and data. We had a rudimentary automated bookkeeping system that maintained our accounts. But historical data and decisions were still recorded in large black ledgers. Not much had ever been recorded, and, as people retired or left the budget office, the remaining memories dimmed and were too often left to the vagaries of minds preoccupied with other pursuits.

One of the pursuits was alcohol, which precluded a number of analysts and their supervisors from having a cogent thought—especially on Fridays after lunch. The office was known for this alcohol binging, so Friday afternoons were often dilatory at best. I did not "drink" lunch, as this became known, and I was the one contacted in emergencies when some issue or other simply could not wait. I also got the verbal abuse directed at me from my colleagues who engaged in the drunken lunches. They felt that I should have told their customers seeking information to expect a call back. For me, the rebukes were part of the learning process. Once in a while, there were casualties: people so drunk that they didn't come back after lunch or that they missed their buses or carpools and thereby had to explain to their families what had happened to them.

The budget office Christmas parties were notoriously rowdy, drunken affairs. I paid, but I never attended. My family would go to Miami for Christmas with the grandparents. I was concerned about the drinking and the mandatory financial surcharge assigned to every member of the office, whether or not they attended the party or even drank. The parties were legendary. This outlandish practice during the Christmas holidays would last about five more years. The culture changed.

Management was chaotic. Each manager led through his own idiosyncratic style. The need to improve processes and do something for staff education or employee assistance was evident. Information sharing was nearly accidental. No one in a leadership position wanted to hear it.

In hindsight, this was really a transition time—not only to more professional management and financial management, but into computerization. The changes and the challenges caused significant turmoil. In the following decade, new staff with better skills produced better results with improved productivity, and the retirement of many of the good ol' boys changed the Friday lunch drinking for the better as well.

I had also become the point of contact for full-time employee equivalents (FTEEs). We had used FTEEs, of course, in our daily budget work and in submitting budgets along with headcount, but the computers that ran our payroll had never before computed an FTEE. Having an actual FTEE to compare against our budget guesstimates was a huge step forward, but also scary in that our own budget estimates— which could be rationalized and debated in a number of ways—would now be compared to an actual. Some of the creative license in our work would be lost. The FTEE data would be reliable. It would truly be an actual.

Two of us were assigned to this task for the VA. I had the medical care appropriation, where the vast majority of VA employees worked. A fine management analyst and future senior executive, Art Hammerslag, had all the rest. It was quite a career coupe for us. I suppose that the old timers thought it would go away. So Art and I kept our flip charts up-to-date, and every two weeks he would brief his executive officers on this new FTEE concept and I would brief the chief medical director, Dr. Crutcher. Incredibly, none of the other top managers were interested in FTEE, so very often it was just the chief medical director and me. He had been brought from the VA medical center in Atlanta to be the chief medical director. The rumor was that he had helped treat Max Cleland, the VA administrator, and Max had been impressed. But Dr. Crutcher seemed to be in over his head. He gazed at my charts and seemed to understand where we were going. The last time I met with him, he said to me, "Fred, you know this job is impossible." I took that as a cue to pack up my flip charts.

The next week the rumors were that the medical school dean at Harvard got credit for the kill because he had called the then VA administrator and the chairman of the appropriations committee demanding Crutcher's removal, and soon thereafter Dr. Crutcher was gone. Dr. Crutcher was probably doomed from the beginning. He came from too far down in the organization to its very top. Dr. Crutcher was a concerned, competent, and caring physician, but he was not a diplomat, nor was he learned in the bureaucratic arts. In vast regions of the nation, a plain-spoken, direct, physician leader is admired. That's much too dangerous in Washington.

What would Drucker think of all of this? He would remind us that hierarchical organizational structures can confuse the simplest of communications. Everyone hears the basic message and puts it into their personal context and understanding. Drucker said that this "aggravates the danger." The danger is that anything a manager says is interpreted as sincere, premeditated, and important. What was important to the top bureaucrats? The absence of embarrassment is easily the bureaucrat's foremost concern. The legions of political appointees are often quite representative of the nation in their background and regional allegiance but seldom have health-care management skills and are always motivated to impress their political bosses.

To the rest of us, the political appointees talked of their skills and power, but too often knew nothing about health care. Sometimes, they viewed this ignorance as a virtue. They seemed committed to taming the bureaucracy and bureaucrats. So they didn't listen well or enough. They took to the power and perquisites of their job as if they were princes born to the realm. If they were educable, they learned too little and too late. So by the time they are useful, too often the administration changes and they depart.

Chapter 7
1980–1981: Getting More Training

As luck would have it, I was awarded entry into the assistant director training program. Someone somewhere decided to do me a favor and assigned me to train at the VA medical center in Miami. Perhaps they noticed that I had graduated from high school in Miami. I took this assignment to be a blessing for my young family, now of two boys and a girl, since we would be moving to the home of my wife's parents and knew that this assignment would only be for a year or two at the most.

We arrived the day after the riots in Miami had concluded. From my wife's parents' home, we could see the smoke rising over the part of the city where the VA medical center was located. On my first day at work, the National Guard was still patrolling the parking lots. The Marielitos were still escaping from Cuba. It was an unsettling and restless time in a crime-ridden community on edge. Still, we were pleased to be there. Our three children dearly loved their grammy and papa.

The Miami VA Medical Center had a warm, comfortable feeling from the very start. Part of the reason was that more than anywhere else in my goofy childhood, Miami had been home. But the larger part of the reason was that my dad had died in the medical center in 1974. He had cancer in the nose, which had metastasized to his brain. He called the bumps on his head cancer berries. I had been able to spend two weeks with him before he passed. He received extraordinary care.

The work at the VA was extraordinary. Everyone opened their arms and hearts to me. Some remembered my father dying there in 1974. An extraordinary director, Tom Doherty, ran the show. We formed a bond that will last a lifetime. His deputy, Andy Montano, was an educator at heart and instilled in me the values of learning on the job and, more particularly, the value of research. I met the chief of medicine, Eliseo Perez-Stable. We were friends until his death. A kind, warm, brilliant, and remarkable man, he personified calm, intelligent, and personable managerial communication for me.

The first crisis at the VA medical center in Miami emerged suddenly. The White House—probably meaning some obscure bureaucrat connected to the White House—decided that the Marielitos should be housed in the Orange Bowl, which was about five or six blocks from the VA medical center. And those powers that be had also decided that the VA would provide their health care. The director, Tom Doherty, stopped this immediately and told VA Central Office in impossible-to-not-understand terms that the VA in Miami would not be providing their health care. Mr. Doherty was, of course, threatened. I was concerned. My director was essentially putting his career at risk in defying both VA Central Office and the White House. Instead, his refusal had caused them to reevaluate their decision.

The VA medical centers were created to take care of U.S. veterans and did not have enough funding to provide care in the way that it should have been done. The Marielitos were refugees—in what was a political attempt by Castro to embarrass President Jimmy Carter. Although the media reported mostly on the mentally ill and criminals included in the Mariel Boat Lift, nearly all of these refugees would establish productive and responsible lives in this country. Even so, putting them in the VA medical center at the expense of this nation's veterans would have been a national disgrace.

A second crisis emerged, and I got to play more of a role in carrying out the director's orders. In the past few years, off-site and nontraditional clinics had been set up to serve Vietnam veterans who wouldn't use the VA. One of these clinics had been set up in Ft. Lauderdale. This vet center or readjustment counseling center had been taken over by a motorcycle gang, who was using the facility to hang out and to conduct drug deals. They intimidated the majority of beneficiaries who really needed its services. The vet center leader had called Tom Doherty and outlined the situation.

Tom's courageous decision was to close the vet center and to send trucks up the very next morning to pack up and store all the furniture and records. The courageous part was that VA Central Office's approval was not sought; no white papers were written. The deed was done, virtually overnight. And from all I learned, it needed to be done. When the new vet center opened, with security much improved, everyone was pleased. Tom Doherty had proven that he was an effective and risk-taking decision maker.

As I rapidly learned, the Miami VA Medical Center was an exciting and vibrant place to work and learn. We had employee-employee fights, patient-employee fights, patient-patient fights, and, once in a while, family-patient fights. This was a true reflection of the community, and, like the community, we were a melting pot of ethnicities, races, and strata of society—with all the myriad variables thrown in for good measure. When incidents are investigated, nobody remembered anything. Our investigations invariably yielded very little in the way of documentation or evidence of what had actually transpired. Many of our employees led difficult lives financially, and, with the crime, traffic, and cost of living thrown into the mix, their lives were stressed. For many of our employees, their jobs at the VA were a respite from their fear- and concern-filled lives.

One day while I was serving as acting director, a group of motorcycle gang members came to see me. The leader of this pack had already been through various VA officials, complaining of stomach pain. He had had surgery some months before at the VA, and, during the operation, the resident surgeon had cut his intestine several times to release a buildup of some kind of gas. I never learned how the gas had been erroneously put there during this veteran's procedure. This error had been extensively examined, but the motorcycle gang leader wanted to press his point and he did. I listened stoically, apologized profusely, and told the man that we would have his case again reexamined by outside experts. He left with his gang. It was only later that I realized how serious that situation was. I was told later by a seasoned VA nurse that very often all that caused such men to moderate their behavior was being with their former comrades in arms. I am convinced that this leader died a violent death or is serving out his prison sentence on death row. I felt his physical threat directly. I felt very lucky that I had not been attacked on the way home that evening. Fortunately, there are few veterans like him.

Another situation that stayed with me while I was acting associate director happened when a nice-looking elderly woman came into the office. She was in tears. She had been through many other staff on her way to get to me. Her husband had died in the hospital that morning. He had served in the Navy for over thirty years. They had had a wonderful life together. But he was still legally married to someone else. He had never gotten a divorce. She wanted to receive his pension. She cried when I told her that there was absolutely nothing that the VA could do for her and suggested that she get a lawyer. The lesson I learned was that long before a loved one enters the hospital, an understanding must be reached on formalizing the marriage, a living will, and funeral specifics.

Former Marines stopped by the office on a regular basis. The director had been in the Marines and had retired from the Marine Reserve. His reputation drew them to his office. They would look at his memorabilia, say a few words to him, and be on their way. Mr. Doherty held the Navy Cross, and many of his visitors were also decorated. One day the president of the Medal of Honor Society came in.

One day, Claude Pepper, the congressional representative and former U.S. Senator, came in to wish us happy holidays. He sent us cards regularly. Now deceased, his legacy lives on in the minds of those who had the privilege of meeting him and in the National Institute of Aging grant that bears his name. To my knowledge, all of these American heroes, the Marine veterans, the Medal of Honor Society, and Claude Pepper, held the VA in very high esteem.

One of the most memorable events in my career happened when we admitted a woman who was a WWI veteran. We processed her, admitted her, started her therapy, and provided nursing services in the same way we would have provided them to any other eligible veteran. I was acting director when the call came in from Jim Christian, the executive assistant to the chief medical director. He said, "Say it ain't so, Fred."

I asked, "Say what ain't so?"

"That there's a Rolls Royce parked in front of the hospital under the canopy," Jim replied.

"I can't do that, Jim. There is a Rolls Royce parked in front of the hospital under the canopy," I told him.

"Why?" he asked.

"Because we admitted Taylor Caldwell, the romance novelist, and that's her Rolls Royce."

Jim continued in his usual calm, professional manner, but there was a certain tightness in his voice that I took to mean that he was very concerned over the possible political fallout.

All of us had heard resentment about the so called Cadillac veterans getting served by the VA. Some of the VA's critics thought these Cadillac veterans did not need services from the VA. Because there were few women who had served, and those who had served were in occupations that generally kept them out of harm's way, it was rare that a woman would incur a service-related injury that would qualify her to be seen by the VA. And at the time, even fewer of these women thought themselves eligible for treatment at the VA.

All of this has long since changed, but, at the time, Jim had every reason to be concerned. I assured Jim that she was an eligible veteran. I asked him how he knew about the Rolls Royce. He said that the OMB budget examiner had been reading the *Washington Post* that morning and had noticed an item about a Rolls Royce parked in front of the Miami VA. I subsequently learned that the day before the *Miami Herald* had published the same item in its gossip column. Unlike the OMB budget examiner, none of us had time to read the gossip column and so did not see the item which asked: "Who's Rolls Royce is it?" I told Jim that we had to park it out front under the canopy because that was the only place we could have reasonable assurance that the car would still be there when she needed it.

Of course, there was more to the story. I subsequently relayed the rest of the story to Jim Christian in VA Central Office and have had the pleasure of telling it many times. Taylor Caldwell was at her mansion in Palm Beach when she had a stroke. The physician at the hospital was telling her husband that she would need extensive rehabilitation. The husband asked, "Where's the best place to get these services?"

The physician replied, "It's too bad she's not a veteran, because the best place would be the Miami VA."

To that, Ms. Caldwell's husband replied, "Well, she is a veteran, and that's where we'll go."

Taylor Caldwell's stay would only last about five days. Her husband was her fifth and considerably younger husband. Her two adult daughters finally tracked her down. The daughters seemingly did not approve of the fifth husband's actions regarding their mother. The husband spirited her out of the hospital in the night.

A few weeks later, a car was stolen from our campus. A Miami Dolphin, an All-Pro, was visiting patients during the annual celebration of the national Salute to Veterans. When he came out, his car was gone. He was pleasant about it. At the Miami VA Medical Center at that time, such felonies were a common occurrence.

One day, the director asked me to take a call that turned out to be from Quanita Edwards, the *Miami Herald* environmental reporter. She asked me if it was true that the research labs were pouring toxic materials down the drain. "Oh no, we follow the most rigid federal guidelines for disposing of toxic wastes," I told her. "I'll check into it and get back to you with what I've found, but I really don't think so," I responded somewhat feebly. Ms. Edwards listened patiently and said that there was report of this from the Miami Fire Department. I tried to reassure her, and we concluded the call.

Alas, I found out that the practice of throwing toxic wastes down the drain in research was common. I talked to the administrative officer in research and the engineering department. We developed a way to cause mandatory compliance with waste disposal requirements. I followed up with the researchers involved. These technicians felt that the associate director's wife had ratted them out. She worked in the research labs too. There was definitely some ill will between the couple and research. Research ironically was Associate Director Montano's cause célèbre. He was saddened, but I learned that research activities had to be carefully monitored. Researchers wanted to do their research, and, for too many years, they saw the regulations and procedures as impediments to doing that.

Another day, I was asked to escort Rob Sweeting, a reporter for CNN, around the medical center. He toured many areas of the hospital. When I was escorting him through the outpatient area, one of our African American clerks said to no one in particular: "Who's the colored reporter?"

Rob pivoted around and said, "I haven't heard that word in a long time." And he smiled.

I thought, "What class!" This reporter could have rebuked us all on the spot.

His report reflected how busy and active the Miami VA Medical Center was.

I was learning how to talk to the various constituencies within the medical center and its community. A big part of that was customer service. So I learned much about customer service through reading and practicing what I read. I learned to say no gracefully. I already had empathy and was genuinely concerned about the issues. I began to keep a list of regulations that could be tweaked by VACO or Congress to ease the burden for those veterans who fell through the cracks. Many years later, the VA established a database for these various complaints and compliments. Some staff truly become burned out from the difficulty of saying no to admissions, to nursing home care, to prosthetics, and so forth—all because of eligibility restrictions.

One day, I was the fourth or fifth person to say no to a small, desperate woman who had reached her limit for caregiving for her husband. She accepted my no with quiet composure and left. We found out hours later that she hadn't taken her wheelchair-bound veteran husband with her. She had left him in a corridor off the main outpatient waiting area. He couldn't really make himself understood, but we put the pieces of the puzzle together and admitted him to the nursing home, despite the previous denial. I was later told that this happened with some frequency.

Caregivers need care and attention before they get burned out. Leaving loved ones who can't communicate in hospitals can have disastrous consequences. These forced choices on the part of caregivers are the terrible consequence of the maze of regulations and authorities, not just in the VA but throughout health care. Despite the fact that abandoning a patient is patient abuse, the often elderly caregivers need more support. Thankfully, programs in the VA exist today to support caregivers and provide respite care for their spouses.

My learning would not have been complete without the able assistance from HR and the incredibly rich mix of issues involving human resources and relations. Our human resources service was challenged by a high turnover among its specialists. The city's problems and cost of living caused the turnover. HR's heavy workload was another reason. The full array and complexity of the HR staff reflected the diversity of Miami.

At any time, the community's issues could spill over into the medical center. An example of this was presented to me early that summer of 1980 when word came down from VA Central Office to terminate all summer employees. Almost all of these summer employees were from the same areas where the riots had occurred. Apparently, the staff director of the House Appropriations Committee, which dealt with Veterans Affairs, had noticed that the Veterans Health Administration was over its budgeted full-time equivalent employee (FTEE) level. This was the cumulative average number of employees on duty and paid, reflecting full-time and part-time and so forth.

We provided a strong rationale for why we should be an exception to this cutback of summer employment throughout the VA. It wasn't good enough. We delivered the message to our summer employees as thoughtfully and tactfully as possible. There were no incidents related to this required action. Nevertheless, it was bad public policy and could have resulted in a severe incident.

All in all, I had some great training and remain grateful to the Miami VA Medical Center and its caring, professional staff for providing me with this wonderful opportunity. I was involved in every aspect of the management of that medical center.

One of the emerging issues that would consume a large portion of my work in the future was centralized electronic data processing. I saw firsthand how centralization impeded innovation and local problem solving. The VA medical center in Miami was fortunate to have received an automated clinical laboratory system. called clin lab, or clinical laboratory. It ran lab results and stored them for most blood tests. It improved the documentation in recording lab results. This computer application illustrated the perils involved in giving too much control to contracts and contract administrators remote to the real action.

Clin lab was universally hated because the negatives far outweighed the benefits. The program was more work and aggravation than it was worth. The required human factors overwhelmed the benefits of automation. Each automated program moved the level of work and understanding to the next level, where insights revealed many other possible improvements and refinements. It taught me how not to do technology management.

In *The Essential Drucker*, Drucker writes that the coming of the computer puts the decision makers further removed from the action. He adds that the decision maker should go and look at the reality. If he does not, then "he will be increasingly divorced from reality." Drucker's book was published by Harper Business, New York, in 2001.

Chapter 8
1981–1984: Chief Operating Officer, I

In 1981 I was transferred to the VA medical center in Dublin, Georgia. I became a chief operating officer, or, as the job is called in the VA, associate director. This assignment was designed to be a feeder position to become a director or chief executive officer. The role allowed me to play a larger part in the health-care activities as a whole and so to make a bigger, more positive difference.

At first, I was able to simply ply my organizational skills to improve the way my part of the organization functioned. The CEO, my boss, would give me direct assignments, and it was my job to make sure these issues were personally handled to his satisfaction. But listening and learning also allow me to think dangerous thoughts—like the idea that my boss could stand a lot of improvement. I entered into this work tenuously and quickly learned that doing it right was frustrating, unappreciated, and highly likely to be misinterpreted.

My view was that I was there to learn and to solve problems. Unfortunately, the leader at that facility couldn't stand to be wrong and therefore deflected his mistakes to me. I eventually came to the opinion that he was a narcissist; in his mind, he could do no wrong. Maybe if the staff and I respected his achievements more, this wouldn't have been so excruciating.

If there were certain areas of the management of the health facility that he could have concentrated upon other than engineering, it might have lessened the negative impact on me and to a lesser extent others. But he always placed himself in the position of critic and never joined in to develop solutions to problems. Perhaps he felt threatened by me. His management efforts were to curry favor among the staff, but also to deliver unto them his solutions, which they were then expected to own. He inflicted tedious, continuous reviews of situations or problems that seemed to threaten him the most. My constant reading of health-care journal articles seemed to threaten him. Unable to control myself, I left articles on the top of my desk with topics such as "How to Manage Your Boss" and "How to Exert Positive Leadership." These never failed to catch his attention.

After having been blindsided by his claims that I had not read any directive or memo in a timely fashion, I started dating them along with my initials. This caused him to begin backdating his reads of these same documents. Nevertheless, I served loyally as a recipient of his blame, and my continued my attempts to improve him (e.g., his very stilted manner of presentation), while frequently backfiring, seemed at some level to be appreciated by the senior leadership of the medical center.

Once, for example, he presented a facility update to service organization leaders, or visiting VA executives. He showed detailed slides—often approximately a hundred of them—to illustrate every minor improvement project in the facility. He seldom talked about patient care or used any data. Our facility had a beautiful avenue of flags, and one day I mentioned to him that including some slides of our very beautiful avenue of flags would be an enhancement to his presentation. He readily agreed. In his next presentation, there were about 150 slides. Approximately fifty of the slides were of the avenue of flags and another hundred or so of his facility projects. It was deadly, droning on and on.

During this time, I was also involved in additional, advanced training provided by the VA to enhance my abilities to take on more challenging assignments. The program introduced me to new literature that certainly increased my understanding of health care. I joined the American College of Healthcare Executives, which also enhanced my exposure to health care and its issues.

The one really dazzling part of this education was a trip to visit my assigned mentor, who was the director of the VA medical center in Albany, New York. I was given the freedom to visit with all of the service chiefs. Most notably, I learned about the decentralized hospital computer program (DHCP). Because of centralization of all computer funding and control of expenditures and no funding available for computers or software in the medical centers, there emerged a loose regional group within the VA health system called the underground railroad, devoted to developing the programming and software that would allow for a true clinical database and information management system.

Albany was among the four or five sites for the VA's clinical computer underground railroad. They were responsible for the lab and diagnostic imaging. The nuclear medicine service, utilizing biomedical engineering trainees or interns from Rensselaer Polytechnic Institute, wrote code using the Massachusetts General Hospital Utility Multi-Programming System (MUMPS) to write its nuclear medicine programming. The other sites used MUMPS as well and formed a cooperative dedicated to furthering this user-developed software to get their jobs done better, including improving patient care.

One nagging source of concern was with human resources service, the providers of personnel services to staff and advice to management. Rumors had circulated wildly about the chief of HR, most likely due to his demeanor and reputation within the broad employee population. They didn't like him, and I was to find out that I didn't respect him either. One rumor had it that he was growing marijuana on our campus and that his family had left him because of his pot smoking. Another rumor was that illegal appointments to government service had been made while he was in charge. So I spent much time running these rumors to the ground and responding to the various inquiries, including congressional.

Finally, I asked the CEO for an external review. He reluctantly agreed. The senior, very able human resources officer who conducted the review found four illegal appointments that had been signed by the human resources officer via his signature machine. Of course, there was no way of knowing who had actually operated the signature machine. The review recommended that the chief be reassigned; however, he was widely known to be the nephew of an extremely prominent congressman with a highly visible and prestigious chairmanship. Despite this, he was laterally transferred to a less-demanding assignment, and various other disciplinary actions were taken on those human resource specialists who had facilitated these illegal appointments.

The next step was to select a new chief of human resource management. Shortly after the new chief's arrival, I found myself outside the day-to-day communications loop for human resources issues. Finally, the recently appointed new chief told me that the CEO had told him to communicate directly with him and only to him. This, despite the fact that the illegal appointments had occurred on my director's watch, not mine. I was the one to finally discover and correct the problem. I have never learned why he did this. Perhaps the CEO would have preferred to let matters lie, perhaps he lied to our superiors and blamed the illegal appointments on me, or perhaps it was simply because his usual preference was to micromanage until something went awry.

In a small town like Dublin, Georgia, it's difficult to separate what happens in the community from the VA. Certainly, race relations were not at the level of other places that I have lived. Trying to be fair to everyone was difficult. This is especially true when many of the highest-ranking VA employees maintained an attitude of racial intolerance that made for some trying times for me and for my family. During my three years in Dublin, I made decisions that probably made the director uncomfortable. Unfortunately, since I was an associate director, he controlled my career.

Having grown tired of some of the social requirements brought on by living on campus, we decided to move off campus, buying a house that was a bargain. The people who owned it had learned that a Black couple from Miami had purchased the house next door. She was an attorney, and he was a public schools administrator. An Indian couple—he was the VA chief of medicine—had already purchased the house on the other side. We moved in and enjoyed our time there, but we were among the very few people in Dublin who would have bought that house, and that was undoubtedly the reason the house was for sale. The Indian family and the Black professional couple were friendly, generous, and were constantly improving their property. Even so, it took us a long, long time to sell that house after I was transferred. The financial sacrifice rolled on for the three long years that it took to sell the house after we had moved.

The Dublin VA Medical Center has a 200-bed domiciliary. This was my first direct experience in managing a minimal medical model facility. Many of the members, as they were called, had mental or behavioral health problems. The domiciliary maintained them at far less cost than any other institutional setting. Some were able to restore themselves to the community and hold jobs. Others paced the campus endlessly, smoking.

One, a World War II veteran, kept a picture of a beautiful Asian girl on his nightstand. It was heavily discolored from the constant cigarette smoke. I wondered about the circumstances that led to his pacing. Was he from Middle Georgia and knew that the love of his life would never be accepted at home? Or had he been unwilling to take the chance? I'll never know.

Another member, called Slick, seemed capable and was certainly affable, agreeing to anything put forth to him. He had been at the Thomasville Domiciliary until it closed in the mid-sixties, a result of Lyndon Johnson's effort to close antiquated VA facilities. Slick moved about the community, often getting himself into photographs that appeared in the newspaper. Sometimes, the newspapers edited Slick out, and all that could be seen was the vacant space where he used to be.

Most of the members were alcoholics, recovering or hiding out. Their wasted lives, regrets, misused talents, and lost ambitions were always apparent. Sometimes, they would act out, betraying their families or employee supports again, and some would end up back with us after they had finished yet another alcohol treatment program.

"Effectiveness must be learned," accorded Drucker in his book. He also taught me that I was a knowledge worker—for whom effectiveness was the primary charge. Knowledge workers were expected to get the right things done. But knowledge workers are often absent from knowledge jobs. I strived to be effective and to do the right things right. It did not seem that many of my colleagues bothered with the study of management through self-directed reading. Some of them simply rationalized their way to why things weren't done by assigning blame, afraid of someone above them taking swift and certain retribution.

In their analysis, doing nothing was OK unless they were otherwise directed. Doing very little unless directed was and is a survival tactic, and it will remain, because only those venturing forth with ideas and proposals get held accountable—and then only sometimes. Effectively learning the Byzantine ways that bureaucracies and their leaders act and react, sometimes in the absence of accurate organizational insight, is also a survival tactic.

Chapter 9
1984–1986: Chief Operating Officer, II

The bureaucracy promoted me to a much larger medical center in Albany, New York. Located in the state capital, the medical center had an academic affiliation, a strong research program, and was in the midst of a management transition. I was not especially pleased with this assignment, but I was certainly anxious to get to it, get through it, and meet the next management challenge. I arrived at the assignment without my family, who stayed so that the children could finish the school year. This allowed me to spend a lot of time getting familiar with the organization.

The gentleman that I replaced never discarded a document. The room was cluttered with papers, directives, folders, reports, and so forth. The window sills were full of papers. The room brightened considerably after I had finished reviewing them all and throwing them away. When I had worked with him in VA Central Office, he had achieved lasting fame by walking around one morning with his zipper down. Several of us had tried to tell him, but he brushed us off by saying, "You guys are always trying to make me look bad." In my view, he really didn't need any help with that. This chief operating officer had preceded the concepts of Lake Woebegone by several years. His direct reports were rated outstanding, way beyond and above average. Even though he was displeased with several of them, he never told them directly. He summoned them all, the good and the bad, and ranted very generally, so no one could possibly take personal offense. This favored tactic was described in my initial briefings with the director and personnel officer. The new CEO, who only preceded me by a few months, seemed unable to understand the management decisions that he made. So my predecessor as chief operating officer had retired, reluctantly, leaving an organization untouched by his views, beliefs, and actions.

The CEO was kind and gracious. He was intelligent and ambitious. He had already taken on the daunting task of changing the middle management and the top clinical leadership of the medical center. The clinical leadership had been changed nearly in its entirety. He had transformed the facility plant's strategic planning by throwing most of it out and implementing projects necessary to make the facility state-of-the-art for the delivery of acute and outpatient care.

The CEO and his wife had me over for dinner. We had a gracious and pleasant evening. I met their two children. Then the chief of staff and his wife had me over for dinner. I met their two children. The chief of the psychology service and his wife had the chief of psychiatry and me over for dinner. The events helped indoctrinate me into what the director seemed to intend to be a kind but firm, hardworking but fun, do-the-right-thing kind of health-care management team.

My first social dinner in town, however, was provided by the chief of voluntary service. We had corned beef and cabbage. I loved it. The voluntary service officer regaled me with war stories, his view on how the medical center should be run, how one of my predecessors had broken her toe kicking her desk in frustration over his antics, his many, many years of alcohol use, and his eventual transition to complete sobriety. He told me of his involvement with the community and his relationship with the local Democratic Party. I left knowing for an absolutely certainty that I had a big problem because of his boastful nature, his impetuousness, and his overwrought passion for "helping." I also worried about the truthfulness of the man's statements, since I perceived that he tended to exaggerate.

That spring, I saw firsthand one of the problems that the chief of voluntary service was creating. I learned that for years he had been collecting all the flowers at the Albany Flower Show and bringing them to the VA. Although this was an ambitious undertaking, the matter had never been discussed by leadership. The chief housekeeping office was particularly annoyed, as it placed extra demands on his staff and introduced all kinds of allergens and potential accidents into the hospital. The gesture was nice, to be sure, but the plants arrived slightly aged and most did not last half a day. This practice, although a time-honored tradition by then, was finally stopped.

My first serious discussion with the CEO was interesting. He told me that he would have never picked me to be his COO. I understood why he felt that way because in some respects we were opposites, but I never knew why he told me that. It seemed counterproductive. Our VA Central Office health-care organization maintained the management right to select associate directors and directors as well as other key officials without any local collaboration, let alone concurrence. This has now long since been changed, but direct assignments sometimes still occur, as VA Central Office exercises its power to know what is best for those in a particular facility.

I told my CEO that I would have never picked him either. This seemed to unsettle him a little, but he ventured on with his expectations for the job that I was to do. There was nothing that I felt was unreasonable or unrealizable in his expectations. And my first impression, confirmed many times since, was that he was a decent, caring, forthright, and dedicated person. He also told me that he wanted me to stay in this new assignment for two years and that the job was mostly about learning how to be a CEO. I left his office better prepared to do my duty, but somewhat perplexed about exactly how I was going to meet his expectations.

The next week I received a call from Dr. John Ditzler. Dr. Ditzler was a physician for whom I had worked in my previous assignment in headquarters. After we had exchanged pleasantries, Dr. Ditzler asked me to become the director of resource management in what was then the Department of Medicine and Surgery in VA Central Office. He was becoming the new chief medical director in the VA. I said I had just been on the job for two weeks. He said not to worry, that this would take awhile. I worried very much. I accepted. I told my family. They were not happy. After about ten days, I summoned enough courage to tell my CEO. He was not happy. My family, who had just joined me in New York, were not ready to move again so quickly. My boss wanted me to stay for at least two years. Ironically, this unsettling set of affairs lasted for two years, at which point I started the job and had another long separation from my family so that the children could finish their school year.

One day while the CEO was out, I was summoned to a conference call at the direction of a supervisor in our VA Central Office, Office of Facilities. The call was about our major construction project, entitled Modify Wards. Modify Wards, like almost all of the VA's construction titles, was something of a misnomer, since it renovated all of the wards, replaced the heating system, and added air-conditioning. All in all, this project would cost more than $10 million dollars. The voices from Washington said to obligate the architect design portion of the project. I questioned this. I was told to do it. There were several people at their end of the conference call, all of them in positions of authority, and only me at my end. I said OK.

I went to my office and immediately wrote up a report of contact, outlining in detail what had been asked of us. I sent copies to the director and the chief of engineering service. I called our chief of contracting and handed him his copy of the report of contact. He wasn't happy and was just as concerned as I had been. He said he would get the contract for the design obligated, and he did. My boss came back and initiated a long series of questions about this transaction. I thank God to this day for the written report of contact.

As this contract passed through the multiple layers of review in our headquarters, the criticism at the manner in which this change occurred affected my work life for several weeks. Helpful folks in VA Central Office and the medical center told me that my career would end. Of course, they were simply speculating, but I feared for sure my career might be stalled at the very least. But, in any case, my boss stood by me, or rather, in front of me. He went to Washington to explain the actual circumstances. He took on much criticism. He never flinched in his position that the unauthorized contract problem was not my responsibility or the responsibility of the local medical center, but rather that of the headquarters staff involved and who had in fact initiated the conference call.

VA Central Office appointed an investigation board to determine the facts of the unauthorized contract and to recommend appropriate discipline. They interviewed me and my contracting officer. They interviewed the people who had been on the other end of the call in Washington. I was later to find out that they all had no recall of the events. They all had no reason to state why the medical center had caused that design contract to be awarded. Only months later did I learn that my contracting officer had gotten a written reprimand. The contract stood, and nothing negative happened overtly for my CEO or for me.

I received a call from one of the health-care specialists who had been on the call, questioning why I testified that he was on that call. How could I be so mistaken? I told him that I wasn't mistaken, and that if he wanted to pursue that line, he would have to do it on his own. I suppose he was afraid that he would be caught in his own lie, but his resentment rang through in every word. Years later, largely because of my habit of reading multiple newspapers on most days, I learned that the project manager for our construction project who had led the discussion on the conference call was convicted of fraud and other counts in federal court. He then fled to Greece and had to be extradited, a process that took two to three years.

While I was working in Albany, a parolee was serving his community service sentence with the VA medical center. He was assigned to voluntary service and essentially worked as a volunteer. He had been convicted of conspiring to rig milk prices in New York State. He was also an investor and developer in real estate. Near the end of his time with us, he donated the wiring of the building for cable TV, which included cable-ready hookups for each patient bedroom and waiting room. This meant that when we were ready to do so, we could have a full cable system without spending appropriated funds.

This novel idea was excellent. I have always wondered why at least some white-collar felons weren't sentenced to serve their time at the VA. It would be a great learning experience for them, and serving those who served would be a daily reminder of the choices and sacrifices made by others. This arrangement, which required the sentence to be served at the VA medical center, was greatly facilitated by Linda Blumenstock, our public affairs officer. An inventive and dedicated employee, Linda made things happen and kept delicate jobs moving in the right direction with style and personal commitment.

In most medical centers, the hiring, disciplining, and other difficult, often resource-driven decision making consumes the day-to-day operations. Often it is the sentinel events (significant adverse patient occurrences), the variances from the norm, upon which employees and the external community become focused. Doing a great job with courtesy and style is often taken for granted. The upsets caused by sentinel events are often what create permanent changes, and hopefully improvements, in the environment of day-to-day operations.

Sentinel events play an important role in leadership. Sometimes managers will not do the right thing because of resistance from their employees. They then try to put the situation back on some committee's agenda, or perhaps they will tweak a process outlined in policy. No one is the wiser until a critical sentinel event occurs. Top management must stay involved and be vigilant in understanding these cases. Good managers make the most of these memorable occasions and realize the gains offered by lessons learned.

During this time, I learned of the work of F. Edwards Deming, one of the founders of the continuous quality improvement movement, first in Japan and then in this country. I resolved to incorporate this philosophy of continuous quality improvement into my management style.

Of course, I still read Drucker. Drucker also philosophized about continuous quality improvement, but he chose not to delve into jargon or the fadish movements that management consultants in general are so prone to market. I do not believe that continuous quality improvement was such a fad. I think that quality improvement is a basic management tool. Drucker believed that we were in a period of management transformation. The recent journey of health care toward improved patient safety and computerized medical records continues the transformation begun by the quality improvement movement. To him, it didn't matter whether it was the emergence of Japan, or computers, or anything else; transforming the organization was the key. With his emphasis on managing information and change as the manager's responsibility, Drucker anticipated the quality movement. He was talking to our top leaders, and, as usual, they were not listening. Fortunately for health care, Dr. Berwick, the president of the Institute for Healthcare Improvement, and others were listening.

During this period as a chief operating officer, I learned to deal with the vagaries of various key personnel. I realized managing highly talented but sometimes erratic and always individualistic professionals took finesse, and I saw how picking the right people for the right job was critical. This is especially so in the federal government, because it is very hard to get rid of a problem employee.

One day the CEO came to me and said that my secretary had

to go. Since she filled in for his secretary in her absence, he told me that he needed someone more talented and more acceptable than my secretary. My secretary was nervous, and she smoked. Those were the two unacceptable traits as far as I could tell. I said I would get her reassigned. In two days' time, I had worked out a reassignment, and, on the third day, I told her she was being reassigned. She cried a little and made a number of jerky movements with her hands, which were natural enough emotions at a time like that.

Just after she left my office, the CEO rushed in and said, "Don't talk to her."

I asked, "Why not?"

He said that his secretary had just told him that my secretary had lost her baby during the night.

I said, "It's too late."

He was visibly empathetic, and certainly he meant well. Timing is so important. Bad news doesn't get better with age.

My former secretary and I stayed friends. She was much less nervous in her new assignment and had some avenues for possible advancement. I picked a new secretary about the time that I was moving to Washington for my second tour. The chief medical director had kept his word and made me his director of resource management. My successor ended up having to fire the secretary that I had hired. Was it me? Was it the job? Was it personal circumstances? I will never know which of us, her accepting the job or me hiring her, made the bigger mistake.

The current vogue phrase is "What is the take-home?" For me, it's getting the job done. Drucker said that the effective person focuses on contribution. He or she works, but he or she should pause to consider the organization's goals. Drucker says that this person will ask himself or herself: "What can I contribute that will significantly affect the performance and the results of the organization?" Thus, an individual's effectiveness is driven by his or her contribution to the performance and the results, the bottom line, of the organization. I gave myself passing marks in this stage of my career but knew that I would have to get a lot better. I began to think of how to improve performance and positively influence the quantitative and qualitative results more and more. And I learned to put the distractions and regrets over past mistakes behind me as fast as I could.

Chapter 10
1986–1990: The Second Time in VA Central Office

I began my second tour in the VA Central Office. Some people in power did not want me to take the job as Dr. Ditzler's resource management director. We had powerful regional directors at that time. The regional directors, for the most part, actively gamed the career development of future directors like me. Accordingly, they caused me to offered medical center directorships in lieu of taking the resource management director's job.

I don't know what they were afraid of, or if they just liked me. I don't think they wanted someone with my knowledge of the budget, comparative costs, and workloads to be in that position. But I kept my word to the chief medical director. In my position, I was head of the department's budget office, of allocation management (the distribution of funds to individual field facilities), and of the resource allocation model, known at that time as RAM.

What the chief medical director failed to mention is that about the time that I was on my way to Washington, he was on his way out. We had three or four weeks of an overlap. I would go in to brief him, and he wasn't interested. I asked him what he would like me to be doing. He reached into his desk and pulled out a parking pass. He told me he wanted me to have it. This entitled me to park across the street from VA Central Office at a discounted rate. I was disheartened to see his lack of interest in my briefing.

The new deputy chief medical director was appointed to his position for four years. He was impressively smart and personable, had been the dean of two medical schools, and was a pathologist. I believed that it was only fair to ask him if he wanted me to continue in the job as director of resource management. I felt it was important for him and the organization to have someone in that role that he wanted. He told me that I would do. I was less than thrilled to hear this ringing endorsement, but at least that meant that I wouldn't have to move right away. I spent most of the next two years wondering why he agreed to have me stay on, but stay on I did.

The man before me had been the resource management director

for about eight years. He became a friend, and he did his damnedest to help me. His instincts had been very good in human relations, management, and the budget. Unfortunately, he was difficult to understand. To say that he spoke as if he had a mouthful of marbles in his mouth would be accurate, but his kindness and sincere caring for the organization and the people in it make it hard to describe him that way even now.

He had not changed as much as he needed. Computers were making the availability of data and information much more accessible, but they were not being used optimally. He still preferred working on issues with gentle persuasion, when, more often than not, no-holds-barred debates and documentation of performance lapses were required. Too many key leaders in the administration and on the Hill no longer held the VA in high esteem and were not willing to fund the VA adequately.

The current organization of what was to become the Veterans Health Administration was not working. We had two spinal columns, or distinct lines of authority and responsibility, often with conflicting objectives, to the chief medical director. The fact that these two lines of authority did not get along and failed to communicate contributed to much misunderstanding and conflict in Central Office. And that misunderstanding led to the assignment of blame. Lucky for me, the favorite place to assign blame was the Office of Resource Management and, of course, its boss.

I tried to establish good working relationships to both lines of authority, and to a moderate degree I was successful. I made inroads with communication by checking every day with my budget analysts to see what they had heard about what was being funded. Nevertheless, the surprises came frequently. My office and I were reassigned from the chief medical director to that of the deputy chief medical director—the person with the direct supervision and responsibility for the two warring spinal columns. This increased the organizational complexity, which made getting things accomplished more difficult—and it certainly increased the communication problems.

My direct, day-to-day supervisor was the executive assistant to the deputy chief medical director. This man, with no budget experience, exulted in his ability to use the deputy chief medical director's clout and authority to get things done, such as getting budget white papers written. I couldn't determine from my limited, pinhole view if some of those things needed doing or if some were items he personally, whimsically wanted done.

The executive assistant required everyone with an issue to go through him or to take it to him first. This meant kicking issues up to his level. This frustrated initiative and problem solving. He periodically initiated witch hunts, seeking to get the "goods" on people who were usually innocent but out of favor and easily targeted. He also usurped the senior executive service grade that I should have eventually received.

This was unknown to me at the time, because I was new to the senior executive service. He took it upon himself and included in his job the higher-level position requirements of my predecessor, thus getting himself promoted to a level or two beyond what his position would have ordinarily qualified for. So, on paper, he was the department's budget expert and spokesman. Since he hardly ever left the building, those very real duties fell to me.

Among the duties of my job was to brief the Office of Management and Budget from time to time as requested. The job of the Office of Management and Budget, or OMB, was to have all the agencies, departments, and so on of the federal government conform to the president's budget by trimming the fat out of the budget. Since the Veterans Health Administration didn't really have "fat" per se, this was a problem.

Most of the time, instead of the agency head being directly responsible to the OMB, the work is carried out by staff, who report the result of the meetings up their various chains of command. The person in OMB who does this is the examiner, or sometimes the assistants. OMB also coordinates with Congress and the Treasury.

As previously mentioned, health care is fragmented into several different appropriation bills and classified as discretionary or mandatory by law. All of this works against the Veterans Health Administration getting an appropriate budget, because it is classified as discretionary and because the examiners don't usually know much about health care. They also don't know—or don't care to remember—that the annual rate of inflation is much more in health care than it is in general. This sets the stage for arguments and constant conflict between the OMB and the VA. I disliked this part of my job very much. I was and am an advocate for the VA. Those analysts, simply looking for something in the budget to cut without regard to mission, are therefore troubling.

Another part of the job that I disliked was going to the Hill to testify at hearings. I would carry the briefing books. It was the responsibility of me and my staff to supply answers requested during the hearings and to brief the chief medical director or whoever else was testifying on the numbers beforehand.

One of the previous chief medical directors had been Donald Custis, MD. Dr. Custis was a retired Navy admiral and a surgeon who was extremely affable. My staff told me that, when the testimonies came back to them, they had to correct virtually every number that came out of Dr. Custis's mouth. But his charm and charisma were much appreciated everywhere he went, and, as a result, Dr. Custis was very popular.

On the other hand, Dr. Gronvald, the chief medical director for whom I worked, never got a number wrong. One briefing, and he would have the right numbers for the right categories in his head and he could articulate them correctly. Accordingly, I only had to open my briefing books twice, and, both times, I could not locate the number that Dr. Gronvald was asking me for. Nevertheless, Dr. Gronvald, because of other personal characteristics, was not very popular. I always felt that this hearing support job called for doing nothing and saying nothing, other than perhaps, "Could I provide that for the record?"

So I had this job, with which there was much to dislike. Weak leadership existed at the top, and dysfunction ruled in many areas of the organization. The pursuit of personal agendas was rampant.

The executive assistant to the deputy chief medical director to whom I reported had successfully gotten his office declared a smoking room. He was a chain smoker. After years of debate, the leadership had finally declared that smoking anywhere in the building was not approved. Smoking was permitted only in designated smoking rooms. This phase lasted only three or four years, but, while it lasted and I was in this job, I got to brief and be debriefed by the executive assistant while he was smoking away in his office. The VA was and is a health-care organization. In fact, the VA's research had been instrumental in discovering the negative effects of smoking. This was something else to dislike.

I mentioned earlier surprises, such as the unannounced funding of a heart transplant unit and how I attempted to head them off by talking frequently to my staff and checking often with others. On one memorable occasion, I was summoned to the deputy chief medical director's office and blasted for having allowed Bob Lindsay, one of the two feuding spinal columns' leaders, to fund a heart transplant program in Salt Lake City. Bob protected his organizational responsibility, that of managing overall operations, with an approach of an overly jealous suitor. I listened patiently, said that I knew nothing about it, and would get the specifics and get back to him. This I did. Bob Lindsay was a dynamic and creative leader, but by design or lack of understanding of the need to communicate, he was positively Machiavellian.

Bob Lindsay had indeed funded that heart transplant program in Salt Lake City. After I questioned many of the players with much more directness, I learned this from his staff and from my very own resource management staff. The paperwork slipped into the resource management, and the budget analyst who processed it did not realize the significance. I wasn't informed. My staff was very sorry but didn't understand why I would be so concerned about this.

Bob Lindsay left within a year to become the director of the VA medical center in Salt Lake City. This, of course, was a conflict of interest. Equally significant, while Bob was the director in Salt Lake City, he provoked Congress to pass a law dubbed "the Lindsay Law." This law prohibits breaking a major construction project into two or more minor projects, thereby decreasing the ability of VA directors to manipulate congressional construction funding. This law would play a role much later in my own career.

The Office of Resource Management was lacking in basic management systems. We had no budget committee. When decisions were made, there were no minutes available. Decisions were made at the chief medical director's morning meeting, to which I was hardly ever invited. Due to a lack of a document tracking system, many of my colleagues felt that anything that Bob wanted to disappear did disappear.

It seemed like Bob created whatever documentation he felt like, or not, as the case suited his fancy. It was plausible that Bob lied to his boss, the deputy chief medical director, about the heart transplant funding or perhaps the two of them were allies in starting the program and therefore blamed me. This set of circumstances would suit the deputy chief medical director, whose plausible deniability remained intact with his superiors. This was something else to dislike about my job.

Another surprise involved the VA Medical Center Richmond's heart transplant program. Apparently, the chief medical director and deputy, with the advice from others, decided to disapprove the director of the Richmond VA Medical Center's request for additional funds to pay for the heart transplant program. They delegated this to me. I quickly had the experts analyze the cost structure of the Richmond program. From this, I learned that Richmond had the longest preoperative length of stay in the VA and was the costliest. I set up the meeting. I briefed Dr. Holsinger, the Richmond director. Dr. Holsinger became visibly upset, reddening in the face and becoming abrupt. He was a fierce and passionate advocate for his medical center. In this case, he was simply wrong and overreacted.

Before I transferred from VA Central Office, Dr. Holsinger was announced to be the new chief medical director. I was pleased, because, compared to recent chief medical directors by virtue of his education and experience, he was the most qualified. But I worried that my previous interaction with him could have career-altering consequences. Happily, it did not. Furthermore, as I write this, Dr. James Holsinger was the nominee to be the surgeon general of the United States. He wasn't confirmed, but I believe he would have made a fine surgeon general.

At the end of the rating period, I received my performance evaluation. I noticed the deputy chief medical director's secretary standing outside my door. She was shaking, and tears were forming in her eyes. I gave her my most reassuring smile. She smiled. I asked her if I could help her. She stopped smiling. She said with a trembling voice, "Mr. Malphurs, they made me bring this down here to you."

I took the manila envelope she handed me. In it was my evaluation.

It was fully satisfactory. There was a one line commentary: "Despite being told many times to communicate significant budget events, Mr. Malphurs continues to fail in this regard."

I reached for her hand and grasped it. I told her, "You and I are the superior beings here. Don't you worry about this for another second. I appreciate your kindness and concern. That's what will make this memorable for me. And, you know, it's always good to know the kind of folks you work for."

She laughed and said, "You are so right, Mr. Malphurs."

For the next several years, whenever I would see her, we would smile, knowing that we were both warriors of the highest bureaucratic order. But it was one more thing to dislike about my job.

The Office of Resource Management had in excess of $17 billion in appropriated funds for which to account. Despite the fact that there was serious dysfunction in the upper echelons of the department and the fact that many of those assigned funds did not have adequate controls, I felt that the office and the people in it did as good a job as they could under the circumstances. We were often in the middle.

A staff office outside VHA wanted information, and the only way we could get it was to request an accounting code change from another staff office. We had to coordinate for both staff offices. This caused much friction and tension. Maybe it was deliberately designed that way, like the regional directors controlling the communication to the field over the budget and being the operating officials who determined budget actuals as well as noncompliance. I thought that this organizational dysfunction might well have been created for the leaders to be able to blame the bureaucracy. This was something Congress and the Veterans Service Organizations were only too ready to believe. Both of these realities covered a multitude of sins, real and imaginary.

Earlier in the book, I mentioned the decentralized hospital computing program (DHCP). These DHCP accounts were nominally under my control, but they were buried in other accounts, and we did not and could not readily inform Congress or OMB of these DCHP funds. The heroes who created this underground DHCP funding should be recognized for their incredible contribution to the VA and to the nation. They probably won't be.

I had already placed a high importance upon communication. I studied journal articles and adopted the management philosophy that one could never communicate enough. I tried to instill this work ethic in my employees. Almost all of them were what Drucker would call knowledge workers. They were bean counters, and most of them were very proficient bean counters.

One of them, Larry Bettes, who hailed originally from Oklahoma, was hardworking, serious, and extremely competent. Federal jobs have to be classified, and the standards at that time were woefully in arrears to what the appropriate classification should have been, particularly in finance, accounting, and budget. Because of this, in order to get Larry appropriate pay for his highly specialized and complex job, supervisors in the Office of Resource Management had to make him a supervisor. They gave him two direct reports. In an office of fifty-nine people, I had nine layers of supervision. One of the truly indispensable people in the building was Larry Bettes. What he knew, no one else knew. What he did, he did competently, professionally, and quietly. He had too much work to do, but he never complained.

At the same time, I had several supervisors who were not like Larry in any way. They fooled around. Sometimes at lunch, reports would come back from various staff that they would drink too much. The staff claimed that they wouldn't remember anything they were told in the afternoon. Anything they did in the afternoon had to be double-checked, if what they did could be found.

After several counseling sessions with one of them, I proposed disciplinary action for him. I had to send this proposal to my supervisors for their approval before going to human resources. One day I learned that my resource management supervisor had been given a special award for outstanding service and that my paperwork had been trashed. The executive assistant to the deputy chief medical director had seen fit to reward his behavior. This supervisor subsequently took an early-out retirement in part because of his continued drinking. Yes, one more thing to dislike about my job.

I have previously mentioned the regional directors. These men were directly aligned under Bob Lindsay. Over the years, their numbers changed from seven to four or to some other number. When Bob left to go to Salt Lake, the successive organizations still had to deal with these autonomous, direct-line field managers. Autonomy is dangerous to all managers who are often lulled into believing that there will never be a day of reckoning. Managers should understand that all decisions are interconnected, and risk management is what should be used appropriately, not assumed autonomy.

I have often seen managers act as if they had autonomy, and certainly many leaders say that autonomy is necessary for things to work right or well. But while I was the director of resource management, only the regional directors appeared to have assumed something like complete autonomy. They held budget meetings, and I would send staff to attend them, as I believed we were expected to do so by my supervisors. Communication was always an essential part of our budget operation. The regional directors would refuse to let my staff into the meeting. It was another thing to dislike about this job.

I was the official responsible for resource allocation. The RAM methodology developed the resource allocation for each medical center and region. One of the regional directors was placed in charge of the resource allocation methodology task force. This group was designed to develop and test changes to the methodology and to write issue papers on these changes for the chief medical director and others to approve. The meetings for this task force were in hotels in Washington or the immediate suburbs. The task force was productive and met until six or seven in the evening for two or three days every two or three months. When the meeting was over, I would drive those of my staff who had missed their rides home. This process would usually take two or three hours, depending on the traffic. No one appreciated this or, in all probability, cared. It was still another reason to dislike this job.

Then one day after two years as the director of resource management, I was approached about becoming the deputy in operations. Once again, we had reorganized, and, with this reorganization, the two spinal columns had been given to report to the same person: my immediate boss in this new organization arrangement. I quickly accepted the new job.

The job as the deputy was everything that the director of resource management job wasn't. It was mostly fun, challenging, and there was much to learn. I worked for Dan Winship, MD, a wonderful human being who was clinically very astute and a fine administrator. I threw myself into the office with gusto, relishing the work and happy to be away from the direct daily operations of the budget office.

There were still the regional directors to contend with, but they reported to Dr. Winship. Of course, most of them went around him and frequently went around the chief medical director too. The then VA deputy administrator always had a friendly ear to lend them. There are exceptions to every rule, and the exception to this rule was Al Washko, who directed the northeastern part of the country. Al was a dutiful direct report to Dr. Winship. Al Washko, in not emulating the antics of his colleagues, created a potentially difficult and acrimonious situation for himself. I call it integrity.

I had an executive assistant named Charlie Koerber. He was gruff but kind and a delight to work with. He was very knowledgeable, worked hard, and had real insight. Charlie had a doctorate from the Vatican. He had been a Jesuit priest and had gotten into health care by running a substance abuse program in NYC, where eventually some-one in the VA discovered him. Charlie would take two briefcases or material home with him every night. He would come back the next morning having mastered the material. He had rabbis, priests, and ministers dropping in on him all the time. I knew that he helped his former parishioners from New York whenever they called. For many years, he supported and cared for two aunts. I have no doubt that he helped numerous VA employees.

Charlie's intellect and sense of humor were often an inspiration to me. Having such a smart and dedicated employee helped me through some of the tougher moments on the job. Of course, I occasionally heard that the regional directors did not like him. Charlie's tough intel-lect and keen insights frequently meant that they couldn't have their way about some clinical situation or problem.

In my new position, one of my jobs was to serve on the uniform committee. This group had been working for many months, trying to sort out a revision in uniform policy. The complaint was that almost all providers were wearing white lab coats. And the numbers of staff members coming into the room, many wearing the same white coats, were believed to sometimes confuse patients. The uniform policy hadn't been updated in some time, so we would meet to argue about the types and colors of uniforms. The most vivid argument came from the nurses who debated the shade of beige that had been chosen for their coats at every meeting. The debate included many facets: respect, status, differentiation, and suitability for the varied professional nursing occupations. Of course, the lightest shade of beige possible was chosen. The men wanted working health-care technicians to have a Ban-Lon golf shirt to wear because they needed the most comfort possible.

I was embarrassed so much time was being spent on this topic in VA Central Office. The rest of the committee would get into substantial and protracted arguments. I would slip out of the meeting whenever I could because I had real business to do before I could go home. I came to understand that it was like the old adage about universities: the reason the political fights were so bitter was that the stakes were so low.

I briefed Dr. Winship. He directed me to announce the plan to introduce new colors of uniforms and styles, reserving white coats for physicians, over the coming Friday's national conference call, which I often moderated. I did this. On Monday, one of the regional directors came to see Dr. Winship. He didn't like the new uniform policy. He couldn't articulate why, but he felt that he had been inadequately consulted with. It is true that I never briefed the regional directors about the uniform change—this being somewhat trivial in my mind, given their limited time in Central Office since they were based in the field. I dutifully announced the holding of the policy on the next national conference call. We gave everyone three weeks to provide me with feedback.

At the end of three weeks, we reannounced the same policy without a single change. (As a footnote, the Ban-Lon sports shirt was not popular at all. A few were spotted on golf courses, and they quickly disappeared from view. Neither were the light beige smocks accepted by any professional nurses, who were among the groups who were supposed to wear them. The nurses quickly reverted to the all-white physician's coat, a practice that holds true still today.) Name tags and badges, which the Joint Commission on the Accreditation of Health Care Organizations requires, replaced the need for differentiation of the nature that we were trying to accomplish. Some patients still get confused, but color coding uniforms certainly wouldn't help.

In my new position, I was assigned to manage the environmental management service. At the time, it was called building management service. This group had responsibility for the housekeeping in the hospitals, its laundries, and uniforms. They also had responsibility for the patients' pajamas. During this time, they managed to greatly confuse the issue of pajamas because they were trying to convert to a much more expensive version that were made with a material called Nomex, which made the pajamas flameproof.

Of course, environmental management service wanted to make them universal. Not all patients smoked, but, in the event of a fire, the patients would have some degree of added safety. The issue eventually boiled down to cost. The pajamas cost three to four times the cost of ordinary pajamas. Eventually, the decision was made to direct the field facilities to furnish these Nomex pajamas for high-risk patients. Of course, banning smoking would have been the cheapest solution. This was a convenient and agreeable course of action for everyone except the environmental management service. Years later, during the fourth year of the Iraq War, I learned that the army was considering going to Nomex combat uniforms. I think that would be a great idea for soldiers in combat. That we as a government haven't already done so remains painful for me.

Performance evaluations are an annual ritual in many organizations. I was tasked to review the regional directors' self-appraisals, summarize the salient points, and then brief Dr. Winship. I recognized this immediately for the unpleasant and thankless task that it truly was. I gathered up the six or seven self-appraisals and read them. One was a page and half typed document of complete gibberish. The standards that were stated were not the assigned standards, and one or two sentences for each standard without a shred of data extolled this regional director's work at the highest possible level. Another was two, two-inch binders with glossy pictures. We had very little data to confirm or deny any of the statements included in the self-appraisals.

The best practice was that of Al Washko, the northeastern regional director. Al's self-appraisal had the applicable standards and his actual performance with data that supported the actual performance. Al happened to be my former boss when I was associate director at Albany, New York, and a friend.

I briefed Dr. Winship, and my original expectations for this project were fulfilled. Dr. Winship certainly agreed with my assessments but gave each of them the usual and customary assigned rating, which was outstanding.

Dr. Winship had a wooden plaque hanging in his office that stated, "Either way will hurt." This was very often the case, since it was impossible to please everyone. We picked our way through the minefields daily as gracefully as we could. All too often, there were forced choices that required some part of the organization to spend more or do more or some variation on that theme. We had a daily conflict in directing others to do the work, or we had to do it ourselves.

The regional directors had deputies who worked in Central Office. They were a mixed bag, and they deemed themselves the heirs apparent to prestigious director jobs in the field. Some worked quite hard; others did as little as possible. Whenever there was an assignment that they objected to, they would simply stall, deny, seek endless clarifications, and obfuscate. Most of the time, the deadline would loom, requiring that I did it or Charlie finished it or we went directly to the field. Charlie's capacity for doing huge amounts of high-quality, analytical work was awe inspiring. We received constant criticism from all areas, so being right and on time didn't negate the criticism very often.

I worked continuously through the day from about 7:00 am to 7:00 pm and often took work home. We all took work home. The work disparity would be driven home each time I had to visit one of these deputy regional directors. They would be on the phone or reading the paper or engaged in frivolous conversation. But Dr. Winship was right. In getting the deputies to do their assigned work or doing it for them—either way hurt. Sadly, there were many such examples of this principle.

EEO cases sometimes crossed my desk. I would have to review them and make a recommendation regarding settlement to Dr. Winship. The process has changed significantly since then, but one case stayed with me as a constant reminder of just how grotesque a situation can become when thoughtless actions and words happen.

The situation occurred at a Maryland VA medical center. A recreation therapist had for many years played Frosty the Snowman in the annual holiday pageant. Everyone agreed that she had the perfect shape for the role. A recently appointed chief of recreation service decided that since this recreation therapist was African American that she should no longer perform in the hospital pageant as Frosty. Of course, he stated many other reasons for his decision.

The EEO case began and moved successively up the chain of command. I recommended to Dr. Winship that the medical center director apologize and return the role to the recreation therapist. It is a good thing when a person owns their responsibility. This woman owned her role as Frosty. Dr. Winship was pleased to make his decision accordingly.

One of the all-stars in VA Central Office was Dr. David Worthen. David was the chief academic officer. He was an ophthalmologist, highly intelligent, and a skilled practitioner of the bureaucratic arts. Academic affiliations are generally believed to have greatly added to the strength and capabilities of the VA's health-care mission. VHA has benefited in numerous ways: research, education, better recruitment of more highly skilled clinicians, and the provision of medical and surgical residents who provided much care to patients and stimulation to the rest of us.

David was a skilled defender of the medical school affiliations. Very often, the new political appointees would come in with the notion that affiliations were bad. They would be briefed early and often by the highest echelon VA Central Office staff, excluding the undersecretary for health, that affiliations were costly, usurped the secretary's authority, and were inefficient. By virtue of this, the Office of Academic Affairs was bombarded with requests for white papers, or briefings with the administrator or his direct reports. David did this brilliantly. His favorite quote was, "Quick, sure, and wrong." This meant that decision makers influencing the administration were opinionated and decisive. They were quick to form opinions, particularly about health care, which none of them had any experience in, were adamant in the defense of those opinions, and were almost always wrong. This doesn't mean that sometimes they didn't get their way, but when they went away, usually their overly simplistic ideas went with them.

An example of this was the push to eliminate all consultants in the federal government. But health-care consultants very often deliver direct care or participate in surgery or unusual procedures. They aren't management consultants. Ultimately, we prevailed, but the cost was huge in the time and energy the organization devoted to what was essentially an exercise in defending the way all organizations practice health care. This time was better spent on other pursuits, but that was the way of the organization, and probably still is. One day David and I were discussing some management idea, long forgotten, and he said that he would ask his neighbor about it. I asked who his neighbor was. He said Bill Marriott, at the time the chief executive officer at Marriott Corporation. I was impressed.

Dr. David Worthen was a valiant and stalwart defender of what is the best in VA health care. He died an untimely death. The VA's highest award for academic excellence is named for this great health-care leader.

Drucker writes about contribution in his book *The Practice of Management*. In the provision of health care for veterans, the VA delivers on its mission and therefore makes cost-effective, high-quality, accountable contributions to society. Organizationally, however, the VA at this stage of my career was erratic—highly effective where brilliant, highly motivated performers like Dr. David Worthen were involved, but in other critical areas, such as building values and developing its people, the organization was remiss.

We had educational programs, and the programs came and went without impacting the real, operating culture of any area in Central Office. Our committees, the Veterans Service Organizations, the OMB, and the VA's political appointees seldom agreed on the fundamental issues confronting the department: finances, organizational processes, the cause du jour, the personal interest groups, the uneven political interest by congressional delegations, and on and on. Worse still, the White House enforced ideological discipline (basing all decisions upon what will get the most votes in a future election, for example), forcing a fit that causes dysfunction and much puzzling about why. Did the ideological discipline come from some political platform or the unfettered desires of some senior staffer in his first real job? Thus, waiting lists in Florida once publicized were unacceptable, despite the fact that the lack of construction, absence of sorely needed clinics, and resources were the primary factors.

So our hard won contributions often submerged into the quarreling of leaders, each pursuing their own agendas, protecting their turf, pushing what they personally felt was the answer to long-standing discrimination, slights, or lack of respect. I am not referring to discrimination against ethnic groups or minorities. All of them are well represented in the VA as patients and employees. Instead, I am referring to the special interests as defined by the lobbyists for health insurance, drug manufacturers, the various professional groups, the Department of Defense, tobacco interests, protecting jobs at the local level, businesses interested in selling or protesting bids, and so forth.

There are mutually conflicting agendas, the greater good getting lost in the competition for resources or power, or someone's advocating that they know what's best for the VA. Often, this latter group is not elected. Too little information about the real issues is given to the public.

Chapter 11
1990–1995: CEO

My mentor and former boss when he was the director at Albany, Al Washko, decided to leave the VA and become the chief operating officer at Deaconness Hospital in Boston. This enabled me to go back to the VA medical center in Albany as director. I never expected to be able to go back and was pleased. Only our youngest, Jamie, elected to join us. The other two were in college: Julie at the University of Florida and Jason at North Carolina State. My wife was pleased we were getting out of Washington—more importantly, getting me out of VA Central Office.

The associate director in my old job at Albany had transferred. The chief of staff, Larry Flesh, was still there. The outstanding chief nurse soon thereafter transferred. Fortunately, we were able to recruit another outstanding chief nurse from within the ranks. The high work ethic of the staff and strong community support was still readily apparent. The budget was decent, the cost effectiveness good, and quality high. There were troubles looming, but, all in all, it was a very good assignment.

The VA medical center in Albany was opened in 1951, and the VA medical center in Buffalo opened shortly afterward. The two buildings were identical: both built in the same eleven-story X pattern with Ys or Vs on the end of each of the Xs. The health-care industry rarely builds identical buildings. The current vogue is to build boxes, so this was an obvious exception. The lack of this standardization is only now being addressed by the VA, which is making a noble attempt to design a standardized, single-patient bedroom. To some extent, in the VA, the lack of standardization is understandable since so many of the buildings and locations were originally donated to the VA.

I believe that the federal government could save millions in expenditures by making patient bedrooms and other spaces in hospital buildings standard. Look at any local community or academic health center, and the casual observer can see the various buildings in no particular order with vastly different configurations of beds, operating rooms, and diagnostic services. In terms of making cost-effective staffing assignments in these buildings, management is made more difficult.

Even in terms of managing heating, cooling, or the air quality, the idiosyncrasies are vast. Since hospitals are also building programs, each addition or modification brings its own changes, which often beget further changes. These buildings are often not conducive to patient flow, staff efficiency, or maintaining a comfortable environment for staff or patients.

When I returned to the VA Medical Center Albany, I quickly realized that the momentum of the changes and general enthusiasm for achieving success had largely dissipated. The CEO in the interim was widely reported to have been aloof, tended to work things out in his own mind, and then would pick someone to implement what he had worked out. This approach negated buy-in. It seemed to me that many of the managers naturally resented this approach.

The anger and resentment grew, as many of his decisions were poor. It also led enthusiastic high performers to submerge themselves into the organization and to hunker down as they quickly learned that this CEO wanted an atmosphere of top-down. His towering, unfriendly appearance made staff reluctant to approach him. His cold, imposing, autocratic rule led to hard times for many of the staff. The associate director, now gone, and chief of staff had performed work-arounds as best they could. But significant events and situations were missed in the general malaise and disappointment.

The team spirit that I had known before had certainly vanished. Although definitely glad to see me back, employees held back, questioning whether the good times, the Camelot of old, would return. Some leaders who had arrived in the intervening four years were not ingrained with the old spirit of can-do optimism. But a critical mass remained. We forged ahead.

The new chief of social work was apparently disappointing others on a regular basis. His staff reported him to be demanding and arbitrary. His social workers would relay their personal dislike of their leader and their increasing anger in private. Their leader was friendly and agreeable to me. He smiled a lot and postured during meetings. I grew concerned over his internal social work issues and lack of true leadership in mental health.

The major construction project was drawing to a close, and this was good news. Having reliable heating and air-conditioning throughout the building was a great asset. The medical center had been shifting from inpatient beds to outpatient clinics during the time I was gone, and this trend continued. There were clinics all over the building. The demand for the elevators had never been greater, and keeping them going was a constant challenge, as was parking.

Change in three key clinical leadership positions also happened. The previous chief of medical service had become VA Central Office director of medicine. He was a dynamic and energized individual whose approach was captured by his desk arrangement: a large picture on his wife in her wedding gown on one end and model of a piranha on the other. His replacement was more level-headed if less charismatic and continued the improvements in the service. The long-serving, beloved, irascible chief surgeon had also retired. His assistant chief was promoted in his place. And the new chief of radiology had finally created some continuity after much turmoil and strife during my four-year absence.

Setting up a quality improvement committee, we quickly reinstituted quality improvement activities on a large scale throughout the hospital. The staff who served on this committee made the cultural and educational change required to make it work. This committee, along with Mary Ellen Piche, the chief of the performance improvement service, took charge and allowed me to step back from a full-time effort in continuous quality improvement.

Change was in the air with regard to the pressures of managed care, and, subsequently, Congress would authorize the VA to bill third-party insurance companies. The quality movement had come to the VA, along with the billing requirements of insurance companies, to make the VA better. The long-held negative perceptions of the VA, widespread in some veterans' communities and some health-care communities, began to crumble.

During my tenure as CEO, I was confronted by two national media events. The first was a network news special from the late 1980s: "If Japan Can… Why Can't We?" This insightful news program really encapsulated why all of management should be doing continuous quality improvement. In Japan's automobile manufacture, continuous quality improve led them to improved productions, faster and cheaper processes, and fewer defects in their cars. I believe that it is as relevant today as it was then. Maybe it's more relevant, because our auto industry continues to lose profits and market share. This news special is a large part of the reason why I am so passionate about continuous quality improvement. This shows the standard of excellence in reporting. And we need a lot more of it.

The second media event was an exposé on the Cleveland VA Medical Center on *Primetime Live*. All of us in the VA were outraged by the unfairness of this report. One vignette that stays with me depicted a reporter who snuck a hidden camera into a patient's room. The patient, identified to the reporter by anonymous VA employees, allegedly was not eating and wasn't being fed. This was totally unethical. Knowing that a completely dependent patient isn't being fed and doing nothing about it except to install a hidden camera is shameful. However, I believe the patient was being fed. I wrote the reporter, telling her this, and to this day I still haven't gotten a reply.

I encountered many troubling issues during my directorship of the Albany VA Medical Center. During each of these issues, there are simultaneously interesting anecdotes, and, as always, the challenge is of delivering quality health-care effectively. I have dealt with each issue separately in the following subchapters due to the complexity of most of them.

Chapter 11.1: An Affair to Remember

The mental health programs continued to rock along. The chief of psychiatry, Dr. Leach, had been brought in several years before to improve care of and the communications with Vietnam veterans. In fact, I had worked with him during my previous assignment as the chief operating officer.

I hadn't been back in Albany long before several individuals complained of the chief being insolent, sarcastic, and bombastic. He was often belittling to other staff. Those who worked closest to him looked repressed, angry, and fearful. They seldom smiled and often seemed nervous or on the verge of tears. They didn't respond with spirit and enthusiasm as they had four years before. My initial inquiries did not yield any insight into why this would be, but the background noise about Dr. Leach soon escalated.

One day when the chief was attending a meeting away from Albany, his administrative officer came down to see the administrative assistant to the chief of staff. The psychiatry service secretary was also off. The two then came to see me and requested permission to photograph and inventory psychiatry's reception area. They informed me that the stacks of documents and mail were several feet high. I gave them permission. The inventory revealed that the mail had not been opened for months, if not years. Journals, memoranda, bills, checks, and all manner of vendor information had just been ignored. Included in the mess were some patient incident reports. Some of these patient incident reports had not been acted upon, thus creating a reportable quality issue to the region. We reported it. The region insisted upon an outside review of the situation. The chief of psychiatry, the chief of staff, and I agreed on a chief of psychiatry at another VA medical center to do this review.

The visiting chief of psychiatry was very cordial and went about his investigation in a businesslike manner. He came to see me twice. The first time to report that Dr. Leach had been intimidating and was not cooperative in his interview and that he was being loud and angry in the presence of witnesses. I wasn't surprised about this, since that was his usual behavior in situations where he was being asked to account for his actions.

In his exit interview, he told me that there were issues with a social worker intern with whom Dr. Leach was reported to be in a romantic relationship. I was somewhat startled at this information. This alleged affair was causing issues with other mental health providers, because they felt that she was being shown favoritism.

He also reported that since files were missing, nothing could be definitely proven relative to the allegation of poor quality for patient incident follow-ups. He gave me a one-page memo and said that he was destroying the backup and supporting documents. I told him this was unusual. He said he just didn't want to be attacked by my chief of psychiatry. He didn't have time to deal with it. I thanked him, knowing that he hadn't finished his job and knowing my work had just begun.

Various staff members brought me anecdotes and rumors about Dr. Leach's acting out his displeasure at this report. He didn't directly admit the relationship and denied he supervised her. Any unfairness related to the social work intern came from others, according to him. I then talked to the chief of psychology, who reluctantly agreed that the chief of psychiatry was intimidating and threatening on occasion, so much so that he had cut off their friendship and had as little to do with the chief of psychiatry as possible. He sent his assistant chief to meetings, for example, so that he could avoid the head-to-head conflict.

I then talked to a nurse who worked in psychiatry as a therapist. She also confirmed this state of events. She said that the social work intern was assigned to psychiatry, which was unusual. She added that no one dared to contradict her clinical case management reports on the social work intern's patients. According to this seasoned professional, other forms of favoritism were also shown her. She concluded by saying that the chief of psychiatry's secretary was pregnant with a mental health patient's baby. I then talked to the chief of social work, who was very upfront: in order to keep his relationship with the chief of psychiatry on a working, collegial basis, he had assigned the social worker intern to psychiatry and would not change that assignment for fear of retaliation.

I ordered an administrative board of investigation to look into the matter of the secretary having a patient's baby. She quickly left on maternity leave, never to return to work. After some weeks, the board turned in their report that stated that the patient admitted being the father and stated that the pair had used the chief of psychiatry's office as their trysting place. The chief claimed to be a victim of this conduct and not an enabler. Most of the testimony was veiled and indirect enough to prevent disciplinary action against the chief or anyone else.

An upsurge of complaints about the chief of psychiatry streamed into my office. I listened and commiserated with the reporters. I consistently told them that I needed documentation and corroboration to ascertain that allegations would be supported to some extent.

A few weeks after the initial board of investigation, the opportunity arose. A nurse had filed a patient incident report alleging that favoritism had been shown to one of the social worker intern's patients. An inpatient had been prematurely discharged because a patient of Leona Tartis, the social work intern, needed a bed. I ordered a second administrative board of investigation. It came back inconclusive, but with enough additional smoke to make me extremely concerned. The chief of psychiatry began to allege that he was being discriminated against because he was an Orthodox Jew. This was news to all of us. It would, however, become a continuing theme.

After a few more weeks, a staff psychiatrist called me from home. He wanted to make arrangements to meet me at an off-campus pizza restaurant. I readily agreed, and we met. This staff psychiatrist reported that he had been threatened by Dr. Leach. His proficiency ratings were going to be lost or downgraded if he did not cooperate by supporting Dr. Leach's opinions during meetings and elsewhere in the medical center.

He felt that he could not do this. He didn't want to leave the VA, but, unless this threat went away, he would have to move. I said that I couldn't do a formal investigation without more corroboration or documentation. He implied that I was honor bound to act on his verbal report, because he could not put it in writing without Dr. Leach acting upon the threat. I told him that I would see what I could do.

I requested that Dr. Leach provide my office with past proficiencies. After considerable stalling, the records could not be found. I ordered another administrative board of investigation, seeking the reason no proficiencies could be found. There were no written proficiencies and no records on the computer. Dr. Leach prized himself as a computer expert, having bragged of his computer knowledge many times in the past. I ordered the computer seized and reviewed by our information resources experts. They claimed that all of the files had been deleted and that they could not be restored. I was disappointed and slightly unbelieving of this report.

I now realize that they too were intimidated by Dr. Leach and uncertain of their own conflicting obligations to management, privacy requirements, and the absence of clear-cut guidance on such issues at that time. Fear in the middle management of the medical center was apparent. The situation generated uncertainty, which was enough to confuse employees and make them distrustful of all management. The board made no definitive recommendations.

A senior and iconoclastic psychiatrist visited my office in a heated rage. This quiet Southerner said that he had found his proficiencies lying on top of the soda machine and watched Dr. Leach in the vicinity, laughing. I calmed him as best I could. I instructed the chief of staff to maintain all of the proficiencies and to get the previous ones redone by the assistant chief of psychiatry as soon as possible.

The work of the steering committee for mental health was being compromised and becoming ineffective. The teamwork and the culture of trust required fell apart. Too many of its members were fearful of coming under attack, professionally and personally. There were reports that past members had left the meeting because of intemperate and demeaning remarks being made about them. Among the alleged statements and insinuations toward others in the medical center was that he would expose all of the nonmarital relationships—past and present, gay or straight.

Two people came to me in the afternoon after Dr. Leach had made this statement, asking me to put envelopes in the safe. In these envelopes would be the disclosure of their nonmarital relationship. I think that these people were intimidated by the threats of Dr. Leach and wanted full disclosure for themselves. Fortunately, the envelopes were eventually destroyed without opening them.

After several visits from various members, I prepared a memorandum, making the assistant chief of psychology the chair and removing Dr. Leach from the committee entirely. This was when Dr. Leach began filing Equal Employment Opportunity complaints and grievances against me. The alleged reason that I was discriminating against him was because of his conversion to being an Orthodox Jew. He had made no known requests for accommodations because of his religion.

A patient complaint came in. A mental health patient alleged that during a group therapy session, the patient who had impregnated the psychiatry service secretary had brought out confidential information that he could have only have learned from his medical record. Another administrative board of investigation had to be chartered. The breach of confidentiality was proven, but the assignment of blame could not be determined. The person to whom to assign the blame was clear in my mind: the chief of psychiatry was ultimately responsible for insuring the office and patient files were maintained properly and protected. I seemed to be the only one around with this view.

After consulting with the chief of staff and the assistant chief of psychiatry, I decided to detail Dr. Leach out of his job as chief of psychiatry and into a staff psychiatrist job where he could be closely supervised and some clinical productivity gotten out of him. The additional productivity was needed because of his inability to recruit and his own staff seeking jobs elsewhere. Leona Tartis, who in the meantime had become a full-time VA social worker, had resigned a few weeks prior. After a few more months, Dr. Leach resigned and charged the chief of staff, the acting chief of psychiatry, and me as forcing him to resign. Ultimately, I prevailed in his EEO complaints and grievances. Then Dr. Leach and his attorney filed a lawsuit seeking damages from each of us, the chief of staff, the acting chief of psychiatry, and me, for $15 million each.

The previous director whom I had replaced had retired from the VA. His aloof leadership style of implementing top-down decisions and making unilateral communications had caught up to him at his next assignment. He hated Dr. Leach enthusiastically. Of course, he didn't want to testify or become a target of Dr. Leach's wrath. The previous director had openly stated that he wouldn't sign Dr. Leach's proficiencies and would have nothing to do with him professionally or personally.

I contacted the VA Central Office's former director of psychiatry and asked him if he would testify about the inadequacies and misfeasance of Dr. Leach. He readily agreed to do so, but this distinguished, retired professor of psychiatry at Yale sadly said that his short-term memory was going, and he was afraid that he might become a liability on the witness stand.

Dr. Leach's lawyer sent interrogatories to each of us. It took two weeks full-time to complete all of the answers to the inch-thick pile of questions. Among the information being sought were the addresses of my adult children. The ploy was designed to provide a wealth of information for which inconsistencies could be identified in later questioning.

Fortunately, the VA asked the Justice Department to represent us. I also had management malpractice insurance, which was great for my peace of mind. Nevertheless, the U.S. attorney decided to settle out of court for the maximum allowable under law: $300,000. The U.S. attorney never consulted me about settling. Over one-third of that went to Dr. Leach's attorney, and the rest purchased him an annuity. Dr. Leach went to work for another affiliate of the medical school. He and his attorney began to put on workshops at the local law school on hostile work environment. They were right in a way: the VA's hostile work environment went away when Dr. Leach did. Dr. Leach and his attorney got their picture on the front page of the local newspaper. His attorney's law firm represented the newspaper.

I suppose that the U.S. attorney had bigger cases to spend their time on. The six administrative boards of investigation, stacked on top of one another, would have been about a foot thick. The VA got rid of Dr. Leach. His staff and the patient care got better over time. His departure from the VA was a blessing and relief for us all. I suppose that there are issues of accountability, both for the VA legal counsel and the U.S. attorney.

My efforts with Dr. Leach received recognition at the next engineering service's luncheon. I was invited and went through the buffet line. I found that the only open seat was next to one of their Jewish employees. We had a fine luncheon, and I deeply appreciate the respect that they showed for my attempts to make the workplace a safer and more rational place to work. Numerous other employees expressed their gratitude.

I asked the regional counsel for advice on what I could have done better. He said that after the first investigation I should have then asked the regional director to set up a board that could have reviewed each of my decisions to establish an administrative board of investigation. This would have taken a long time. In the effort to see that everyone gets due process and those processes are fair and impartial, the work, and the environment in which the work must get done, suffers. I hope that the importance of the real work and the negative impact of protracted investigations, hearings, and so forth on the skilled employees and staff doing that work get more recognition throughout the federal sector.

Chapter 11.2: The Nuclear Regulatory Commission

The Nuclear Regulatory Commission has broad oversight and enforcement powers over all things nuclear in this country. All hospitals, because of nuclear medicine, radiology, and research must be in good standing with the Nuclear Regulatory Commission (NRC) to maintain the license that permits them to handle radioactive isotopes. Included in the multitude of requirements is being able to pass unannounced inspections.

One morning I received a phone call from an NRC inspector. He announced his presence in the hospital. He said there would be an exit interview at the end of his day. About twenty minutes later, I received a call from Dr. Nutt, the chief of nuclear medicine service. Dr. Nutt admonished me for not having notified him of the unannounced NRC inspector. I declined to accept the admonishment and said that we had to be in a constant state of preparedness for such inspections. He hung up.

The chief of staff, Dr. Flesh, and I had a brief conversation. I passed along the phone call from Dr. Nutt. He said that he would check into how the inspection was going periodically during the day. The NRC inspector called a few minutes later and requested that Dr. Flesh join him. Dr. Flesh told me that the inspection was not going well.

Later that afternoon, Dr. Flesh and I had another brief discussion. He said that he didn't have time to fully explain, but all the radioisotopes couldn't be found. If he didn't find them all, according to the NRC inspector, we would be shut down. I told him the priority was finding all the radioisotopes and doing as much damage control as possible; I could be briefed later.

During the exit interview, the NRC inspector was livid. His anger and hostility toward our radiation safety officer and our chief of nuclear medicine service, Dr. Nutt, couldn't be contained. Dr. Nutt, a board-certified nuclear medicine physician and chairman of the radiation safety committee, had become our acting radiation safety officer at about 9:30 am. Our official radiation safety officer had eloped from the building and resigned from the VA at about 9:15 am. Our inspector had started touring with the radiation safety officer, and, at each research laboratory, he would ask the staff who this man was. No one knew. The radiation safety officer should have been doing his own inspections and periodic training for all radioisotope users. When confronted, the radiation safety officer resigned. The NRC inspector complained that our radiation safety officer couldn't speak English at all. This was all news to me.

In his briefing, the NRC inspector had turned to Dr. Nutt, because he had the credentials to be a radiation safety officer and was the chairman of the radiation safety committee. Dr. Nutt, despite his years of service to that medical center and years of experience in nuclear medicine, couldn't seem to help the NRC inspector either. That was when the NRC inspector put in the call for Dr. Flesh, who by the end of the day found every isotope except for one that he believed had been properly disposed of some time before. Before the exit interview was over, I had to put into writing that Dr. Flesh, who was also board-certified in nuclear medicine, was the acting radiation safety officer and the chairman of the radiation safety committee. Now I was livid. I had profound gratitude to Dr. Flesh for saving us, but he also supervised the clinical services and so should not have been so trusting of Dr. Nutt.

The hospital was entering yet another period of budget cutbacks. Faced with eliminating all the temporaries, freezing hiring, and a myriad of other disagreeable tasks, I decided that we didn't require the services of Dr. Nutt. After careful consideration and numerous consultations with various experts, I learned that, since Dr. Nutt was working on a part-time basis, I could simply terminate his services, which I did.

No matter how badly any particular employee performs or how unlikable he or she is, when he or she is terminated, it seems to bring out a certain number of people who feel that the termination is wrong. The numerous people who support the termination rarely speak up. In addition, the physician being terminated can play on the sympathies of other physicians. This always seems to engender a certain amount of support. From what quarter this assistance will arise is always hard to determine. Since I had valid reasons: the budget has to stay balanced; this physician's productivity and decision making was much less than acceptable; and, in talking to the chief of staff, it appeared that making the staff nuclear medicine physician the chief of service, we could get along fine clinically without Dr. Nutt.

The VA has a nuclear medicine service at the national level. All of the other clinical disciplines are represented as well, either in VA headquarters or at some VA site in the field. These program managers are responsible for the care and feeding of their field representatives. In this case, the VA chief was in Ann Arbor. He undoubtedly fell for Dr. Nutt's impassioned plea that he was wronged. As it turned out, there is a body of laws designed to protect the whistle-blower, or in this case a person who provides testimony.

Dr. Nutt hired a lawyer and filed the necessary paperwork to allege that protected whistle-blowing activity on his part had been violated on my part: specifically, I had terminated him. The protected whistle-blowing activity was his testimony to the Nuclear Regulatory Commission at two field-based hearings that they conducted over the Albany VA Medical Center's violations of NRC policies and procedures. Now Dr. Nutt's testimony was simply that he was wrong; he had made a mistake because he didn't know any better and begged for their mercy. Somewhere along the way, unbeknown to me, the NRC interpreted this as management deliberately failing to provide adequate resources to the radiation safety program, thus setting up Dr. Nutt for failure in his capacity as chairman of the radiation safety committee and as acting radiation safety officer.

During these hearings, the chief of staff and I learned that we were the only persons in attendance in person or via conference call without an attorney. In attendance were representatives of the VA Office of Inspector General, the VHA nuclear medicine program, and the NRC had multiple representatives and attorneys present and in Washington via conference call. The regulations concerning whistle-blowing in NRC matters were in the Department of Labor laws.

This situation seemed very wrong to me and still does. I realized that I needed to become an expert on the NRC regulations and laws as soon as possible. I studied these regulations and laws. Since this case had been accepted as a whistle-blowing violation, I was able to secure VA representation. I knew that my VA attorney, who was otherwise a very capable attorney, would not be devoting as much time and attention to this case as I would since it was personalized to me. When he and I met in conference, I told him that I felt that there were two significant determinations on my part that we should use. First, Dr. Nutt's case had been untimely filed, by a matter of a day or two, but nonetheless not within the allowable time statutorily. Second, by the NRC's own standards, any board-certified physician in nuclear medicine automatically possessed the qualifications to be a radiation safety officer. My attorney looked glum nevertheless. I also felt since we were dealing with a heretofore unknown situation to either of us that there were no reasons for optimism.

This court day finally arrived. My attorney had come by train from the VA regional counsel's office in Buffalo. The administrative law judge had come from Washington DC. Dr. Nutt's attorney was resplendent in a suit that I could never afford. He had been an assistant deputy attorney general in Washington. With them was the senior partner of one of Albany's most prestigious law firms. The senior partner was a state senator and very active politically in the community. I did not think that I could get more concerned about my case, but, in these unhappy circumstances, I did despair.

My attorney was dressed for just another day at the plant. He had wrinkles over his wrinkled, mismatched sports coat, shirt, and pants. It looked like he hadn't shaved recently. Just when I didn't think it could get any worse, he got into a conversation about minor league baseball with the administrative law judge. I despaired some more.

The state senator made his apologies and left. I was first up as a witness, and, as soon as my brief questioning and answering was over, I was excused from the proceeding entirely. In the adjacent room were several nuclear medicine technologists waiting to testify on behalf of Dr. Nutt. As I was to find out later, the new chief of nuclear medicine was holding them accountable, thus making them work harder, and, because of this, they missed Dr. Nutt and desired to have him back. I despaired some more.

That afternoon, my wife and I went to the airport and proceeded to the gate, where we bumped into the administrative law judge. I smiled and nodded acknowledgment to him. He appeared to be stressed and tired. I despaired some more. My wife and I went on the same plane to Washington. Fortunately, we did not sit together and didn't see each other on the ground in Washington.

Several months flew by before the administrative law judge's decision in this case was published. I prevailed. The case turned on the untimely filing of the whistle-blower claim. I was grateful. I knew, however, that the NRC had learned something from the case as well. Because I continued to study their rules and regulations, I learned that they had backed off the rule that any board-certified nuclear medicine physician could be appointed a radiation safety officer. Now they had to approve the nomination. I had continued to study the regulations because I wanted to be ready for the appeal. Happily, there was to be no appeal. Dr. Nutt returned to federal employment with the Food and Drug Administration. Nobody from the FDC ever called me for a reference.

I have often wondered what turned the administrative law judge's mind in finding in effect for me. Was it my folksy, baseball-loving attorney? Was it a safe way to avoid finding fault with the NRC? Was it my complete innocence in the matter? It wasn't the latter. Justice was served, as it always is. Justice in my experience is sometimes wrong, but justice is always rendered, right or wrong. I am just glad that the breaks came my way this time. Five years after the unannounced NRC inspection, I received a letter from the NRC exonerating me completely for any violation of their regulations.

About the time the decision was published, an employee came to me and asked if I would like to read the decision online in one of the legal databases. I did. He also said that there was another *United States v. Malphurs.* I was shocked, because the name is rare. We looked that case up. It involved my grandfather, Ernest Napoleon Malphurs Sr., who at the time of the case was running for sheriff of Palm Beach County. No one in the family had ever mentioned that Grandpa had been involved in a case that was ultimately decided by the Supreme Court!

It seems that in campaigning for office, Grandpa visited several

Works Progress Administration (WPA) projects in Palm Beach County. He told the employees that they owed their jobs to him and they had to vote for him. The supervisors of these federally funded projects thought that was wrong and so brought a legal action against him for violating federal law. The Supreme Court ultimately decided that he had violated appropriation law. By the time the Supreme Court ruled, Grandpa had lost the election and was out of his previous employment as the police chief of the city of West Palm Beach.

Chapter 11.3: Let There Be a Light

Albany is a fascinating town. Besides being the state capital and the site of several universities, it remained a holdout of the old-style Democratic machine politics. The mayor, Erastus Corning, had been the mayor for decades. When I arrived back in town in 1990, he was dying in a hospital in Boston. Several people had briefed me on the need to get along with the Democratic machine, and I certainly desired to do so.

The main entrance to the hospital did not have a traffic light. Being located in what was called the University Heights section of town, there was traffic constantly flowing down the busy street that the VA's main entrance intersected. At peak times, such as when the nurses got off the afternoon tour, the wait to get out of the VA was many minutes long, with traffic backing up into our parking lots. There had been numerous accidents. In addition, the aging veteran population and their drivers were also at risk due to the lack of a traffic light. Compounding this scenario was the fact that there were a multitude of students using this street, and usually speeding. I decided to request a traffic light.

Several people pointed me in the direction of Assistant Albany Police Chief Thomas Coleman. They also warned me that he could be difficult and would almost certainly say no. I had been told that Chief Coleman had done the Democrats in the mayor's office many favors over the years, and so they were beholden to him. I set up a meeting. It did not go well. He told me that there was no way the VA deserved a light at that intersection, that there were already too many traffic lights in that area, and that his budget was impossibly tight. I was polite and expressed concern over his budget. I also told him of my aging clientele, the numerous accidents that had occurred there, and that the nurses, an increasingly difficult to recruit occupation, complained of that intersection, particularly after working a full shift or overtime. When they went home, they were tired and were placing themselves at some risk.

I went back to Chief Coleman after a few weeks and asked him to reconsider. He refused. I said that there was lots of community support for veterans. He said he didn't care. I was probably too snide and may have been a little obnoxious in my statements. He seemed defensive at first and then got a little belligerent. He called in his two traffic engineers, both of whom looked like college students. Of course, they readily agreed with the chief's assessment, saying a light there would make matters much worse on University Heights and for the VA as well. I thanked them all, telling them that I didn't agree and would continue looking for a solution.

A few weeks later, the McDonald's restaurant that had been under construction opened, and it had a traffic light newly installed. I called Chief Coleman. He was still highly negative and not embarrassed over failing to mention that McDonald's was getting a traffic light. I was angry and let him know it, saying something about priorities in the city. He countered that the light was necessary for economic development and that McDonald's was, most importantly, a tax payer. I said that VA was very much needed in the community and provided extraordinary economic benefits. I asked what did McDonald's did for the city. He said they paid for the light. I asked how much the light cost. He told me $17,000. I asked if I paid for the traffic light would there be any other obstacles to getting one. He said he didn't think so. He should have simply told me that in the first place. I told him I would get back to him soon.

When I got back to the VA medical center, I quickly called a couple of colleagues in the VA who I thought might have the answer. One did. He said to get our chief engineer to work up a purchase order for the traffic light. I did that. Six weeks later the light was installed. I received numerous thanks. I was especially gratified by a registered nurse who had coke bottle lenses in her glasses. She told me that she so hated to make that left turn on her homeward commute that she drove around the block in the other direction. She also said that she would always love me. That was nice too. Chief Coleman, on the other hand, seemed to glare at me on those rare occasions when I saw him at a parade or other community event.

Chapter 11.4: The Seven Dwarfs

One day on my way into the medical center, I passed the area where our engineering service arranged for flowers from the spring until fall. There were tulips to begin the spring season. This reflects the rich Dutch heritage of this part of New York widely saluted by the various communities and, in this case, the VA. Our grounds crew did a great job keeping the little remaining green space we had looking good. This helped to humanize the VA medical center, especially since most folks knew little about the VA. Having the grounds looking good was a way to provide a positive image to the VA in the public's mind. It also provides some peace and comfort for patients. The efforts of the VA's landscaping crew definitely were worth the small cost and provided a huge benefit to our patients and our employees. Sadly, many hospitals have lost all of their green space, and some attempt to provide one inside. We provided live plants inside too, but we were careful to avoid allergens, safety issues with water or leaves on the floor, and the like.

On this day, I spotted the seven dwarfs. They were artfully arranged behind the tulip bed and were freshly painted. One of the dwarfs had a purple face. Snow White was not with them. I wondered about this and made a mental note to talk to the chief engineer about that when an opportunity arose.

The opportunity arose quickly enough. A few days after first spotting the dwarfs, I inquired of the chief engineer. He laughed. He said, "One of the carpenters who does demolition work on his own time found them on a job. He brought them to the VA, the painters painted them, and then they put them out by the flowerbed on the side entrance."

I asked, "Why was one of them purple?"

He laughed and said, "The maintenance crew wanted one of them to be Willis, the general foreman." I said Willis is black. He laughed and said that they wanted Willis to be purple. I said OK. I was thinking in the back of my mind that this could be a genuine loser of an Equal Opportunity complaint, but I knew that Willis was highly respected. The next time that I saw Willis, I checked with him. Willis laughed and said he was proud to be represented by the purple dwarf.

One day I was doing rounds in surgery and the operating rooms. The head nurse, Helga, ran a tight ship, and I really didn't expect to find much that was wrong. Out of the corner of my eye, I spotted surgical residents moving into the OR. One of them was a dwarf. I went back to worrying about an EEO complaint immediately. While the dwarf was on the VA residency, I saw him from time to time. I once inquired of the chief of surgery service about how the young man was doing. He said he was doing fine. I quit worrying about it. Years later, on the show *60 Minutes*, I saw a segment on the dwarf surgeon. He was in practice in Baltimore, specializing in orthopedic surgery to lengthen the legs of dwarfs. Although he doesn't know me, I am forever grateful to him for never making an issue about the dwarf statues.

The dwarf story goes on and on. I would periodically be asked why there were dwarfs out by the side entrance. I would tell them the story. Most of the medical school leadership, veteran organization leadership, and visiting dignitaries thought the dwarfs were all right, and some thought they were fun.

One day the chief of the infectious diseases section came running into my office. Out of breath and anxious, he asked me, "Where are they?"

I said, "Who?"

He said, "The dwarfs!"

I told him not to worry and that I would find out what happened. After I found out, I called him with the happy news: the dwarfs were being repainted after a hard winter. He was much relieved.

Chapter 11.5: The Fatherland

One morning, I received a call from Peter Reagan, MD. Peter was then the chief academic affairs officer in VA Central Office. I had worked with Peter over the years and had grown fond of him. At one point, he had been the acting president of the University of Buffalo in addition to many, many other prestigious academic appointments. He asked me to check up on a childhood friend for him. I said sure. Peter told me that they had grown up next door to each other in New York City and that I would find him very interesting. He was worried that his friend was sicker than he was letting on.

I asked the folks in medical records to flag his chart for the next time he was in the hospital. Sure enough, in a few weeks, I received a call saying that Rudy had been admitted. I went to the ward and inquired of Rudy. He had cancer but seemed to be doing all right. The prognosis was decent enough considering, maybe two or three years to live a relatively normal life. I went in to speak with Rudy. I introduced myself. Rudy more or less grunted. I asked him how he was doing. Rudy more or less grunted. I told him that I was a friend of Peter Reagan. Rudy sat up immediately. He asked how Peter was doing, and I said fine. Rudy lifted his eyebrows while he narrowed his eyes into slits, expressing his doubt about my report. I said that I had seen Peter and talked to him over the telephone in the last couple of months. Peter and his family were doing fine. For Rudy, that seemed to close the conversation. He rolled over. I told his back that I wished him well and hoped that his hospital stay would be brief.

I learned more about Rudy as time passed. He and his family had immigrated to New York City in the late 1930s. When war was imminent between Germany and the United States, Rudy's parents, being Nazis, went back to the Fatherland. Rudy had been about eighteen. He was promptly drafted into the German army. He served in the infantry and fought in France, where he was captured by the U.S. Army. After being a prisoner of war for a while, Rudy somehow managed to convince the army that he was a U.S. citizen, was perfectly fluent in German and English, and wanted to join the U.S. Army. This was permitted, so Rudy became a U.S. soldier. During the Battle of the

Bulge, Rudy was captured by the Germans. But this time, Rudy did not tell them that he had been in the German army and remained their prisoner of war until he was repatriated.

Over the next few months, Rudy was in and out of the hospital. Most of the time, I was not able to see him. Gradually, Rudy faded from my active memory until one night, at about 2 am, I received a call from the VA medical center's administrative officer. I instantly set up in bed. George, the administrative officer, was laughing, and there was some background noise that I couldn't make out. George said, "There's a note in the file to call you about this patient Rudy."

I said, "Sure, what's going on?"

George continued laughing. "I have the manager of the Governor's Motel on the other line, and he's begging me to send an ambulance for Rudy."

I asked if Rudy needed an ambulance.

George asked me to hold on. "The manager doesn't really know. He says that Rudy and his partner are having a helluva row, screaming at each other." George added, "The door to their room is wide open, doors are slamming, the whole motel is awake, the police are there, and the volunteer fire department is on the way." George continued laughing.

Since I lived in Guilderland, New York, not too far from the Governor's Motel, a notorious hot sheet motel with hot tubs, mirrors on the ceilings, and an all-red décor, I listened for the sirens, and, sure enough, I could hear them. George asked me what I wanted to do. I said to authorize the ambulance. George asked me if I was sure. I said I was. This authorization was not quite in keeping with the regulations, but the public scene and the fact that the VA was known to be involved in the incident essentially made the decision for me. George said he would get back to me.

George called back and said that the ambulance was on the way. Still laughing, he added, "The manager is very grateful."

I said, "I'm sure."

George did say that there was one small problem. I reluctantly asked what it was. He said Rudy was dead. We were to learn later that Rudy died of a massive heart attack, no doubt in part caused by his cancer. George said, "I have to say that we aren't supposed to transport dead people. But I think that you should still authorize this."

I told George that I definitely agreed. I thought that Rudy would be considered another dead on arrival at the VA, and that was what happened. No further related investigations or criticisms came my way.

I never called Peter and told him of the hysterical demise of his friend. I just told him that Rudy came in DOA. I thanked Peter for letting me get to know Rudy. And whenever George caught my eye, he would burst out laughing.

Chapter 11.6: The Secretary's Visit

For many years, Albany and a significant portion of the surrounding area had been represented by Congressman Samuel Stratton. Sam was a polished and convivial person who never failed to be supportive of the VA and the local VA medical center. While I had been associate director in Albany from 1984 to 1986, I had gotten to meet Sam and was in his company on several occasions. Sam had been an intelligence officer in World War II and served as an interpreter of Japanese at the time of Japan's surrender.

Unfortunately, Sam left office during my absence from Albany due to sickness. In fact, he had Alzheimer's and died. In his stead, Mike McNulty was elected to office. Mike McNulty and several congressmen from surrounding districts, in a bipartisan effort, got the law passed naming the Albany VA Medical Center for Samuel Stratton. It was well received in the community and at the VA. The veteran community and the staff of the VA medical center fully supported the renaming.

Sam Stratton certainly deserved the honor. To accomplish the renaming, the protocol demanded that we invite the secretary of Veterans Affairs. The secretary had the right of first refusal. We in the VA had much work to do. Others had to be invited as well. We had to agree on a date. Among the notables who would be invited were the congressmen in our primary service area, the governor, the mayor, the city councilmen, state representatives and senators, and community leaders, such as the dean of the medical school. We established a committee and went to work.

We got a local TV news anchor to be the master of ceremonies. We also needed VA chaplains to lead the opening prayer, benediction, and closing. We got a Baptist church choir to sing. And, eventually, the secretary of Veterans Affairs agreed to be the featured speaker. Of course, the late congressman's extended family, most of whom no longer lived in New York, were invited. In short, for the community and veteran organizations, there were high expectations. This was to be a widely reported event in the city.

The big day arrived. Linda Blumenstock, the Albany VA Medical Center public affairs officer, had made all the arrangements. She thoroughly went over the program with everyone. The family and congressional representatives were to meet in the auditorium an hour before the dedication ceremony. A painting of the late congressman was to be unveiled in the lobby. The speakers, the choir, and the other notables were to be out in the tent on the grounds for the ceremony prior to its beginning. Refreshments were served in the auditorium and the lobby. The medical center was crowded with people, despite the drizzle in the morning.

We knew that the secretary was to be driven from Vermont, where he had spent the evening. Of all the VA medical center telephone numbers he could have called, he called the police office to report that he would be a little late. His driver had missed a turn. The family and crowd gathered in the auditorium, and, except for the absence of the secretary, the event seemed to be off to a fine start.

The secretary's driver called again. They needed directions. The secretary could be heard yelling in the background. The police sergeant who took the call quickly reported to Linda Blumenstock and me. We were concerned, of course. Linda's assistant gave the secretary driving directions. Several of us reviewed them to make sure that they were clear and accurate. We waited in the lobby, increasingly nervous.

About thirty minutes late, the secretary arrived. He was livid and short with us as we tried to get him to the auditorium to meet with the late congressman's family, the congressmen, and other dignitaries. He refused. He asked where the police office was. We took him to the door. He slammed the door, asking that we not bother him. His driver meekly went in the office. Our police sergeant was in the office and stayed there.

Through the police sergeant, we learned the secretary had made numerous phone calls, fuming about the lack of good directions and the fact that there was no one to meet him when he arrived. About ten minutes after the scheduled start of the formal program, the secretary came out. He was still abrupt, brusque, and looking put upon, but we all hoped that he had calmed down. Still, he clearly did not want to meet and greet anyone. I escorted him to the tent, where hundreds of people were waiting.

Linda Blumenstock, meanwhile, debriefed the driver. The driver told her that they were late leaving Vermont and did not have much trouble finding their way to the VA medical center. Once there, however, they had made a right instead of a left and went into the main entrance of the Albany Medical Center and Hospital, our primary affiliate and the academic health center directly across the street from the VA. Of course, no one there knew him, and they certainly didn't greet him. Finally, someone there figured out that the secretary needed to go to the VA and helpfully directed him.

In the meantime, I was introducing the family and our distinguished guests. The master of ceremonies did a beautiful job, especially in not calling attention to the late start or the reason why. He was the perfect host: warm, friendly, and gracious. Our chief chaplain delivered the perfect benediction. I then introduced the secretary, who opened his remarks with a preacher joke that was in very poor taste. The African American Baptist choir visibly recoiled. My chief of chaplains turned red, and his entire body tensed. The secretary's few words were not worth recalling. He barely mentioned the late congressman, nor did he say one complimentary word about the VA or the Capital Region of New York. I was relieved when the program was over.

I had to escort the secretary until he departed. He made it clear that he did not want to meet any of the local veteran leadership. I had introduced one of our local veteran service officer commanders, and the commander got short shrift from Mr. Derwinski, the VA secretary. He quickly turned away from them. I began thinking of him as Mr.

Dumbwinski. I was also afraid that I was going to end up calling him that if I wasn't particularly careful.

Fortunately, Linda Blumenstock brought two young Polish physicians to introduce them to the secretary. These two physicians were without-compensation researchers, in this country and at the VA to learn how to do research in chronobiology, part of which is the timed, sequenced delivery of medications in a complimentary manner with the body's biorhythms. The Polish physicians wanted to ingratiate themselves with the secretary because they had girlfriends in Poland for whom they wanted to get visas. They thought that the secretary, because of his former State Department connections, could assist them. And I think the secretary did assist them in that regard.

Finally, the secretary got into his car and departed. The local media's coverage was good and appropriate for the occasion. Everyone seemed pleased and willing to overlook the secretary's inappropriate joke and behavior. All of us at the VA medical center, especially me, breathed a huge sigh of relief.

The legend of the secretary's visit grew, however. At the next dean's committee meeting, the dean, who had been recently appointed and was still seeing a very few patients, told the assembled group an anecdote he had heard from one of his patients. This patient, a former Veterans Service Organization state commander and staunch Republican, had attempted to introduce himself to the secretary. The secretary snubbed him and turned to the two Polish physicians and said in Polish, "I can't stand anymore of this crap. I'm getting my driver and leaving." The former state commander had been an interpreter of German and Polish during WWII and understood what was said perfectly. I enjoyed hearing the dean tell this story in several other venues before my career took me elsewhere.

In fairness, Secretary Derwinski did one good thing for the VA, although at the time, I didn't agree with it either. He summarily decreed that every VA medical center would have a patient advocate. I had until then resisted the notion that we needed someone to serve as the patient advocate when it was all of our jobs. Of course, I was wrong. The global "everybody" who is to do the right thing on every occasion just wasn't realistic. It's also counterintuitive that these same employees would keep accurate data about their customer service mistakes. I have always tried to empower every employee to fix whatever the issue is when the veteran in front of them has presented it and still do.

We hired a patient advocate. With a formal program, this woman, formerly the director's secretary, also helped to educate me to the need. The patient advocate tracks complaints and categorizes them, thus providing management with useful information. The patient advocate that we selected had been an outstanding employee her entire career until she had been promoted out of the director's secretary position. This woman was pretty, statuesque, and charming in personality and demeanor. Many veterans who were in quite a rage by the time they got ushered in to see her were so stunned that they forgot what they were annoyed about. And many times, they went away happy that she would take care of the problem.

The saga of the VA Secretary Derwinski ended a couple of years later when he tried to orchestrate the provision of care to nonveterans at selected VA medical centers, where his staff had determined that there was excess capacity. The deal was to pay the VA for this care through the use of Medicare funds. Eventually, even though the secretary had been publicly billed as a masterful politician, this maneuver led to the service organizations demanding his resignation. I think rightfully so.

The VA health-care system has been denied reimbursement from Medicare for years. This arrangement dates to 1965, when the two committee chairs involved decided that there would never be a time that Congress would not fully fund veterans health care. There was also a sentiment at that time in Congress that Medicare would use the veterans' lobby if Medicare paid for their care. The potential for the powerful veterans' lobby to be unleashed for reasons other than the support of veterans' health care frightened many. Things have drastically changed in the intervening forty years.

I think what really did Secretary Derwinski in was that he was publicly advocating the use of Medicare in VA facilities but did not advocate Medicare reimbursement for veterans to use the VA at a time when large numbers of them couldn't or wouldn't use the VA for eligibility and numerous other reasons. I can certainly attest to the fact that the VA health-care delivery budgets were tight (and getting tighter) during this period. Still today, there are the so-called Category 8 veterans, who were excluded until early in 2009 from VA enrollment and care based on an income level set unrealistically low.

Chapter 11.7: The Award

I was frequently asked what kind of manager I was when I transferred from one VA facility to another. I had always responded that I was a participative manager. By participative manager, I mean I tried to be inclusive of others in soliciting ideas and in making decisions. But I felt I needed more material to better respond to that kind of question. I had been reading Drucker and various articles concerning the transformation of the Japanese economy. One of central elements of the Japanese effort was continuous quality improvement. My education on continuous quality improvement was deepening. As a result, I was very interested in getting a comprehensive continuous quality improvement effort going at the VA medical center in Albany as soon as I could.

Fortunately, I was left the legacy of Al Washko. His efforts at participative management and organized problem solving had been abandoned by the top-level management of the medical center, but some of the middle managers and others in the medical center still were believers and practiced the art of participative management to the extent that they could.

During the intervening four years, in which the director who replaced him implemented a top-down management scheme with a controlling yet remote leadership style, significant issues began to emerge within the medical center that no one wanted to present to the director. And so those who wanted to take advantage—and fortunately they were very few—deliberately did their own thing, to the detriment of the entire medical center.

So in an effort to bring the organization back into the practice of participative management, we set up a small committee of true believers in continuous quality improvement (CQI). We set up education programs for all. I was publicly adamant that the principles and practices of continuous quality improvement were going to be the way that

I would lead the medical center and its employees. In private, whenever I was confronted by someone who questioned my leadership principles or dismissed CQI, I told them that I was unalterably committed to it, and their job was to either get rid of me or leave. I respected their choice, but we did not have time to debate the relative merits of CQI. Sometimes I would ask them what school of management they would advocate instead. There was never a good answer to this question.

The VA had established the Carey Award for quality. The award itself and the requirements and principles that the award stood for were modeled after the Baldrige Award. The Baldrige Award was the nation's highest award for quality. The winners were extolled in meetings and conferences across the country. I found pleasure in reading about them, even though none of them were in health care, and it would be years before a Baldrige Award was created for health care specifically.

We decided that we would apply for the Carey Award. This decision required us to work on the presentation of our journey and to show graphically that we were using the criteria to improve the organization. We sent the report off without much hope that we would accomplish anything by applying, beyond getting feedback that would help us in future applications of CQI and being able to tell our story more precisely.

John F. Kennedy said, "The great enemy of the truth is very often not the deliberate, contrived and dishonest—but the myth—persistent, persuasive and unrealistic." To me, CQI is the truth. It requires hard work and conscientious application of initiative to make CQI apply to all areas of the medical center. Changes in rules, regulations, court decisions, personnel and equipment, and new designs or systems brought to bear because of advances in medical technology all combine to make health-care management challenging. I believe that the VA's unique health-care delivery system will be increasingly studied and emulated. This is because almost all the physicians are employed, systems are in place throughout the health-care delivery network that standardize business practices, and the early adoption of patient safety practices and its automated medical record.

JFK's quotation clearly demonstrates the difficulties that we will have in truly reforming health care. The hard work of reengineering our delivery systems will require that we change our attitudes toward what we ideally believe that the system should be and the truth of what it is: fragmented, episodic, expensive, burdensome to providers and consumers, and, perhaps most of all, unfair in many, many aspects.

CQI is the platform upon which I chartered the continuous improvement of my medical center's efforts. Becoming more efficient leads directly to better planning, better use of resources, better understanding of the dynamics of change, and better customer service. Of course, there are a multitude of management consultants to help. Health-care providers spend a fortune on these consultants. The benefits are hardly ever measured. Instead, the CQI tools are readily available, and what is needed is a management willing to implement those tools and the CQI processes.

There are many pressure points in any health system. Many health-care executives use consultants to make change happen and to provide some defense for themselves against the inevitable critics and, when things don't exactly work out, the board. Real leadership requires personal commitment and accountability. The need for systemic improvement in health care is reality. Waiting times to schedule an appointment and at the time of the appointment are critical customer service criteria. The admission and discharge processes are nearly universally cumbersome, inept, unnecessarily time–consuming, and far too variable. These are a few examples of the challenges that we face. The best solutions come from subjecting ideas and solutions to relentless testing and criticism. The best solutions need constant critique. CQI done well in a meaningful way captures learning for the organization.

One day I received a phone call from the deputy undersecretary for health. She told me that we were the recipients of the Carey Award. I was overwhelmed. I immediately called the CQI committee and key staff and informed them. We had many decisions to make: how to inform the media and when, who to go to the award ceremony in Washington, how to tell all of employees and our community about our recognition, and so on.

Some decisions were made for us. An enthusiastic volunteer heard about the Carey Award and immediately called the newspaper. A positive article appeared the next day. We were told that we could bring eight people to the ceremony. It was hard limiting ourselves to eight, but we did. Our employees were informed through memoranda, posters, and e-mail. Of course, we had a party to recognize those who did the hard work and to celebrate. We were the first VA medical center to receive the Carey Award.

The crowning moment in our effort to improve health-care delivery through CQI came at the next dean's committee meeting. The medical school dean, Tony Tartaglia, went through a description of our affiliate's efforts to install a CQI system. Tony went on at some length, describing the many visits that their committee had made around the country, visiting those health-care systems that Albany Med's research of the literature had shown had exceptional programs. Then the dean said, "And then the committee decided that they might as well visit the Albany VA. And they came back and reported to the executive board that the very best implementation of CQI that they had seen was at the Albany VA Medical Center." Needless to say, it was one of the proudest professional moments of my career.

Chapter 11.8: The Fisher House

The Fisher House is a personal care comfort home similar to a Ronald McDonald House. The Fisher Foundation awards these homes and sees to their construction for the Department of Defense hospitals and the VA health system. The VA medical center in Albany was the first VA to receive a Fisher House. The story is intriguing and reflects the truth of Margaret Wheatley's statement: "The things that we fear most in organizations, disturbances, imbalances—are also primary sources of creativity."

The Fisher Foundation was established by the Fisher brothers, who owned and operated a large construction and real estate development corporation in New York City. All of the brothers were originally construction workers who literally clawed their way to success. The brother who was responsible for starting the foundation had been a bricklayer. We learned that the Fisher Foundation was responsible for the *Intrepid*, the retired Navy aircraft carrier berthed in New York City. In addition to numerous contributions in the New York City area, they had funded the tall ships to visit New York harbor.

We also learned the Fisher Foundation had donated many facilities, mostly personal care comfort centers, to Department of Defense hospitals and to the service academies. Some of these hospitals, such as Walter Reed in Washington, or Wilford Hall, the Air Force hospital in San Antonio, had two Fisher Houses. The foundation had also built the Jewish Chapel at West Point.

The story of how our VA medical center became involved with the Fisher Foundation is an interesting one. One day the assistant chief of engineering came to see me. He said that there was a person representing the Fisher Foundation that had been found walking the grounds. After he identified himself, the Fisher Foundation representative asked a lot of questions. He said he was asked to do an assessment of the grounds and the medical center. I brought in the chief operating officer and chief of staff and key staff personnel. No one knew anything about this. We quickly did our research on the Fisher Foundation. We called, and no one at the Fisher Foundation knew anything about the VA and certainly would not comment at all about their interests in the VA medical center in Albany.

We were anxious to find out more about the Fisher Foundation's interest in us and to learn their next move. We would not have to wait long. A few weeks later the foundation called to set up a visit for an architect and an engineer from the construction company that the Fisher Foundation used. I escorted them around the campus. Our engineering staff answered their questions and explained VA building requirements. We also explained our unique mission and answered numerous other questions. The architect was clearly interested in trying to emulate the Dutch architectural heritage in Albany, some of which was demonstrated right across the street.

The next step was alerting VA Central Office and trying to find out what we would have to do to accept the possible donation of a Fisher House. This was incredibly complex and time-consuming, in addition to being very frustrating. Anything new that happens in a vast bureaucracy is a problem for the legal minds and others who feel that they must protect the VA against any possible transgression. I would have thought that VA Central Office would have stopped everything else to facilitate the donation. I was, of course, was wrong. Even so, we persevered.

The Fisher Foundation attacked VA Central Office as well. Probably disbelieving that anything could be so complicated, they were given potential roadblocks. Instead of praising the Fisher Foundation and pushing through the project, VA Central Office raised all sorts of questions and objections. The fundamental question appeared to be that the VA's mission did not allow for the VA to accept a donation that would be primarily directed to veterans' families and not the veterans themselves. I felt that this theory was wrong, because the veteran in the hospital would clearly be benefiting from having his or her family closely available to visit. Eventually, it all worked out. I always felt that the Fisher Foundation took a political route to make it happen. I am so glad they did.

One of the requirements would be to establish a nonprofit corporation to manage the house and handle fundraising. In this, we were ahead of the game; we already had one. We had previously established the nonprofit VetCare to legally support donations to employee education.

Finally the construction started. We were thrilled. The Fisher Foundation had its own ideas about the construction. Our engineering folks strongly felt that there should be a full basement. This was, after all, the furthest north that any Fisher House had been constructed. We didn't get a basement, but we did get a crawl space with lots of additional gravel to protect the foundation of the house.

We all eagerly anticipated the dedication of the Fisher House. Because of the long list of special people who had to be available, the dedication date was set for late October. This was problematic because of our possible weather that late in the calendar year. We couldn't find a tent company in our area willing to risk their tent in the weather. The Fisher Foundation found a tent company in Maryland willing to risk it—the price probably made it a good decision. Personnel at the Fisher Foundation made numerous suggestions and inspections to make sure that everything was right. On-site managers determined that a row of bushes, although neatly trimmed, were in the wrong place for the dedication, so they removed the bushes and replanted them afterward. We in the VA were amazed by the world that the Fisher Foundation executives lived in. It was a sharp contrast to the fiscally constrained, conservative-in-most-activities—especially celebrations—world that we lived in.

The day for the dedication arrived. We were anxiously anticipating what the day would bring. We had practiced, rehearsed, and planned to make the day perfect. The weather was decent, cool, of course, but no precipitation.

Everyone from out of town made it. Dr. Thomas Garthewaite, the deputy undersecretary for health, came to represent VA Central Office. We were pleased that Tom was the one appointed. He represented the VA beautifully. He was a sharp clinician, a decent person, and, since he was a graduate of Cornell, cared about New York and knew enough about our operation to make valuable, insightful comments.

At the dedication ceremony, Tom sat beside one of Mr. Fisher's personal friends and a board member of the foundation, Mike Stein. The conversation that Tom had with Mike was classic in defining the different worlds of the Fisher Foundation and the VA. Tom asked Mike where he was from. Mike replied, "Rome."

"Rome, New York?" Tom asked.

Mike shook his head. "No. Rome, Italy." Not only was there an ocean between us ideologically, but it seemed culturally as well.

Mario Cuomo, the governor of New York, was the featured speaker. He was eloquent. In his speech, he extolled the virtues of the Fishers as people who had ascended the ladder of success and left the ladder in place to help others. Mr. Fisher had said privately that one of the reasons he wanted to build a Fisher House in Albany was to put one under the nose of the governor. Whatever the reason, the Fisher House generated enormous positive goodwill and publicity for the VA.

After the dedication ceremony, one of the rarest of events in all federal government occurred. The VA paid for a catered lunch. We were limited to about fifteen people. We assembled in the director's conference room. We watched Mr. Fisher and waited for him to begin eating. He said that he couldn't eat without a drink and requested a Johnny Walker Black scotch. We sent our assistant director trainee,

Mike Moreland, along with one of Mr. Fisher's aides, to buy a bottle. We made small talk. About fifteen minutes later, they returned with a pint of Johnny Walker Black. Mr. Fisher smiled. He drank. We ate.

After everyone had gone, I learned that Mike Moreland had paid for the whiskey. The nearest liquor store wasn't open. Mike went to the garage next door, which was in the same building, and got the manager there to call the owner. Fortunately, the owner promptly appeared. The aide had no cash, so Mike bought the multimillionaire his scotch whiskey.

Chapter 11.9: We Can Never Do Enough

The patients were always one of my primary fringe benefits. I enjoyed talking and interacting with them, even the few who were so disagreeable and/or dishonest that their actions and words were really self-defeating. But the vast majority did their service, worked all of their lives if they could, paid their taxes, and were in general good citizens. Hardly any of them considered themselves heroes. All of them did things that they never would have done outside of service and went to places that they never would have gone without the military sending them there. They were draftees and volunteers. The VA mainly serves the privates, seamen, and airmen, not the officers as a general rule. They are plainspoken, down-to-earth, concerned about each other, and proud of their service to the country, regardless of what that service was.

They are as a rule afflicted with the disabilities that occur with greater frequency in all men under twenty-five years old in this country: loss of limbs, traumatic brain injuries, paralysis, neurological damage, and the psychological and physical traumas of war. Added to this is the damage done by inadequate diets, long-term exposure to combat or incredible stress, and exposure to extreme weather. They survived.

Many of them aimed to be like John Wayne: Tough it out. Keep your head down. Don't complain. Do your time. Go home. So often they did not tell anybody about their injuries. They just wanted out. They weren't lifers, and, at the time of their injuries or infections, they were often nineteen or twenty, physically in great shape, and did not give a thought to the consequences of their injuries, infections, or the rest of their service experience on their bodies and minds when they would reached sixty or seventy.

Several veterans have told me that their service-related injury was a broken leg, suffered while playing softball or baseball on base. I heard it so often that I began to wonder just how tough a game they played in the service. I concluded that in many cases that was the cover story. They may not have liked to discuss the real injury suffered in combat. Or more likely, they didn't want their sweethearts, mothers, and sisters to worry even more about them. The cover story seemed to work, so they stuck with it.

I met Patsy one day in the nursing home care unit. I had seen him in a wheelchair at the Pearl Harbor Day ceremony. His real name was Pasquale Bambrela. He always had a smile on his face. He was a Pearl Harbor survivor. He was frail and died soon after I met him. I was told that when Pearl Harbor was bombed, he spent long hours in a hellish, blackened hole deep within his ship before he was saved. That may have been the reason that he was always smiling, permanently relieved by his redemption after the nightmare of uncertainty and approaching death.

A young draftee in Vietnam was patrolling with his infantry unit. He was nineteen and proud of his service to country. He had been in the country for about four months. On this particular patrol, the Viet Cong found them first. There were loud artillery explosions all around the unit. The young man was knocked out while crossing a shallow stream. He lay facedown in the water for a few minutes—long enough to be brain injured when his comrades found him. Rehabilitation failed. He remained in a coma. He required constant care. Of course, the VA would provide such services to the young man until his death. But his parents were dairy farmers in upstate New York. They insisted on taking him home. They cared for him for over thirty years. Then one day, Pa had a heart attack and died. Ma carried on with the dairy farm and caring for her son.

I met the mother and son when they were admitted to the Albany VA Medical Center. The mother had had a stroke and wasn't in much better condition than her son. The mother was a fully eligible veteran and so was her son. There could be no greater honor than to provide them high-quality health care. Like many such stories, I don't know how this one ended. I wish I had had the time to stay in touch. I include this story to show another example of kind of men and women that the VA serves.

Due to the large numbers of returning soldiers from Iraq with concussions, I will close this section with the story of a veteran who received a concussion in Vietnam. He was standing near a landing zone inside a fortified camp, where he should have been relatively safe. An artillery explosion occurred about twenty feet away from him. He received a concussion but was not entirely knocked out and seemed to quickly recover. He returned to the states and worked for some twenty years as a manufacturing draftsman in the Catskills. The plant closed, and he began experiencing joint pain. He received pain therapy from numerous VA medical centers. He also received psychological counseling.

In spite of this treatment, he insisted on having his legs removed because of the pain. First they were removed below the knee and then below the hip. When one VA surgical team would refuse to operate on him, he would go to another VA. When I met him his legs were gone, as were most of the fingers on his hands down to the first knuckle. The VA provided him with funds to buy an adaptive van. Despite his giving the VA the exact specifications that he required, there was always some safety problem or another with these vans. He wrote letters to Congress that often on the surface had to do with improving rural care in the VA but always carried another message about his personal concerns. After I lost track of him, I heard that he was seeking to have his gall bladder removed. This man showed me that there are veterans who are not seeking mental health care but who need it.

Chapter 11.10: The Secretary Who Cared

Jesse Brown, a combat-wounded veteran, was appointed by President Clinton to be the secretary of Veterans Affairs. He was originally from Chicago and had been a veterans' advocate for many years. He came to New York on many occasions. He was a dedicated veteran advocate, and he surrounded himself with medical center directors, especially for big conferences or meetings of veterans that happened in the state.

Jesse Brown came to Rochester for the dedication of our new outpatient clinic. Ironically, the clinic had been in the federal building downtown in a terrible space that was chopped up and impossible to organize effectively. The federal building housed the federal courts. The federal courts had a huge appropriation to rebuild many of their courtrooms and offices, and Rochester was one of the ones chosen. So the federal building asked the clinic to move out. It was an unintended blessing. I am sure that they were also delighted to get all those veterans away from their newly palatial and prestigious building, not to mention recouping a lot of parking. Sometimes, the right things happen for the wrong reasons.

Rochester is an interesting town. With Kodak, Bausch and Lomb, and other corporations, it had substantial wealth and great educational institutions with the University of Rochester and the Rochester Medical School. For about forty years after World War II, it also had a single rate for health insurance. Every citizen of Rochester paid the same for health-care insurance, because the big corporations underwrote the cost. Largely because of this, Rochester had never had anything more than a VA clinic. In essence, they didn't need a VA hospital because everyone was covered. I was told a story that might also have had a bearing on that.

Supposedly, the dean of the medical school had served during WWII and for a long time thereafter hated Franklin Roosevelt and somehow conceived that the VA was socialized medicine and didn't want one in Rochester. One day at a meeting, when someone made the innocent comment that Franklin Roosevelt was his own worst enemy, the dean replied, "Not as long as I am alive." So during the fifties and sixties, when a new VA medical center could have been had, Rochester didn't want one. However, when the crisis in health-care financing hit in the nineties, they desperately wanted a VA medical center. Of course, their timing was horrible, and they were fortuitous to get a new clinic. Like many other cities in the Northeast, Rochester closed hospitals and the HMOs lowered their payments to academic health centers like Strong Memorial, the Rochester Medical School's primary academic affiliate.

On the day of the dedication of the VA Rochester Outpatient Clinic, Jesse Brown was the main speaker. Outside the clinic, a veterans' group had arranged for Jesse to be ambushed by the newspaper and one of the local network affiliates. They had three or four wives of veterans who were in the nursing home at the VA medical center in Canandaigua, NY. The wives and their veteran representatives complained of cutbacks reducing the care that their husbands and fellow nursing home patients were receiving.

Jesse handled the situation beautifully. He came across as a caring, thoughtful person and not as a heavy-handed bureaucrat. He talked to the wives and reassured them. Then he got the VA medical center directors into the room, along with the service organizations' leaders, and gave us his marching orders. He told the VSO leaders to tell him every single problem with the VA. There weren't many. Part of the problem was that many of the staff of the VA medical center in Canandaigua had an "us against the world" attitude. They didn't much care about performance measures or productivity standards. They have changed a great deal in this regard, but, at the time, many of the employees and some of the spouses, volunteers, and people in the community were scared about their VA being downsized or closed.

During one morning meeting, a night nursing supervisor was standing in for the chief nurse. She recounted the night's events, concluding with a report that someone who looked a lot like the man in the picture on the wall in the lobby had been on the nursing home care unit on Sunday. We inquired anxiously about which man on the wall in the lobby. The pictures were of the president and the secretary of Veterans Affairs. She said, "The black one." This meant Jesse Brown had come to the hospital unannounced, didn't ask for any special favors or consideration, and had left telling the nurses that they were doing a great job.

In a environment where so many politicians need to be "handled," "helped" and/or "protected," Jesse was totally comfortable with veterans and VA employees. He was also unfailingly kind and gracious. Having been around him many times in many different situations, I saw an audience waiting patiently for the main event to be over so that they could be with him. Jesse said that these people huddled around him were his relatives. I saw so many of them, on so many different occasions, that I can't believe that he had that many relatives in upstate New York when he was from Chicago. He gave them time, took pictures with them, hugged them, and showed them a special love and attention that I am certain they reciprocated.

Chapter 11.11: Clinton Health-Care Reform

Early in the first term of President Clinton, the administration initiated work on health-care reform. Health-care reform was a central part of his pledge to the American people. Work started almost immediately under the leadership of the first lady, Mrs. Hillary Clinton. This was an exciting but daunting task that I felt was necessary for the country. I hoped that the VA would be included and wondered if there would be a way for me to become involved.

A few weeks later, I received a call from VA Central Office. The young lady said that she was calling on behalf of Dr. Elwood Headley, the associate chief medical director for ambulatory care. Dr. Headley was interested in having me participate in a task force to determine how the VHA would change because of health-care reform. I immediately accepted.

About a hundred of us were called to Washington for the kick-off meeting. There we learned that we would have to work for seven or eight weeks with time off only on the weekends. We were briefed on the Clinton health-care reform proposal and told that some of us would be asked to participate in the White House group as well or instead. Before I went home, I had been summoned to talk to the assistant secretary for policy and planning, who invited me to join the White House group. I was astonished but provided the information he requested, which included a brief summary of my career. At the next week's meeting of the VA health-care reform task force, I was asked to go to the White House that weekend and begin work. I had only brought enough medication for the week, and, since one of the meds was for high blood pressure, I had no desire to stroke out over the Clinton health-care plan. I told the contact that I would have to excuse myself to go home that evening and would come back as soon as a flight could get me back to Washington on Saturday morning. The contact abruptly said that wasn't OK; they needed me at 8 am on Saturday. I said in that case I would not be able to join the group; going without my blood pressure meds for an indefinite period of time just didn't seem prudent. I could have called my doctor and asked her to call in a prescription, but just didn't think of it. She hung up. And I never did get to join that special task force.

I was assigned to the finance work group, and I was named co-chair along with the VA Central Office director of finance. We assembled our group quickly and started the briefing process to bring everyone on the group up to speed as quickly as possible. The briefings included health-care financing, VA health-care costs and budgets, and the assignments of the other groups, including marketing and insurance and the Clinton health-care plan. We were semisequestered in the Washington DC Techworld complex. We worked diligently.

We arrived at what I think was a quality product. Without a detailed description of that effort, I can summarize our work in the phrase, "All money is green." By that I mean that all the health-care funding would go into one big pot, including the VA's health funding. All the myriad divisions, floors, ceilings, limitations, restrictions, and so forth would be removed. These obstacles are bad enough in the VA health care, but in the private sector, these legally based but frequently arbitrary restrictions introduce complexity into health-care decision making and restrict any organization's ability to take care of the whole patient when the eligibility doesn't provide funds for that purpose.

One big funding pot introduces a new bureaucracy that probably would be best done some other way, but this self-inflicted problem continues to exist. There are too many payers, too many layers in the payers, too much opportunity to deny or restrict based on fund availability, for example, as opposed to the patient's need. In addition, the "all money is green" concept would allow health care to become a more low-cost solution without the specialized and earmarked funding for specific diseases. Since most health care being provided is for chronic ailments, it would allow for a new database to make further recommendations as to the real demand—for example, for mental health care or obesity rehabilitation.

We had a running joke we called "You can't do that." The assigned VA attorneys would frequently tell us or some other group, "You can't do that." It seemed most of the time they were focusing on existing legislation rather than being aware of the art of the possible in terms of improving health-care delivery. Sometimes they would contradict one another; for example, one would tell us the VA couldn't advertise, and another one would say we could.

I believe that all health-care advertising should be restricted to purely informational, not sponsoring golf tournaments and signage at football stadiums. Our goal was to create for the VA the same legal abilities as the private sector. We proposed that the VA could bill and collect from Medicare and HMOs. We also proposed that the VA be allowed to fund raise in the same manner as our private-sector counterparts.

Health-care reform was an interesting experience. Sooner or later the nation will be back to considering health-care reform. The overall expense of our health-care system will—if it hasn't already—become detrimental to our economic competitiveness.

Chapter 11.12: The Bus Lady

One beautiful spring day, Linda Blumenstock, our public affairs officer, called the office. My secretary interrupted me in a meeting. I asked her what it was about. She just said, "It's about that bus lady, and she said you would want to take her call."

I was a little perplexed about who the bus lady was but agreed to take Linda's call. Linda was bubbling over with excitement. She quickly said, "Rosa Parks, the woman who started the Montgomery bus boycott is here visiting her nephew." Then she said, "Would you like to meet her?" I said of course.

We got to the patient's room, and there stood Rosa Parks with a genuine smile on her face. She was glowing at her nephew. He was a large man, probably 250 pounds and maybe six foot four, with arms like a steelworker's and a bull neck. I was quickly escorted outside the room by her personal manager, an elegant, young black woman who was polite but firm and unequivocal about her role in protecting Rosa. I assured her that we meant no harm and told her we had many employees who would be honored by the fact that Rosa Parks was in the building. We took a picture, and I left Rosa alone with her nephew.

One of the joys of being a health-care executive is the unexpected. The chance to meet famous people and modern-day heroes is an incredible fringe benefit. It also points out that you never quite know who the patient in the bed might be or who loves them. We have many such heroes, and it was my great honor and privilege to serve them for over thirty-seven years.

Chapter 11.13: The First Detail

Taking a detail in the VA means taking a different job on a temporary or interim basis. In my career, I have had many details as I came up through the ranks. These were brief and were not formalized, meaning the detail was not produced and signed by the approving official to commemorate the event. In the executive ranks, however, details become official and are documented. I received a call from my supervisor, Barbara Green, the eastern region director, who asked if I would accept a detail to act as the director of the VA medical center in Beckley, West Virginia. After consulting with my family, I accepted.

Beckley was a small town in rural southwestern West Virginia, about an hour south of the capital of Charleston. It was hilly country, and the VA medical center sat on top of a hill that had been leveled off. It was isolated in that its only access was a narrow road that had been built about thirty years before. This was not a good access to a medical center. Because of accidents, emergency vehicles, bad weather, and other possibilities, having two ways to get to a medical center should really be the minimal standard.

It was a small, general medical and surgical hospital—definitely a change of pace from the large, tertiary, academic health center that I led in Albany. Much of the medical center was new: outpatient areas, some of the diagnostics, and the canteen. An interior design consultant under contract had done a fair job of selecting furnishings and colors but had selected too many fake plants, almost all of which had fake thorns on them. These plants were often in the way, and anybody who brushed too closely was likely to get snagged. This was a hazard for old, fragile, or mentally confused patients.

There was a nursing home and inpatient units in the old part of the building. In the older part of the building the color choices seemed a bit odd or worse. The director often had the last word on every project, including color selection, I was informed. This accounted for the baby blue and pink colors in the nursing home. The staff in the nursing home hated the colors and the fact that they had no input in deciding them. The director's office was also in new construction. It was spacious, by far the largest office that I had ever been in. New furniture, bookcases, and a computer couldn't quite fill it up.

The staff, especially the nurses and clerical staff, was very good. Their main problem and mine was that most of the leaders of the administrative activities and a few of the clinicians did not appear to be so good. A weak, journeyman associate director who I knew from my time in VA Central Office, a secretary who was never occupied with work, and the cronies of the former director contributed to the situation. The chief of staff, however, was a pleasant surprise. His name was Mark Shelhorse. He was well educated, had excellent experience, was highly insightful and energetic, and he was a psychiatrist. This came as quite a surprise because the facility had no inpatient psychiatric beds. I quickly formed the opinion that we could turn this facility around and in a short time make it much better.

Mark Shelhorse had a positive, proactive attitude toward improving clinical issues: improving quality, accountability, physician productivity, and the facility's response to the assigned performance measures. After he briefed me, I knew that he had his hands full. He was aggressively seeking solutions, including recruiting better-trained and more qualified clinicians. One problem that Mark had identified was that some physicians requested consults on virtually every patient. This practice frequently delayed treatment and increased the cost of care. The former chief of staff, who had gone into private practice, was one of the most used consultants. Often his specific expertise, infectious disease, didn't seem to fit any justifiable reason for a particular consult. He was close to the recently retired director, who still lived on the grounds because he was on sick leave pending retirement.

The former director was a legend in West Virginia and had served in Beckley on three separate occasions. He was a dynamic and personable figure. Because of his personal charm, his reputation as an effective administrator had remained intact. But the local perception was that he had stayed too long and had become too much of a micromanager during the last few years.

Despite numerous illogical and problematic clinical decisions, he had allowed the former chief of staff to stay in the job for far too long. Over the objections of others, the previous chief of staff had hired two physicians who had reportedly been fired previously by the VA. One, an internist, had been fired from the Beckley VA Medical Center! There apparently had been promises that he would reform, but it seemed to me that he hadn't. The other was a surgeon who had left a VA in Ohio, where reportedly he had been terminated from the staff. This surgeon had been accused of malpractice, and Beckley had hired him on the grounds that it was difficult to get surgeons to come to West Virginia. The VA's district counsel reported that there were multiple malpractice claims against him. The surgeon was detailed to the library. The former director had approved these hirings. The director had gradually and inevitably transformed his excellent public and community relations into a cauldron of seething resentment and suspicion. He seemed unaware of this.

One of the first ceremonies in the auditorium that I went to was the incentive awards presentations to recognize those outstanding employees who had received superior performance awards. I was to personally give them their certificates, shake hands, and have my picture taken with them. Most of the audience was sullen throughout. During some of the presentations, there were openly negative remarks being made from the audience.

During a break, I consulted with the chief of staff. He quietly explained that some of the service chiefs only rewarded their "pets," and the biggest awards were reserved for the clique that drank coffee with the director. I asked the personnel officer about the strangely hostile atmosphere. She tried to put a rosy glow on it that we were trying to change negative attitudes by having such ceremonies. I told her that I doubted anyone's attitude would ever change based on what I was seeing. I finished the ceremony knowing that some administrative changes in middle management and processes would have to be made.

I had been of the opinion that the quality of care in the VA was as good as anywhere and better than most. My sojourn at Beckley convinced me that there was at least one exception and perhaps others. The two senators, two of the most powerful in the Senate, and the local congressman were deluged with constituent complaints. I was to learn that the Office of the Inspector General had visited the medical center and had written a report. The medical center was supposed to have a copy of that report. I began the search for it.

I was sickened that the VA had enabled the mess to continue for far too long. In spite of the many fine employees, the mess continued because the magnitude of the problem was unknown to them. The director had been trying to pacify the regional director and the congressional delegation. When the mess became public, only then did the regional director and VA Central Office start to cast about for an immediate change.

That evening, I finally discovered the VA Office of Inspector General (OIG) report. It was scathing. To say that the OIG report stated that the surgical program was a shambles would have been an understatement. No one at Beckley had seen it except for the director. They had no knowledge that it had even been written. In the course of looking for it, I also found correspondence from the congressional delegation that was pointed and critical and that may have never been answered. If it had been answered, the answer was complete denial of the allegations contained within.

I also found two Office of Personnel Management (OPM) employee satisfaction surveys. Essentially, they both said the same things: morale was terrible, employees had little if any respect for their leaders—especially the director. In the comment portion of the surveys, there were many negative statements. The statements criticized care in certain areas of the hospital, declared their desire to retire on disability, and expressed the notion that favoritism was the only way to get promoted.

The following morning, at a staff meeting called for the purpose, I discussed the reports with leaders of the medical center. The findings were mostly about morale issues, especially the ill will felt toward the former director and his closer advisors, a group of four individuals who were allowed to operate as they desired. My staff and I decided to increase recognition for employees and explain the issues for the hospital.

One Friday, I gradually got sicker as the day progressed. Finally, at about 2:00 pm, I went to the employee physician. In Beckley's case, the employee physician and the chief outpatient physician were one and the same. I was seated in an exam room, and the employee physician said that he would be right with me.

A few seconds later, a senior clinical leader came to see me. He said that my clinical need would show why his service, which had requested two additional positions recently, deserved them. I had denied that request on the grounds that the service had not provided a productivity analysis. I told him that his saying that to me under these circumstances was highly unethical. After hearing this, the senior clinical leader scooted rapidly out of the room. Soon thereafter, a laboratory technologist came in to draw my blood.

After she had drawn the blood and departed, there was a knock on the door. I heard the chief of staff's voice and asked him to come in. He rushed into the room with a worried look on his face. He said, "Fred, I wish you had come and got me."

I said, "I think it's just a urinary tract infection. I shouldn't need to bother you."

He said, "As long as you're here in Beckley, please come and get me first." He quickly asked for my symptoms and called my personal physician in Albany to get the name of the antibiotic that she had prescribed for a previous infection. He then got the employee physician to write the script. We took it to the pharmacy, where it was filled, and Mark sent me home.

When I went for my routine follow-up visit to the employee physician, he was in his office preparing to eat lunch. He had a handful of paper towels and was carefully layering them across the surface of his desk. I waited for this process to be complete. He asked me how I was doing. I said fine. That was the sum of his care for me. I was fascinated with his display of obsessive, compulsive behavior though.

Beckley was a town with a quiet, charming facet and a rough and tumble facet and with some of everything in between. It is Senator Byrd's hometown, and his mastery of the federal appropriation process shows up clearly in Beckley. Beckley boasts a new addition at the VA, a state Mine Health and Safety Academy, an armed services induction center, and a rather large IRS office. There may have been other federal establishments as well. I felt that they were well placed. The economy and the town certainly needed revenue.

The coal mines nearby Beckley had a high degree of sulfur, and, because of environmental concerns due to the difficulty of removing the sulfur, the coal mining had moved further from Beckley. This led to a high unemployment rate. West Virginia had a high enlistment rate, as its young men and women frequently chose the military as the path to a better education and better opportunities.

The mental health and addiction needs of the veteran population that the VA medical center in Beckley served were paramount and neglected. Of course, the chief of staff, Dr. Shelhorse, fully understood this and had understood it from day one. His wife, also a psychiatrist, had been denied employment by the previous director on the misplaced grounds of nepotism in the face of an increasing demand for mental health services. Her credentials were also impeccable.

Changing the shape of the medical center to accommodate psychiatric patients would take a minimum of a couple of years to modify wards that would remove elements that might allow patients to harm themselves or others, to train the nursing staff, and to hire the other mental health professionals that would be required.

What Beckley did was often fruitless and always frustrating. When a drunk or decompensating veteran showed up in the ER, and the ER physicians determined that he or she needed psychiatric care, the physicians would call the neighboring VA medical centers to determine if they had inpatient room and could take him or her. This process would also be required for medical and surgical patients who had a problem that the VA Medical Center Beckley had neither the expertise nor the equipment to handle. The neighboring VA medical centers were all hours away. These were Huntington, West Virginia; Salem, Virginia; Pittsburgh, Pennsylvania; and Cincinnati, Ohio. Sometimes the ambulances had to go all the way to Richmond to find a bed. Very often, by the time they got to the other VA, the psychotic episode was over or the patient was no longer intoxicated. The determination then was that the patient didn't need admission, and back they'd come.

The need for mental health professional staff was a problem that manifested itself in other ways as well. Shortly after I got to Beckley, I was on my way to the canteen and passing the corridor the led directly to outpatient services. In the middle of this corridor stood a veteran screaming at the top of his lungs at the patient advocate. The patient advocate, a grandmother and genuinely kind, caring person, was quietly absorbing this verbal, profane punishment. I quickly walked down to them. The veteran saw me coming and departed. I asked her what this had been about. She said that it happened all the time. "Not anymore," was what I said.

I called the VA chief of police and asked him if he knew about the verbal abuse the staff was taking from certain veterans. "Yes, indeed," was his response. I asked why. He said, "It's always been this way. The previous director told us in no uncertain terms that there would never be a veteran arrested at this VA on his watch."

I instructed him to change that process immediately. Veterans who were verbally abusive to staff would at the very least be escorted to their car and told to come back when they could be civil. Things got much better for our bedraggled patient advocate.

My secretary continued to be a puzzle to me. She got the work done that I assigned her. Her desk stayed clear. She sometimes seemed uncertain when she walked into my office. I actually thought that I had somehow offended her. She never lost that nervous uncertainty that an employee with a new supervisor sometimes exhibits. She walked slowly and carefully. She was also immediately alert whenever I spoke. But in the press of business, I let any concerns I had rock along.

After I had been in Beckley for about two months, she came to see me. She said that she was retiring. I said I hope that it was not because of me or something I'd done. She said no. For years, she had had declining vision. She had been to all of the academic health centers in the general vicinity, including Ohio State, seeking something that might improve her vision, but everything had failed. So she was going to retire and live with her sister. I told her I was sorry. I had had a blind secretary and didn't realize it. I think this shows that a determined person can hide disabilities, addictions, or a myriad of other personal problems in the workplace without the supervisor realizing it. We all need to make sure that we have effective employee-assistance programs and that they are utilized.

I am grateful for the Beckley experience. I used skills that I hadn't used for years. I got to know a dedicated and resourceful group of employees and a deserving group of veterans. The employees wanted to improve. The veterans wanted and deserved a high quality of care. I was proud to be a part of them. I still think of them often and wish them the very best. An excellent director was appointed soon after I left, and the good folks at the Beckley VA Medical Center continued to improve.

Chapter 11.14: The Sing-Along

Whenever a deputy secretary comes to town, it's a stressful experience for the medical center director. A conference of the state Veterans Service officers was being held in Saratoga Springs, a beautiful and historic town about an hour north of Albany. The state director of Veterans Affairs was excited about his visit. The two were rumored to be pals, and the deputy secretary had once hosted a state directors of Veterans Affairs conference in Little Rock when he was the state director for Arkansas.

The conference was primarily for training of the benefits counselors who were located in every county of New York. Speakers were brought in, and, as usual, I was invited to update the group on what was happening with the VA. Having the deputy secretary there was a coup. The

New York State director was busy planning the festivities that would occur after the training sessions had concluded for the day. The deputy secretary enjoyed sing-alongs, we were told. So everybody who could play an instrument was asked to bring it. There was alcohol and other refreshments. The secretaries who normally worked in the state office were asked specifically to come to the training and to stay late.

On the Friday before the conference, I received a call from a person on the secretary's staff. She was cordial but firm. The secretary wanted me to stay until nine o'clock in the evening the night before the deputy secretary was to leave to go back to Washington. This was the first and only request of this kind that I have ever received. I was already somewhat concerned but agreed.

I picked up the deputy secretary at the airport and brought him and his staff person to the VA medical center. We toured the medical center. He was kind and gracious to all the staff and enjoyed interacting with the patients. There were two incidents that are worth reporting.

First, on the rehabilitation unit, Deputy Secretary Buford enjoyed the homelike surroundings and the fact that the staff had come to work wearing costumes because it was Halloween the next day. One of the nurses had dressed up as Dolly Parton. Mr. Buford thought that was funny, and the patients really enjoyed her costume. Part of every such visit is picture taking. Many of these pictures go to the staff, who treasure them as a memento of the time a big shot from Washington came to visit their ward or clinic. Initially, Mr. Buford was agreeable about getting his picture taken with Dolly. After it was taken, his mood changed, and he told the photographer that he wanted that negative.

The next incident happened in the outpatient clinic. He asked a patient in a wheelchair how long he had been waiting. The patient, who looked very sick, weak, and exhausted, said that he thought about two hours. Mr. Buford flared up and asked me why the patient had been waiting for two hours. I didn't know and went to the desk clerk and asked him. Before I could get back to Mr. Buford, the patient said that he really didn't mind waiting; the staff had been very kind to him, and he knew he was being taken care of. I wanted to kiss the patient. The desk clerk told me the physician who was consulting on the case was on his way down to see the patient.

The conference started the next day in Saratoga. Mr. Buford made the usual kinds of remarks: extolling the sacrifices made by veterans, explaining the budget choices were the best that could be made under the circumstances, and praising the effort and concern President Clinton was making over veteran issues and budgets.

After the conference agenda for the day ended, I moseyed over to the hospitality room, where I found one of my employees, an RN who took care of most of our high-profile veterans and who attended all the veterans conferences and conventions in our area to make sure that if any health issue arose, we could promptly take care of them. Due to their preexisting conditions and, in some cases, the drinking that some of the members did, it was not uncommon for a health issue to arise.

After some guitar playing and singing, it was time for dinner. Mr. Buford spoke again, the state director spoke, and the president of the state Service Officers Association spoke. I was watching the time, because I had every intention of leaving precisely at nine o'clock.

When dinner was over, I went back to the hospitality room. I chatted with the folks there. The secretaries from the state office were there, looking ill at ease. My VA RN was there, and she told me frankly that she didn't like what appeared to be going on. I felt ill at ease also. It seemed painfully apparent that Mr. Buford and the state director were intending to drink and party with the secretaries. I agreed and told her I was leaving at nine. I didn't have the courage to confront the deputy secretary or the state director. She smiled and joined in the singing. At nine o'clock we both left.

The next morning, there was a little article in the Albany newspaper about a high-level Washington official partying in Saratoga the previous evening. The Saratoga newspaper was more explicit. I felt the need to report this incident to my supervisor, the regional director. I did this just in case there were any political inquiries that became directed at her. I told her, "Barbara, for what it's worth, here's what the two newspapers are reporting. My instructions were to stay with the deputy secretary until 9:00 pm, and I did that." I also told her who had asked me to stay with Mr. Buford and suggested she call her. I never learned whether she made that call.

The denouement was that nothing more occurred about this

incident as far as Mr. Buford was concerned. However, the gossip was that the young ladies from the state office had filed Equal Employment Opportunity complaints over the matter.

Chapter 11.15: Conferences to Remember

VA executives are required to go to many, many conferences. Over the course of a career, there are very few that standout in my memory. The first conference to remember came as a complete surprise. An invitation to the formal dinner of the biannual conference of the Medal of Honor Society came in the mail one day. Their meeting was to be held in Saratoga Springs in July. This was the first and only time that I have been invited to this highly select group of veterans.

Several of us were also honored by being in the parade that the city of Saratoga Springs put on in honor of the Medal of Honor recipients. The march was festive: kids lining the route waving the American flag, bands playing, and lots of patriots, in uniform and not, who came out to honor the Medal of Honor recipients. Several other veterans' military organizations were there too. Navy battleship or cruiser reunions for the people who had served on them, ex-POW groups, and Veterans Service Organizations were there solely for the purpose of recognizing the recipients of the Medal of Honor. Of course, many of the recipients belonged to these other groups. I was reminded of many charms of small-town America, but I suppose any town in the county would have gone all out to recognize these American heroes.

At dinner that night, there were probably about fifty recipients in attendance. A few were still in military attire, two or three on active duty, but most wearing their uniform in retirement. At my table was a retired Marine colonel. He now lived in Jupiter, Florida. He brought his wife with him. She appeared to have Alzheimer's, and he was constantly attentive to her. He was a farm boy from Idaho who joined the Marines after World War II. He had gone to Officer Candidate School and was commissioned. He was a major on a very cold, bleak hilltop in Korea when his brigade came under assault. Waves of attackers, with artillery shells constantly raining down, went on through the night. The major constantly had to reorganize his lines and defenses. When dawn broke, he was the highest-ranking, surviving officer on the hilltop. It was such an honor to be with him.

The speakers that evening were Andy Rooney from NBC, Mike Wallace from NBC, Senator and future Senator Mr. and Mrs. Bob Dole, Governor Pataki, and an FBI agent who spends his time tracking down illegal and fraudulent claims of people who have asserted that they hold the Medal of Honor. There were people at my table who were there solely to get the autographs of the recipients. Others were attending because they had once known a recipient and wanted to be there to honor their memory.

Another memorable conference was a long-planned affair. Several of us from the VA went to the national conference of the Gold Star Mothers. All the notable politicians in the Albany, New York, area showed up. There were corporate sponsors. Members of the various Veterans Service Organizations ushered the members of the Gold Star Mothers to their seats and waited on their every need.

As I sat at my table, a special event came back into my memory. At a previous Veterans' Day parade in Albany, I had finished marching and was standing in the reviewing stand. As I watched the marching groups go by, my eyes drifted to the crest of the hill, where I saw the Marine Corps Band drum major just coming into view. He was a bull-necked African American, and he was proudly and appropriately strutting, leading his excellent musicians in the parade. As I watched him, I saw him catch a glimpse of the Gold Star Mothers, whose car was parked near the reviewing stand so that they could watch the parade in greater comfort. The drum major led his band to the car of the Gold Star Mothers, and that's where he stopped the band and the parade. They serenaded the Gold Star Mothers with three songs. The Gold Star Mothers were smiling through their tears. It was a wonderful moment. At this dinner, after I had said hello to all the Gold Star Mothers, I waited with some trepidation for the featured speaker.

The featured speaker that evening was a Medal of Honor recipient from Rochester, New York. I knew him, even though we had never met. I knew him because he used the VA to receive his health care, and I wondered if he would say anything about the time when we had delayed his compensation and pension appointment for a very long time.

Fortunately, he didn't say a word about that, but rather explained why he didn't do what it was his Medal of Honor citation said he did. Of course, that caught everyone's attention. He had been an army ranger medic and served in Vietnam. When his outpost came under attack, an explosion threw him to the ground. He was unconscious for a time, and, when he regained consciousness, he couldn't move his legs. He edged his way to the sandbags guarding the command bunker.

A Montagnard soldier serving with the Rangers came and got him. The Montagnard picked him up and carried him to where a soldier lay injured and needed care. The medic supplied that care. The Montagnard picked him up again, only to be shot and killed. Two more Montagnards were shot and killed in the same manner. The medic went on to say that his citation said that he went from injured ranger to injured ranger without mentioning the Montagnards. He later regained his ability to walk and went on to become a guidance counselor. I was so honored to hear this soldier's story. He could have bashed the VA in the process and didn't. The VA medical centers in western New York and Syracuse collaborated to get this man's exam after a year of canceled appointments and missed opportunities. The two medical center directors personally intervened to get the job done. And they would have done the same for any veteran, not just one holding the Medal of Honor. Whether the Medal of Honor write-up was a mistake or an omission doesn't matter. Whether our delays involving his exam were a mistake or an omission doesn't matter. Get the job done. Recover quickly and get the job done.

The VA sponsors an annual event entitled "Salute to Veterans." This event features live entertainment, visits from dignitaries, professional athletes, entertainers and others. In addition, a national Salute chairman is chosen, usually a veteran. Past chairmen have been Ernest Borgnine and Charles Durning.

In Albany, during the governorship of Mario Cuomo, we had the governor's wife, Matilda Cuomo, as our special hostess. With a warm and generous smile on a beautiful face, Matilda lit up the lives of our patients and employees. She was there at the special invitation of the state director of Veterans Affairs, who was a patient of ours. During one of the various tight-budget periods, we at Albany, like so many other VA medical centers, cut off the so-called lowest-priority veterans. One of those cut off was a professor emeritus of romance languages at St. John's University who claimed to have introduced Mario and Matilda. That night at the event, I asked him why he wanted to receive care at the VA. He said, "This is where my buddies are." The ceremony with Matilda continued on with his bright and shining face. He would read his annual special poem tribute to Matilda, but I was always sad about the unfair circumstances that made my job tougher than it needed to be and denied this veteran his choice for where he wanted to receive care.

Chapter 12
1995–2002: Network Director

We had a new undersecretary for health in Washington: Dr. Kenneth Kizer. He came from California, and he was a board-certified emergency room physician among other certifications. During this time, some in the administration and Congress were saying that this was the VA's last chance to reform itself. The concept of giving veterans vouchers and having them choose their own providers frequently came up. The published assumptions were always that the VA was an overly expensive health-care system, antiquated, bureaucratic, and unmanageable. Dr. Kizer arrived in Washington at a critical time in the VA's history.

Moving with incredible rapidity, Dr. Kizer immediately set a tone of expecting positive change. He made many of those changes himself. Always arguing from an expert knowledge of data and managed care, he set about creating a climate that embraced change. He was asking a lot of questions, proposing new ideas, and making changes, despite a loud chorus from his critics and detractors.

Before long, he created Veterans Integrated Service Networks (VISNs). Furthermore, he was going to announce the jobs for those positions not only internally, but externally to the federal government as well. This was a radical departure from the norm. This change alienated many of my colleagues, but I was intrigued and hoped that I would be able to go after one of these jobs.

Dr. Kizer presented us with a prescription for change that covered virtually every aspect of our business. We were going to do more outpatient care, open more clinics, close inpatient beds, and really do managed care by aggressively reducing the length of stay and by improving quality, performance, and customer service. This looked like an impossible task. Many of my colleagues wondered out loud if they were being set up for failure.

The job announcement for network director came out, and I applied for the job. The job announcement covered all twenty-two of the networks. I studied up on managed care and learned as much as I could about the issues related to moving inpatient care to outpatient care. The VA had traditionally exceeded the averages for length of stay in nearly every category. If you could reduce these lengths of stay to the norm, significant resources would be freed up to spend on treating more veterans in lower cost settings in outpatient. In addition, Dr. Kizer had set targets for reducing long-term care beds. The VA had inpatient nursing home beds, contract or community nursing home beds, and a category called intermediate beds, which were long-term and in most settings indistinguishable from nursing home beds. I thought that the network director job was the new frontier for the VA, a chance to be in the forefront of positive change on a large scale, reinventing the VA health-care system.

I was fortunate enough to be selected for an interview, and I flew to Washington. It was a sultry, hot day there, and my interview appointment was at 5:30 pm on a Friday afternoon. I arrived early and was shown to the undersecretary's waiting room. There, much to my surprise, was my supervisor, Barbara Green. We chatted. I always bring something to read, so waiting doesn't bother me too much, but I could tell that, as her appointment time kept getting farther and farther behind, she was getting annoyed. She fidgeted, rolled her eyes, and crossed and recrossed her legs. She pursed her lips and checked her watch repeatedly. On Friday afternoons at 4:30 pm, the cooling systems shut down as an energy-saving measure. So it was warm and uncomfortable in the waiting room. Eventually, she was asked into the interview.

Once she went in, I began to study a list of the ten points that I wanted to make with Dr. Kizer. I wanted to give him the impression that I really wanted the job, which I did. However, I really didn't want to move from Albany. The site selections for the twenty-two network offices had already been made, and Albany had been chosen to be one of them. Therefore, if I was selected for Albany, I wouldn't have to move. This was important for two reasons: first, my family and I had already moved twelve times for the VA. Second, in a year or two, my wife would become vested in the New York State teacher retirement system, a considerable feat considering how much we had moved, and she loved her job.

At about 6:00 pm, Barbara came stumbling out. Her head was down, her body was rigid, and she didn't acknowledge my presence in any way. I went into the conference room with Dr. Kizer. Dr. Jule Moravec, who had been chosen to be the chief network officer and thus third in command of the Veterans Health System was there, and a very senior minority associate director was on the speakerphone. This was the interview panel. Dr. Kizer had a list in front of him, which must have been the questions constituting the patterned interview. I pulled my index card of the ten points I had made out of my pocket and placed it before me along with a pen.

Dr. Kizer proceeded to ask me questions. Sometimes, he would follow up with a multitude of other questions. He asked me when I was sitting in my rocking chair in retirement what would I look back on as my proudest professional achievement. I answered, "The continuous quality improvement (CQI) effort and journey that we have made at the VA medical center in Albany." I kept coming back to continuous quality improvement in the rest of my answers. Neither Dr. Moravec nor the associate director on the telephone ever asked me a question. I was glad when the interview was over. I had made all ten of my points. I thought I may have dwelled on CQI for too much of the interview, but I was satisfied with my performance. My suit was drenched with sweat. I went out into the slightly cooler Washington air very glad that the interview was over.

After a couple of weeks, Dr. Kizer called me to tell me that I had the job. He seemed pleased, and I certainly was. He told me that the job was for the network in Albany. I was thrilled. I thanked him profusely, and he said, "Thank me after we get the job done." I did then as well.

Back at the Albany VA Medical Center, I quickly made plans to transition to the new job. Fortunately, I knew all the supporting folks, so I set up a team to screen and interview applicants for the ten positions that I would have in the network. This was not enough, but it was a start.

We were also contending with a continuing resolution. This meant that the folks who were selected for jobs other than where they were already at couldn't move, no new employees could be hired, and so forth. In other words, except for the fortunate few of us who were already in place, progress in establishing the network stopped. In December, with the continuing resolution not being extended, the Speaker of the House of Representatives essentially held the federal government hostage. We were told that it was part of his Contract with America.

The VA medical center was one of the few federal agencies to continue operations, having been deemed essential. As we were part of the federal executive board, the board met at the VA. Most of these executives had been furloughed along with their employees, so meeting at the VA gave us all a chance to organize assistance to help employees who were struggling during the holiday season without a paycheck. Many of our organizations helped federal employees with cash assistance and moral support. The Vietnam Veterans of America were first and foremost among those organizations providing assistance.

The staff we selected were health systems specialists by title for the most part. I was having difficulty in finding a chief financial officer, a medical director, and a chief information officer. After reviewing countless applications and making scores of phone calls, I selected a chief of staff from another network to be the medical director. He was an internist and had gone to school in Canada with training, among other fine places, at the Mayo Clinic. I convinced a friend, Mike Moreland, who was an associate director at a smaller facility in Pennsylvania to become the chief financial officer. I knew his quantitative skills were excellent. I convinced a young health systems specialist who was transferring to us from the El Paso Outpatient Clinic to take on the responsibilities of the chief information officer.

The chief network officer, Dr. Jule Moravec, asked us for organization charts. I had formed a somewhat negative opinion of the traditional organization charts, which don't reflect the way that the work really gets done and leaves the customer, in this case, our veterans, out of the picture. These charts also put everyone into a box and reinforce the strictly hierarchical nature of most organizations. There was some literature to suggest that organizational charts could be done in a concentric fashion, with the mission at the center and the rings of interest as represented by the key parts of the workforce being rings around that center.

The nucleus of people who had arrived in the office had also recommended that the office be paperless. We thought that the network office, if it started paperless, could remain so because all of our work would be on computers. This led to a decision to not have a secretary position. We were naïve of course, but felt with everyone in the office being computer literate and expected to produce their own documents that we would have more time and talent to take on the ambitious changes that we knew lay ahead of us. We polished up the organization chart and sent it in to Dr. Moravec.

Pending final approval, we went ahead with committing all the office jobs, save one, which was the one that could be converted to a secretary if the organization chart was not approved. In the interim, Dr. Moravec would call and ask me how things were going. He was interested in how we were functioning without a secretary. The truth was that it was too early to tell, but I told Dr. Moravec something like, "So far, so good."

On about the third call, or perhaps the fourth, Dr. Moravec politely let me know that our organization chart would never be approved. I was not shocked but pretended to be. I cautiously inquired as to why, thinking that it was because the chart looked a little like Mickey Mouse's head and they wanted a more traditional view. But I was wrong. He told me that we would have to put a secretary on the organization chart. I agreed to the change. Some of the folks in the office were irate about having to put a secretary on our organizational chart, but they quickly got over it.

In the first town hall meeting that I moderated as network director, the second question that was asked was, "Why do you hate secretaries?" I realized then that the paperless office proposal had been a bad idea. I had never thought I was demoralizing a key group of employees across the network (i.e., the secretaries). I reviewed for everyone at the town hall meeting what our thinking had been, and I was sure to tell them how much I actually loved and depended on secretaries. I also told them we had been wrong.

My staff and I were flooded by paper, much of it from VA Central Office, some duplicative of what they had already sent electronically. Even without paper, we would have needed secretaries to be the interface persons for all the electronic messaging, directives, and assignments that come in, must be tracked, and so forth. I always have appreciated the kind and gracious manner in which Dr. Moravec approached the rectification of what he saw and knew to be a problem.

All of us had much learning to do about e-mail. We still do. One of the central issues that I see is that e-mail is so easy, direct, and instant. Prior to e-mail, we had to dictate or compose in word processing, and prior to that in pen and paper. This extended process led us to be more thoughtful.

There was a prioritization process that prolonged the preparation of a memo or letter. The thinking involved was was it worth the time to write and send a memo, or can I just make a telephone call? For those communications that actually left the medical center, there were several reviews. Often, by the time the memo got written, things had changed, tempers had cooled, and the issue or miscommunication was clarified. E-mail often allows for extended issue development or dialogue to occur and permits lots of input. Too often there is too little thought put into the preparation of the e-mail. A practice that I developed was to write a response or initiative in my notebook and let the issue develop in my head before I would go charging into an e-mail response to a potentially difficult situation.

Dr. Kizer, the undersecretary for health, and his deputy, Thomas Garthewaite, both used e-mail to a great extent. For a manager, there is nothing quite like receiving an e-mail from the organization's CEO or chief operating officer. Dr. Kizer sent us proposed policies and directives with short turnarounds. He forced learning in the organization and taught us a lot about how to prioritize. In the previous organizational scheme, the proposed directives and policies would serially go around the organization and then to the regional directors, so unless an issue was absolutely critical, the directive or proposal took weeks or months to reach the field. And there was an attitude in many senior executives minds that they had the authority to modify it as they saw fit—with the idea of improving it and making it better. That attitude helped to defeat the system-wide implementation of change on a fairly frequent basis. Furthermore, it led directly to VA Central Office thinking that all its field facilities were doing things one way, when the reality was that there were multiple versions of the procedure or practice in place with always one, two, or more that hadn't seemed to have gotten the message at all.

The new concept allowed Dr. Kizer to forcefully implement his will on the organization. In fact, the new directives were orders that had to be carried out. The Veterans Health Administration had been a decentralized organization in the extreme. While this encouraged innovation, there was neither enough innovation to justify it nor enough lateral communication to spread the innovations, and there was not a single platform from which everyone could rely and build upon.

Dr. Kizer also taught me that the formerly tried and true processes of continuous quality improvement were not going to work in this new management environment. So we took the continuous quality improvement and made it fast track. Sometimes teams would report in two to three weeks instead of the usual six to eight weeks; sometimes we took their data and implemented changes that we hoped would work; and sometimes we simply had to take matters into our own hands. We learned that we could move the system upward through stages or phased changes. This was because even minimal changes made the data we collected different.

We stumbled over our five sites, causing sometimes slight, unintentional variations in the data collections or the interpretation of what was to be measured. We were frustrated by the simple collection of required reports to VA Central Office. These same factors—individual interpretation, different views of common definitions, and differences in how our computers were set up and programmed—drove us to realize that organizational changes and our new management processes had to occur and quickly.

Dr. Kizer's *Prescription for Change* was the template that guided us. The *Prescription for Change* suggested that we try service line organization. Our network's executive council discussed this, and we arranged for non-VA health-care organizations to brief us on their lessons learned. After this and much internal discussion, we elected to give service line organization a try.

This meant going back to VA Central Office to get approval of our new organization that would cover the entire network and cut across all of the existing functional organizations. The few service lines that we had learned about were product specific (i.e., cardiac care or imaging services). We were about to change a tried and true organization to an experimental design. A new organization meant we would have to learn "on the fly" and have the courage and insight to make changes quickly and adroitly.

A great many supervisors in the network viewed these changes with trepidation and outright alarm. Even so, a critical mass of us were committed to the attempt. We knew that the radical changes being driven by Dr. Kizer to improve our performance and quality would require a more streamlined organization that transcended the former top-down, functionally based organization.

Before 1995, the VA was a very decentralized organization. Our critics, and there were a great many, frequently expressed the notion that the VA health-care system was a loose confederation of occasionally warring fiefdoms. Internally, our quality and performance experts and many of our senior executives knew that our quality and access were plagued by multiple variations. Most of us knew that making changes, even simple changes, was achingly slow and erratic in implementation.

Most importantly, some of us knew that the quality of our management was extremely variable. All of the previous management culture was rationalized by the fact that we were always short of funds, sometimes critically so. We rationalized that we in the VA had a higher degree of difficulty in that we did not have the management flexibilities (a streamlined and flexible hiring process and a quick, sure termination process) of the private sector. All of our human resources tools were and still are slow and frustrating.

New York State, including the piece that I led in upstate and the other New York network which had the rest of the state, came under some intense criticism for the changes we were attempting to make. The changes were going fairly smoothly in upstate, but there was a constant barrage of criticism directed at our sister network to the south. The New York congressional delegations expressed its desire to meet with Dr. Kizer over the changes. They asked the secretary for a meeting, and he directed Dr Kizer to meet with this group. Dr. Kizer then asked my colleague and me to meet with this group at the same time.

I thought initially that Dr. Kizer simply wanted us to say that we needed to do what we had been assigned to do (e.g., reduce the length of stay in acute medicine). At the morning of the meeting, I arrived, somewhat anxiously studying my notes for possible answers to probable questions. My colleague arrived. Just before the meeting was to start, Dr. Kizer arrived. He looked like he had just jumped out of the shower, but, other than having his long hair slightly wet, he looked like a man on a mission. His demeanor was stern and intent. His eyes looked ready to challenge and be challenged.

We entered the large conference room. Most of the representative delegation was there. They sat on one side of the table, and the three of us on the other. Dr. Kizer gave the *Prescription for Change* overview. He then invited my colleague to speak. Then he invited me to speak. Then we answered questions. During the answer to a question prefaced with the notion that the VA should expect longer lengths of stays, Dr. Kizer's very direct, undiplomatic, but seriously correct answer enraged the congressman who had asked the question. I thought he was going to come over the table at Dr. Kizer.

I silently blessed Dr. Kizer for his forthrightness but questioned his lack of political correctness. The hard, cold truth is such a precious commodity in Washington, and we do not honor it nearly enough. The VA health-care system is better by far for the transformation he led. The congressman, who at one time was a serious contender for the Speaker of the House position, hopefully learned something and did not reprise against Dr. Kizer.

James Autry has said, "A paradox of management is that too many managers take themselves too seriously while too few take management seriously enough." Those managers who do take themselves too seriously also want autonomy. Employees and managers want autonomy. But autonomy doesn't really exist for anybody in an organization. The result of assuming autonomy is an easy trap of ego and entitlement that softly ensnares managers who aren't carefully examining and reexamining their ideas, motivations, expectations, decisions, goals, and objectives. To really measure your direct reports' work intelligently without personally criticizing their efforts to maximize their own and the organization's performance is a skill that appears to be a lost art. Dr.

Kizer never took himself too seriously, and he had to change a whole lot of managers who no longer took management seriously enough.

During this time of installing our new service line organization, I remembered an article I had previously studied. I circulated copies of this article to the key staff working in the organizational design for our network for service lines. "Balancing Corporate Power" from the November–December 1992 issue of the *Harvard Business Review* talked about Federalist principles and how they applied to corporations. This article reinforced the principles that we needed to guide us. It told us that an alliance must be held together by trust and common goals. Managing by trust, empathy, and forgiveness energizes and supports those who are away from the center. In our case, the network office was the center. The center trusts but verifies, motivates, and structures the actual work.

Federalism's principles include the following: (1) places power at the corporation's lowest point; (2) interdependence spreads power around, avoiding the risks of a central bureaucracy; (3) a proper federation needs a common law, language, and currency—a uniform way of doing business; (4) separation of powers keeps management monitoring and governance in separated units; (5) twin citizenship, in our case network and facility, ensures a strong federal presence in all parts of the organization. This article also convinced me that we should practice our management to the greatest extent possible as a democracy and not as an autocracy.

The most critical task of the new organization was to select the personnel who would provide the leadership for the service line at the network level. We wanted skilled managers who would make the necessary changes with the least amount of disruption. Some of that disruption would inevitably be with the medical center directors who were losing some of their power and authority. They would not have the same level of their previously assumed autonomy. Their new role would have to become more flexible and responsive. Instead of being top-down leaders who didn't need to consult with anybody before they made a decision, in the new organization, they would have to consult, negotiate, and be articulate and persuasive enough to win other network leaders over to their point of view.

Needless to say, this was a new day for our medical center directors. This personal change in the way each leader viewed his or her job and his or her function rippled throughout the organization. All supervisors, including the medical center directors, had to become more knowledgeable about the facts and the data. This was critically important to our success and was also an abrupt departure from the norm, which was to generally rationalize our way to decisions.

To avoid threatening any of our leaders, I made the promise that no one would lose his or her job due to restructuring. Then we had to hire the leaders of the eight service lines that we had decided to implement across the network. These service lines were medical/surgical, behavioral health, diagnostics and therapeutics, and long-term care and geriatrics. The fifth service line was all of the administrative processes of registering, admitting, and discharging patients along with managing patient information. Our chief information officer was at the top of all the information employees, programmers, and technicians across the network. This was the sixth service line. The same principle applied to financial employees and purchasing and contracting employees, the seventh and eighth service lines or, in other terms, network consolidated centers. We left the human resources, environmental management, and engineering employees under the medical center director.

Selecting the leaders of these organizational components was a deliberative, time-consuming process. We found some all-stars, and we made some misses. Becoming a service line organization was a fundamental change in the traditional way that health-care organizations were organized. In the VA, each medical center essentially followed a table of organization that had functions, such as finance. Each functional area constituted a service. In the private sector, these are frequently called divisions or departments. Nursing is the largest service by far. Its employees are spread out over the medical center and essentially work in every aspect of clinical care, and some administrative areas as well. Service lines reassign all the personnel who work in mental health, for example, to mental health. This would include all of the various kinds of nurses, technicians, psychologists, psychiatrists, social workers, rehabilitation specialists, and so on.

At the essence of this change is the principle manager or supervisor, who manages a service line that produces health-care services for the ultimate consumer. In the functional arrangement, the service supplies personnel to work in each clinical area, but the ultimate responsibility is frequently confused by the inability of Service A to provide enough hours for the clinical services to meet demand. Another example is the problem employee who the service would rather not deal with, so that person is assigned wherever they will cause the least disruption. And there are countless other suboptimizations that go on in the traditional or functional arrangement. In some specialized activities, all parties work for the same boss with the same goals and objectives with none of the ulterior motivations—at least not as many of them.

In the case of Network 2, we came to the opinion that, in addition to this organizational restructuring, we would also have to assign budget and line authority to each service line. This was a radical departure from the norm and one which the medical center directors did not appreciate at all.

We agreed to do a six-month shadow budget, meaning we would keep the books in the traditional top-down way and by each of the service lines. This meant that the director would not be the ultimate decision maker in budgeting. It also meant that the director would have a much different role going forward as a senior consultant, coach, mentor, and educator. The director would also play a network role as the deputy network director for a particular activity, such as behavioral health care. All of us felt some trepidation as we went forward, but we were committed to the journey.

In the case of behavioral health, we achieved remarkable success on all fronts. We hired a marvelous leader, Scott Murray, who immersed himself quickly into the activities of mental health (soon to be called behavioral health) across the network. He was actively involved in selecting the local mental health-care line leaders. He was intimately involved in setting up the reporting mechanisms and all related quantitative data collection and analysis.

We were also downsizing to stay within a tight budget. Much of the required cutbacks would have to come from behavioral health in the network. This was a sensitive task, because the Vietnam veterans were especially vigilant about mental health care, particularly post-traumatic stress disorder (PTSD) and suicide prevention. In our process of discovery, we found that we had six inpatient substance abuse treatment units. If you will recall, we only had five medical centers, so one facility actually had two units! We also had an inpatient PTSD unit. All of these units were costly and inefficient.

Dr. Murray also quickly grasped the importance of excelling at our assigned performance measures. Dr. Kizer had assigned each network about thirty or so measures that primarily covered primary care in outpatients but also included a number of measures in behavioral health. Under Dr. Murray's leadership, we closed all the inpatient substance abuse units except for one and made that one a polysubstance abuse unit. In addition, Dr. Murray and the western NY behavioral health leaders turned the very expensive inpatient PTSD unit into a residential unit, while also starting a number of other enhancements that were applauded by our veteran community.

Dr. Murray became a national leader in behavioral health, widely recognized for his many contributions. When this network was established, Network 2 was last in the then-measured attainment of performance measures. By the time that our behavioral health service line was fully implemented, which occurred in less than a year, Network 2 was first in performance measure attainment among all the networks. We invented many best practices!

Long-term care was another natural implementation for service line organization. Long-term care personnel do not widely cover other areas of the medical center, and their workload presents unique issues that lend themselves to a dedicated management and analytical team at the network level. Long-term care, much like behavioral health in the academic setting, often suffered in the assignment of resources.

We reviewed a variety of methods to determine the optimal assignment of resources from the network. Having a Health Services Research and Development (HSR&D) researcher involved in this task helped us immensely. Using expertise at his disposal, the researcher developed a model that produced budget data for each service line based upon national VA data, specifically categorized by the service lines as we had organized them. Of course, we were downsizing and reallocating, but the work of our researcher, Dr. Gao, provided us with financial and cost guidelines that greatly assisted us.

In long-term care, the cutbacks were severe. We eliminated over 2,000 beds and placed those patients into community settings. We eliminated all of our intermediate care beds, a category that the VA used to house patients who were too sick for the nursing home but not sick enough for acute care. In fact, almost all of these patients could easily have been discharged, and that's what we did.

With all of the field's reorganization and downsizing, VA Central Office in many respects continued business as usual. The Central Office organization was still filled with silos and traditional leaders. This meant that any change (e.g., an organizational shift taking line responsibility away from a chief of social work, for example) was resented by the director of social work. Priorities changed; what the director of social work in Central Office wanted in the way of information was not the operating information that the service line for behavioral health needed to make better decisions. The revolution going on in the field was visited upon them. An example of this was one day when I received a call that it was time to replace the telephone system at Albany. Since we did not want the particular telephone system that was the current low bidder, we declined—an almost unheard of occurrence in the VA. When the time rolled around again, we insisted upon doing this project as a network so that our equipment was standardized at all sites.

Another example is the facility planning that had been done entirely by the five individual medical centers. We closed 2,000-plus beds, since care was more effectively and efficiently delivered for most of those patients either in the outpatient setting or at home. All of the approved construction projects for Network 2, a tightly controlled process in VA Central Office, were to modify wards. Essentially, this meant that inpatient wards would be renovated and modernized with improved privacy for patients. Since we didn't know for sure how many acute beds we would need and we were not exactly sure where those beds should be, I ordered all of the projects canceled. Once again, doing the right thing was not celebrated, nor was the network rewarded.

Dr Kizer did downsize the health system administration part of VA Central Office. He deserves our everlasting credit for taking this difficult and challenging process on. We in Network 2 were about to find out how difficult and how challenging a transformation could be.

The acute medical, surgical, and primary care service lines proved from the beginning to be the most challenging. This was the part of the VA health-care system that was most closely affiliated with our partners, the medical schools. From the beginning, there was intense suspicion and disagreement about any of the proposals put forth. The clinical service chiefs involved: neurology, medicine, surgery, and their component parts: cardiology, CT surgery, pulmonary, ICUs, and so on were the most drastically effected and were the most concerned.

Our search for a network medical, surgical, and primary care service line leader did not yield an ideal candidate, and the one we selected did not last. We had to reassign him because he was not implementing systems to meet the assigned performance measures or other quality targets. He had an excellent analytical mind but did not have the motivation to be a change agent for the acute care needs of the veterans in upstate New York. In spite of him, we managed to get the attention of the primary care teams in the network.

Including primary care in our medical/surgical service line was probably a mistake. Most other networks and medical centers made primary care separate. We were a smaller network and didn't think that we could afford the overhead for another service line at the network level. Fortunately, by including primary care, we avoided some of the conflict that others experienced. We discovered that the cost and staffing variances in medical and surgical programs was enormous. The variation in our primary care settings was also gaining attention. When we got an effective care line leader and reporting system in place, the medical/surgical service line was energetic in eliminating these variances and improving and monitoring performance measures across the board.

In addition to the three or four leaders that we were forced to reassign, numerous mid-level managers decided to pursue their careers elsewhere or chose to retire. This had the enormously beneficial effect of opening up jobs for excellent clinicians and administrators who had been buried in the organization. These people relished the challenges and the opportunities. This was an unexpected side benefit of reorganizing and downsizing.

The fourth service line was diagnostics and therapeutics. This included rehabilitation medicine, laboratory and pathology, radiology, nuclear medicine, pharmacy, and prosthetics. The VA is a one-stop shopping service for health care. Prosthetics is a critical part of this one-stop shopping, since so many veterans require braces, wheelchairs, stump socks, crutches, and so on. Admittedly, this is a catchall category without much opportunity to reduce duplication and streamline.

Another way we achieved significant reductions was the integration of our database across the network. The Veterans Health Administration has developed a marvelous automated medical record, previously known as DHCP, now called VistA or Computerized Patient Record System (CPRS). These programs allow managers to actively seek lower-cost alternatives and to standardize drugs and other products. By virtue of the consolidated network database, we were able to centralize some staffing in support of all of these activities, greatly streamline network reporting, and reduce the cost of our operational information resource management staff.

The fifth service line included the customer interface parts of administration and medical records. Enrolling, eligibilizing, and collecting insurance information were the principle activities. By reengineering this process across the network and standardizing the interface with the veterans to the extent that we could, we improved customer service and member services. In the process, we became the first VA organizational component to be accredited by the National Committee for Quality Assurance (NCQA), the organization that accredits health maintenance organizations (HMOs).

By having an integrated database, we were also able to significantly clean up inconsistencies in the information we had regarding our veterans. Some veterans frequently used more than one VA facility. We were able to enroll them properly, put them into the appropriate eligibility category, upgrade our insurance information, and standardize data requirements via templates.

Budget cutting is a painful process in which all of us became experts. The debates over where to cut were energetic and contentious.

Of course, we cut staff drastically; we had over 800 employees avail themselves of early out retirement authority. We also had reductions in force for several hundred more. These reductions in force, or RIFs, were especially traumatic, because, as careful as the planning and review was, you could never know for sure who would end up having to go out the door. This was because of bumping. A veteran or a person with more years of service and the same qualifications could bump into a position of someone with less years of service or who was not a veteran. It had to be done, but those of us involved would probably still say that it was the hardest thing we ever had to do in our government careers. Each time a new initiative came to us from VA Central Office and that initiative required additional resources, we would have to reduce staffing and funding somewhere in order to accomplish the new initiative. Our reward was that we stopped being a "loser" network in three years— even though we had to pay the additional costs associated with all the employees approved for early outs and reductions in force. We were proud as a network at having done this difficult task. I never heard of an employee who did not secure adequate employment elsewhere. We provided significant job and career counseling to ease their transition. As a result of our reorganization, downsizing, and staff reductions, we lifted the dark cloud off our network. We had improved significantly, and we had the data to prove it.

Many different organizations in the VA audited, reviewed, and criticized Network 2. Our neighbor networks in the Northeast rationalized away our success. One of my colleagues said to me, "Fred, you're so lucky that you had that budget gun pointed at you. You had a reason to change that the most of the rest of us did not." I laughed at the time rather than confront her, but almost all of the Northeast and Midwest had the budget gun pointed at their heads, and they didn't change, or at least not fast enough.

One of these networks to this very day has never been a gainer under the resource allocation model. For all of these years, a floor of resources has been applied to this network that enables it to limp from one year to the next. This is a sad and completely unnecessary situation for the employees, staff, and patients of this network. For the last several years, it has also lost workload in the form of veteran users.

The purpose of the resource allocation model is to level the playing field. A network in the Southwest should have the same financial ability to treat patients as any in the Northeast. There has been research that shows that the lengths of stay and the incidence of certain kinds of procedures are higher in the Northeast. The cost of care is higher in the Northeast and lower in the Southwest. In the case of Network 2, however, we reduced the cost of care from the highest in the country to the second lowest. I think that it is because we learned to use the data and to make the data more reliable. We also learned not to confuse ourselves in the analysis of data. We came to an understanding, though some directors reluctantly so, to agree on the sources and methods of analysis prior to the analysis beginning. In the past, varying analyses reflecting various points of view and biases were common in VA.

Now we simply have VA Central Office giving us the numbers and data without being able to review and test those analyses, but this is still an improvement over the bad, old days. It is also a sign that Dr. Kizer's wonderful journey of discovery and improvement is sadly temporarily concluded.

The act of sending the funds south also led to resentment and alienation by those networks losing or, more accurately, not gaining enough funds to maintain the status quo. These networks were largely in the Northeast and Upper Midwest. Despite the fact that the South in general was severely underfunded for years, the variances became even more pronounced and to an extent exist to this very day. The market share of eligible veterans is one way of measuring the degree of underfunding. Waiting lists, which have become virtually illegal and unacceptable, used to be another way. The disadvantages of operating high-patient-demand, tertiary health systems in the face of shortages of several hundred thousand square feet of space is yet another way of measuring this.

Network 2 received many positive accolades. It received the first Kizer Award, the quality recognition modeled on the principles of Baldrige and specifically for networks. It was the first network to receive the Carey Award, the VA's highest award for quality, also modeled on Baldrige. The network was recognized as having a number of best practices. After we had gotten to the top of the performance measure attainment list, we stayed there.

Dr. Kizer had his first performance review with me at 11:30 pm in a conference room of a hotel where the VHA executive leadership council was being held. Another network director had his performance review after my appointment. At the time, I really wanted to be in bed. Now I realize the importance of that meeting. I am sure that Dr. Kizer would rather have been in bed asleep as well. He reiterated his understanding of Network 2's data and the challenges that it faced. I fully accepted that he knew my data better than I did and certainly agreed with his analysis of the problems. He had many critics, but to me his sharp, focused attack on the problems of the VHA has made him a hero. Other less-contentious approaches could have been taken and no one would have thought less of him.

While the Kizer voyage of discovery was happening, there were side issues and tangents that deserve full discussion. I will cover some of the more interesting of those issues in the following sections.

Chapter 12.1: The Admonishment

Planning for minor and major construction projects can be problematic. I have previously mentioned that I canceled all of one year's funded construction projects. Once we had a chance to review the data and become familiar with all of the facilities, we knew that we had major needs in several categories of construction. None of the canceled projects would have met any of these needs. Construction projects were tightly controlled and rigidly administered by VA Central Office. Whether a project was a major or a minor classification was determined by congressionally set dollar limits. Field-based engineers did most of the planning and writing of the justifications for projects, which were rated and ranked according to the severity of the need. Despite this, politics entered the equation. States with an active, VA-alert congressional delegation tended to do better than those without.

Those states that are represented by congressmen who become chairs of important congressional committees tend to get more and larger projects that those states not similarly situated. During President Jimmy Carter's administration, he and his administrator, Max Cleland, seemed to bend over backward to avoid the perception that they were disproportionately helping Georgia, their home state. The net effect for the VA medical centers in Georgia was almost certainly that they were receiving less construction funding than they would have otherwise.

Another exception to this rule was the appropriation subcommittee that handled the VA, chaired for several years by Jim Walsh of Syracuse. Although VA Medical Center Syracuse received some minor construction projects in these years, its needs and Congressman Walsh's powerful position could have combined to award it much more. To Jim Walsh's credit, he did not take undue advantage of his position.

Without a doubt, the total pool of funds requested by the administration and granted by Congress for many, many years has been too meager to even pretend to keep pace with growing workloads and the need for updated facilities.

Another factor in the construction process in the VA has been that some of our senior facility directors were suspected of conniving to get projects awarded. Some directors were former engineers and this, combined with the experts running the construction process in VA Central Office, led to an overly technical and inbred process. Never leave any management process exclusively, or even mostly, up to the subject matter experts. And when the funding pool is not commensurate with the pent-up demand for construction funding, then some folks may decide that they should game the process.

One day in my office, I got a call from VA Central Office that VA Medical Center Buffalo's project for installing air-conditioning in that building had once again been turned down. I was angry. I felt that the scoring process did not accurately account for the fact that Buffalo was probably the only academic health facility in the United States that was not centrally air-conditioned. Despite Buffalo's chilly and long winters, the need for modern central air-conditioning to protect medical equipment and maintain a consistent environment inside the building for patients was clear. Operating maintenance costs alone with all the window units hanging off the eleven-story building would justify the capital expenditure.

I called the director at Buffalo and directed him to split the air-conditioning major construction project. I knew that there was potential trouble for doing this because a creative VA senior executive named Bob Lindsay had gotten a law passed expressly forbidding project splitting. I thought that because the project had failed to meet the cut in VA Central Office for eleven years running, that it was time to take a different approach.

Most VA medical centers of a certain vintage suffered from infrastructure problems, mostly notably electrical. In the case of Buffalo, their basic electrical systems had to be totally redone, greatly expanded, and updated. This cost, which was significant, was included in the total costs of the project whose short title: "Install Air-conditioning," was misleading as to the real scope. I told the director that the decision was mine and advised him to use any opportunity he had when interacting with his local congressman to advise him of the change and the need for his support.

A few weeks later I was advised by the chief network officer, Ken Clark, that the matter of the air-conditioning project in Buffalo had been reviewed and the splitting of the project was to be investigated by a committee. This committee was established to make recommendations for several construction projects at several VA medical centers that for one reason or another had come under suspicion.

When I got the letter advising me of this, I saw that one of the projects to be reviewed was "Build Out Swing Space" at the VA medical center in San Diego, California. It was probably coincidental, but the past deputy administrator and future secretary of the VA lived in San Diego. Some kind of political greasing had to have happened to get San Diego's project past numerous others with critical needs. I was incensed and still am. Swing space can easily be leased and cannot compete against a project needed for environmental reasons, such as Buffalo's, or to correct deficiencies cited by the Joint Commission on the Accreditation of Health Care Organizations (JCAHO). There was nothing I could do about it but wait for their verdict. I knew what that verdict would be.

More than a year later, I was summoned to the Office of the Deputy Under Secretary for Health for Operations and Management

(DUSHOM). This title, created by yet another reorganization, was a replacement for what had previously been known as the chief network officer. At the time, I was on yet another detail. The DUSHOM apologized and complimented my gracious acceptance of the construction project review committee's recommendation that disciplinary action should be given to me for ordering the splitting of Buffalo's project. I signed for it. As of this writing, the Buffalo VA Medical Center still does not have central air-conditioning. Work has started on correcting their significant electrical deficiencies. This project was split successfully at some later point. Competition between proposed construction projects and competing priorities within financial limits was the reason the air-conditioning was not completed as of this writing.

Yet more importantly, the executive branch and Congress needs to quit ignoring serious construction deficiencies in the VA. VA health-care facilities need to have their real needs met. The demands of rising workload and the pressure of tight budgets, coupled with ever-increasing new initiatives makes facility management too demanding in the face of critical physical plant issues. The wonderful VA staff and patients of western New York deserve better.

Chapter 12.2: The Reprimand

A fellow network director at our national executive leadership council meetings approached me about taking one of his directors into Network 2. At the time, I was very frustrated with the leadership of the VA medical center in Canandaigua. The director there was thoroughly informed and educated about management and leadership, but his implementation of the difficult decisions that had been made by the leadership council was less than desirable. Increasingly, we were implementing these decisions by remote control. In any case, the idea of taking a director interested in coming to Network 2, Darryl Jones, billed as a hard-charging, get-the-job-done kind of guy grew steadily on me.

I knew Darryl Jones from meetings, and he had had an interesting career, never staying in one job beyond approximately two years. We were told that he had settled now that he had children, and his wife had relatives in the Rochester area. Despite the reservations of some of the staff in the network, I approached the director in Canandaigua about a swap. Since he and his wife were from the west, where the new job would be located, he readily agreed to the switch. The deed was done. Our new director at VA Medical Center Canandaigua was Darryl Jones.

Darryl continued to talk a good game when he reached Network 2. He was positive and enthusiastic about the changes that we thought needed to be made in Canandaigua. We were soon to learn that his actions and words at Canandaigua were notably different than what he was reporting. The VA Medical Center Canandaigua had the largest of our outpatient clinics, the new clinic in Rochester. Various managers reported that Darryl stirred up trouble there. The VA medical center in Bath, which was periodically rumored to be merged with Canandaigua, also reported concerns about unsanctioned trips he made to Bath without my knowledge. When confronted about these incidents, Darryl blew them off, saying that he was just familiarizing himself and blaming any concern that the network or I had on the fears of change and deliberate misinterpretations of others.

In December of Darryl's first year in Network 2, I issued a formal counseling and asked him to improve his communications within the network. I had appointed Darryl to hear the grievance of a physician in Albany. Darryl looked into the grievance and never spoke to the physician concerned. I don't know really whether he spoke to anyone about it. He had called my chief operating officer and asked him whether he should speak to the complaining physician. The chief operating officer had asked me. I had said yes. I suspected that Darryl asked his local human resources officer and they had said he didn't have to. That was true in the bureaucratic sense. The physician who filed the grievance was a world-renowned oncologist and clinical researcher. He ultimately left the Albany VA Medical Center. Of course, when the matter exploded, Darryl blamed me by saying that the oncologist was my friend, which he was. I told Darryl that there were abundant management and professional reasons to interview the complainant and that he and I would expect the same if it were us. Darryl didn't agree. He wouldn't or couldn't interview the physician. It seemed to me that he refused or simply couldn't acknowledge having made a mistake. He raised smoke screens after being confronted by others, passionately defending his reasoning.

This may be an example of having too much flexibility, a management concept that is highly desirable in complex situations. In customary situations, this flexibility provides managers the opportunity to do the wrong thing. Given that the network director said that the grievant should be interviewed and human resources said that he didn't have to be interviewed, what would a rational person charged with this task do? The answer to that question was obvious. Despite its clear-cut nature, Darryl grumbled. This was the first of many cases in which he turned a straightforward, minor assignment into an unpleasant, angry, and completely unnecessary dustup.

In April of his first year, Darryl went to VA Central Office to be interviewed by Dr. Kizer, the undersecretary for health. Darryl had applied to be a network director. Some vacancies had opened up after the initial selections chose to retire or left under undesirable circumstances. During the course of the interview, Darryl told Dr. Kizer that he planned to integrate the VAMC Canandaigua with the private sector. Dr. Kizer was concerned by the response, and he asked his chief of staff to call me to see if this was true. It wasn't.

Because Darryl increasingly had to be given specific instructions, he was often openly verbally combative. When I counseled him about the lack of his attendance and his union partners at a network labor management council, he forwarded the message on to the labor officials at the Canandaigua VA Medical Center. The union then complained to me, saying that Darryl should not be counseling them. He claimed he was building trust with them and defended his right to forward the message, since it wasn't marked confidential.

In April of Darryl's first year, I had a conversation with my supervisor, Mr. Ken Clark, the chief network officer. Ken wanted to know how things were going with Darryl, especially since his former supervising network officer had given him a glowing review. I responded with a quote from one of my key operating managers: "Darryl thinks he's a management Roger Clemens. The reality is that he couldn't make his high school team." I quickly agreed.

Also in April, which was midyear for performance review purposes, I received an e-mail from one of the network service line leaders. Her local service line leader had sent her an e-mail complaining of Darryl. When they were leaving a coordinating committee meeting, Darryl had distributed materials that no one had seen before. In the document, her role as well as others was questioned, and among other things the document said that the service line leaders should have no organizational responsibility for labor management relations. No one had previously heard of this document, and it did not reflect any policy or directive of the network. In fact, it was the opposite of what everyone understood to be the case. Once again, I had to counsel Darryl, who clearly resented the intervention, saying that I was undermining the medical center director. I told him that I disagreed.

The previous director at the Canandaigua VA Medical Center had requested (and I had endorsed that request) that Canandaigua host the Golden Age Games. These are Olympic-style games organized and financed from year to year by the national office of the Veterans of Foreign Wars (VFW). The VFW cosponsors the games with the VA. The games result in a huge gathering of veterans from all over the country. The games provided wonderful public relations with the entire region as well as the community.

At the end of April of the same year, I received a call from a national representative of the VFW. He had contacted the coordinator at VA Medical Center Canandaigua, who worked directly for Darryl. The coordinator reported that he couldn't get anything done because the director, Darryl, had vetoed all of his attempts to get communications out to the network facilities, to line up community support, and to kick off a fund raising drive. Once again, I called Darryl and got him to promise that he would remain personally involved until the conclusion of the Golden Age Games. I directly contacted all the facilities, however, to line up their volunteers, block out the dates of the games, and see what they could generate in the way of donations.

In June of that year, I received another call from Dr. Kizer's chief of staff. This time the issue concerned the University of Rochester affiliation with the VA medical center and its Rochester outpatient clinic. The chief of staff, or Miller Time, as I called him, was not his usual cheerful self. I privately named him Miller Time due to his penchant from suddenly closing up his desk and stating loudly, "It's Miller Time." I should also add, however, that he would close up his desk anywhere from 6:00 to 9:00 pm—sometimes later. He deserved that beer after the workday he routinely put in.

According to Miller Time, Darryl had told the vice dean for the University of Rochester Medical School that his plan was to integrate with the private sector health system, that the dean shouldn't worry about putting medical residents in Canandaigua, and that he should lean on Dr. Kizer to get more resources to support the affiliation in Rochester. Furthermore, Darryl stated that the university should lean on the congressional delegation to facilitate this. The vice dean had put Darryl's comments immediately to the test. Darryl himself had previously been counseled about this integration with the private sector idea that he had launched with Dr. Kizer when he was being interviewed.

Darryl defended his actions as merely giving the medical school and congressman a courtesy brief, failing to understand or appreciate that neither his supervisor nor Dr. Kizer nor the secretary of Veterans Affairs had approved the concept—not to mention that this was a scheme that was sure to launch a firestorm of veteran objections.

I didn't trust the vice dean because in my first three months in the network director job he had taken several actions that were disagreeable to me. The Rochester outpatient clinic had been realigned to the VA medical center in Buffalo. This was a problem, in that Buffalo had a different medical school affiliation, and management was tuned into its media market and veterans issues in Buffalo. This left Rochester with an inadequate amount of top leadership time to genuinely deal with their issues. For these reasons, early in my administration, we had realigned Rochester to Canandaigua.

Then, one Friday early in December, the vice dean called me to say that if I didn't get all of the University of Buffalo medical residents out of the Rochester outpatient clinic that day, he was going to pull the University of Rochester's cardiology residents on Monday. I told him that I wasn't going to pull Buffalo's medical residents and asked him to reconsider pulling his cardiology residents. He declined. I called the director at Buffalo and asked him if at all possible to stand by on Monday with cardiology residents and attendings to meet Rochester's clinic appointments. Attendings are the supervising physicians actually in charge of the patient's care and the resident's education. The VA medical center in Buffalo responded enthusiastically. A few weeks later the University of Rochester's cardiology residents returned to the Rochester clinic. Now this was the person in whom Darryl was confiding. Darryl's assessments and judgment were now widely suspected by nearly all network officials.

In July of Darryl's first year, I received a call from an EEO investigator who was so angry that she was almost crying. When she calmed down, she explained to me that she had reached an agreement with an employee to settle his EEO case. This type of informal resolution is fairly common and is often the best and cheapest way to resolve EEO issues or complaints that employees feel that they have. In this case, she then called Darryl Jones to brief him on the matter and to get agreement as to the proposed resolution. Darryl readily agreed. What the resolution was is immaterial to this discussion, and I am not sure that I ever heard what it was.

Many days went by, and the employee confronted his supervisor, who was enraged that the resolution hadn't been discussed with him. They both called the EEO investigator and complained vociferously. She then called Darryl to politely remind him that he had agreed to the resolution. He denied it and reminded her that he was the director in Canandaigua. I apologized profusely and said that I would get Darryl to straighten matters out that day. I called Darryl and explained to him that he was to implement the proposed resolution that day and to apologize to both the employee and the supervisor. He reluctantly agreed.

In early September of that year, I received an angry call from a staff person in the newly elected congressman's office in western New York. He was incensed that when he had called the associate deputy secretary for police and security in VA Central Office that the associate deputy secretary had yelled at him and told him to go to Hell. I said I was sorry but had no control over the associate deputy secretaries in the VA.

He sniffed. I asked, "What was the problem?" He explained that he was representing an employee unfairly being terminated from the VA medical center in Canandaigua. "Oh, really," I said, immediately sensing that Darryl may have created a problem. The staff person explained that a police officer was being fired but had never been taught the proper procedures. This was going to be a hardship on the congressman's constituent.

I paused and asked my secretary to get on the phone to human resources in Canandaigua and get everything they had on this faxed to me immediately. The congressional staff person said that he had talked to the director, Darryl Jones, who had completely agreed with him and said that he had no control over the matter; that it was being railroaded by the network office. I asked for a name. He told me. I sent for Linda Weiss, a sharp health systems specialist on my staff. I assured the staff person that I would enthusiastically and intensely look into the matter but advised him that he could not and should not represent a VA employee. He remained too loud, demanding, and belittling toward me and the network office. After his outbursts, I told him that he worked for the legislative branch, and, as such, he could inquire, write, complain, and do any number of things, but he could not represent a VA employee in any official administrative proceeding. He said he would speak to the congressman about that. I said everybody involved in this matter, including the state police, were his constituents. I noted that the congressman ran the risk of alienating far more people by this advocacy than just one person. He calmed down.

As I was hanging up, my secretary appeared in the door to tell me that the associate deputy secretary for police and security in the VA Central Office was on the line, upset and demanding to talk to me. This usually quiet and reserved professional talked to me for about ten minutes. What did that director of mine in Canandaigua think that he was doing in overruling the associate deputy secretary and not firing this police officer? Why was my director complaining to the assistant deputy secretary for labor relations? he wanted to know. He explained in excruciating detail the situation with this intermittent police officer. "Intermittent" means that the officer worked as scheduled and was not in a full-time, permanent position and thus not entitled to union representation, nor did he have any other avenues of appeal.

This officer had used the VA computer to access the New York State Police database on a personal matter involving friends involved in a divorce. Their friends found out and complained to the New York State Police, who had terminated the access of the VA Medical Center Canandaigua to their computer files. I assured the associate deputy secretary that we would terminate the police officer and that I had just counseled the young congressional staff person to get out of this matter and stay out of it. He thanked me.

I then talked to Linda Weiss, the health system specialist responsible for day-to-day operations of Network 2. She had already been through all of this with Darryl. She had in fact directed Darryl to fire this police officer for unauthorized access of police databases and for misusing that information in a matter that had nothing to do with the VA. This should have been clear to Darryl, but for some reason, he felt his perquisites as a director were being infringed upon. Once again, he showed that he would immediately take the matter to the highest levels of VA and discussed the matter with two assistant deputy secretaries in order to get official blessing for his decision, which he knew would not be approved by me. Once again, a stream of very angry people left in his wake.

About two weeks after the police officer episode in Canandaigua, I was detailed to be the acting network director in Network 1, the New England network. A network director hired from outside the VA in New England had resigned, in lieu of being fired for a multitude of sins, leaving the network in some disarray. I agreed to accept this detail for six months. I left for Boston as soon as the paperwork was signed by the secretary.

As a result of this detail, I reluctantly agreed to give Darryl a full satisfactory rating for his first year in the network. Anything else would have required that I stay in the network to directly monitor his performance. My absence would not change anything about Darryl's performance or his behavior.

In January of the new rating period, which began on October 1, Darryl was again under the supervision of the acting network director in Network 2. I was somewhat aware of this, and certainly I agreed that Darryl deserved the reported counseling, but I was fully engaged in the large, dynamic, and at the time troubled Network 1. Again in January, the Network 2 public affairs officer reported that Darryl had made a congressional contact that he failed to inform the network about. That March, I sent an e-mail suggesting that Darryl be notified of a proposed unsatisfactory rating. I was not contacted very often during the six months that I was acting network director in Network 1. During this period, the relative lack of incidents provoked by Darryl had more to do with the kind, sensitive manner of the acting director than it did with any improvement on Darryl's part. Still, there were occasions when Darryl's maverick actions caused notable problems.

My medical director and, while I was gone, acting director, was Dr. Larry Flesh. We had worked together for a long time. Larry was frequently reluctant to initiate action. It was often reported to me that he would complain of how my intervention created problems for him, but with the wisdom not to tell me. Larry is a wonderful person but expects that everyone will respond to his caring, nagging way of counseling them. Of course, some simply take advantage of him and the situation.

Darryl frequently boasted of his leadership and improvements in labor management relations in Canandaigua. During August, both local unions voiced their disbelief and anger at Darryl for his toxic communications to them and to others. The number of labor issues rose to the degree that members of the network had to spend considerable time and energy in Canandaigua to resolve issues. Although Darryl attended most of the network labor partnership meetings, his participation was criticized by those management officials in attendance. He also seemed to not implement ideas and agreements that came out of these network meetings. Various communication flare-ups occurred, with Darryl being proven to be misinformed on several occasions. In essence, nothing changed in Darryl's behavior while I was in Network 1, with the exception that his behavior wasn't documented. Toxic was how most of the leaders in Network 2 came to describe Darryl's communications.

During his tenure in Network 2, Darryl frequently called

congressional committees, local congressmen, the state director of Veterans Affairs, and various people in VA Central Office, including the secretary of Veterans Affairs. He would then drop their names as being in support of some concept of his. Although counseled on many occasions, Darryl defended his contacts with these officials as being part of the director's job. Although he never advised the network of his calls prior to his making them, he was not embarrassed by what many viewed as his continued attempts to undermine others in the network. I can only reluctantly speculate on Darryl's motivation. This is important to keep in mind as I discuss the culmination of events leading to the reprimand.

On July 28 of that year, I sent Darryl an e-mail which read in part:

> With much trepidation and some considerable personal pain, I am writing to express my concern over your verbal participation in the executive leadership council yesterday during the Bath VA Medical Center request for proposals discussion. First, let me say that I fully support your right to say whatever you want to say in whatever forum. Second, I need to say that many people in this network have expressed their dissatisfaction to me about your communications to them or to others in meetings and one–on-one. Third, I am convinced that there is a problem that needs your full effort and commitment to resolve. Fourth, my concern will be reflected in your appraisal. Fifth, my apologies for using e-mail. I find it impossible and personally disagreeable to talk to you directly.

I went on to discuss how his perception of his communications was radically different from anyone who listened to him, including veterans who attended his town meetings.

In July, I called him to inquire about his efforts regarding the Golden Age Games. Darryl again denied any problems and threatened to call the VFW and others in power to explain to me his efforts. I talked to him about personal accountability and team building, both areas in which he was lacking. I told him that he fell below acceptable standards in management development and strategic planning. I told him that we were out of time to correct flaws in how the games would proceed.

The games were successfully held during early August. On the following August 13, not ten days after counseling Darryl at some extended length, I had to send an e-mail out to all employees in the network correcting, amending, and praising them for their gallant efforts at holding a very successful Golden Age Games. Darryl had simply sent his congratulations to the employees of VAMC Canandaigua. The games would not have been successful without the overwhelming support of the entire network, especially the leadership of the Service Employees International Union and employees from around the country who in many cases used vacation time to be there. And an eternal debt of gratitude to baseball great Maury Wills, who provided the icing on the cake!

In September, the Darryl pot boiled over. Two separate incidents culminated in my deciding that Darryl had to leave the network—or at the very least step down from being a member of top management.

The first of these incidents involved a nurse with considerable additional training in counseling veterans, particularly those with post-traumatic stress disorder. The chief of staff at Canandaigua during a routine medical record review discovered that this nurse was creating potentially billable charges for his services at a state prison. This somehow was immediately blown up by Darryl into fraudulent billing charges, practicing beyond the scope of the nurse's license, and alleging that the network was behind a conspiracy to up-code and therefore collect more funds through third-party recovery and get more workload credit in the VA's resource allocation process. Of course, Darryl did not call me. My introduction to this matter was through Congressman Bernie Sanders of Vermont, calling the office to complain about convicted felons receiving bills from the VA in New York. I don't really know who was behind this. The motivation, I can only guess, had something to do with creating embarrassment for me and deflecting blame onto others who worked for the network.

A short while later, the VA's Office of Inspector General called on the same matter. When the matter was carefully and calmly reviewed, we discovered that the nurse, on his own volition, had entered the codes for his work with veterans at the prison, expecting to receive personal workload credit. No bills for insurance companies or veterans were ever generated. The nurse should have had the medical records that he generated signed and approved by a physician supervisor but had not. His supervisor was willing to sign after the fact on all of the nurse's workload. Because of the hoopla generated by Darryl, despite the fact that the congressman and the inspector general were well satisfied by our fact-finding, the Vietnam combat veteran nurse took an early retirement. The veteran community fully supported and applauded his efforts and resented what they viewed as a forced retirement.

The second, much larger incident occurred when the VA's External Peer Review Program (EPRP) visited the Canandaigua Medical Center. A licensed practical nurse (LPN) was directed by her supervisor to scrub the medical records chosen for review. *Scrub* is a commonly used term to describe efforts that are made to clarify and prepare records for audit. In this case, the LPN set about clumsily and obviously changing the records in such a way that, if undiscovered by the EPRP reviewer, the medical center would have received greater credit than deserved. The person in charge of performance improvement at Canandaigua called and then faxed a report of contact describing the finding of the EPRP reviewer. We immediately reported the matter to the Office of Quality and Performance in VA Central Office and to my supervisor, the deputy undersecretary for operations and management.

Insisting on an external review of the incident, we immediately set about correcting and clarifying the language used to prepare for these external reviews. These reviews are used by the VA to prepare the actual achievement on its myriad performance measures. Of course, Darryl or someone called the VA Office of Inspector General, who also joined in the auditing effort. The VA widely used a blue sheet upon which to record and organize data in each reviewed medical record. The EPRP reviewer stated that he would no longer accept the blue sheet. VACO had not mandated the use of the blue sheet, but it was a widely accepted best practice. We said we would no longer accept him as our reviewer, since this was a standard and acceptable process, and one for which we didn't have a readily acceptable substitute.

In the meanwhile, all of the concerned records were sequestered for the two audit teams that would be assigned to do separate audits. We also found out that the VA medical center in Buffalo had been concerned about the EPRP reviewers comments and unsubstantiated complaints about them that they were led to believe came from the chief of staff at Canandaigua. Darryl discovered that the blue sheet had never been approved by the medical records committee or the medical staff at Canandaigua. The interpretation of all of this by Darryl was that they were victims of a ruthless network, driven to any measures to look good to VA Central Office. I thought he should have been involved with activities at the medical center and proactive enough to know what was going on. The failure by management to take the initiative to prevent the numerous blowups that were occurring was a great concern to all involved.

The investigations by all parties exonerated the network staff. They did make some useful recommendations that we implemented. Unfortunately, during this episode, colorful language entered the debate and the record. Darryl was described by others as an alarmist, an accuser, a blamer, and a whistle-blower. This last word especially would be tantamount to a death blow in our efforts to make Darryl account-able for his actions. All of us at the network level believed sincerely that what our mission needed was a leader, a manager who solved problems, a leader who created an environment where other managers felt free to discuss their concerns, a leader who enhanced and encouraged effec-tive communication by his or her actions. Instead, Darryl created an institution driven by fear and uncertainty. Since Darryl was considered by most to be unapproachable, he did not know what was going on at his medical center. His management style was to pontificate, complain, and deflect the blame unto others, most frequently, the employees.

On November 2, I called Darryl and told him that I was proposing his non-recertification as a senior executive. During the administration of the first President Bush, a process of recertifying federal senior execu-tives had been created. It was subsequently done away with early in the administration of the second President Bush. I was advised by staff that he would claim to be a whistle-blower and that I would be at risk for proposing this. I felt that we had ample documentation. Since Darryl had called numerous officials in the executive and legislative branches, I was well aware that there would be personal risk. At first, Darryl agreed to a settlement and a downgrade to a GS15, then, after a few days, he backed out. His proposal for non-recertification went to the Veterans Health Administration's executive resources board. His attorney made a lengthy rebuttal of our arguments. I countered. Subsequently, the board recommended approval to the VA executive resources board, and ultimately the secretary approved the non-recertification. In a few weeks, the Office of Special Counsel accepted Darryl's case as a whistle-blower and the non-recertification as retaliation for his being a whistle-blower.

I attempted to put Darryl on a performance-approval plan until the action on the proposed non-recertification was concluded. The Office of Special Counsel intervened, and I was ordered to rescind the performance-improvement plan. Then the Office of Special Counsel, the federal government office that holds jurisdiction over whistle–blowing, came to Albany to investigate my actions. Because of the last incident, Darryl had filed a complaint with the Office of Special Counsel that he was being proposed to be non-recertified because of the EPRP incident. I collected my two years worth of material on Darryl, providing it to the two investigators.

In the EPRP case, several of us had used the word *whistle-blowing*. We had, of course, mentioned whistle-blowing because that was part of Darryl's modus operandi. When confronted with an issue, his immediate motivation was to proclaim his innocence in the matter. This would be followed quickly by using the name of some high-level official as having approved his course of action. The high-level official would never be in Network 2. Therefore, Darryl became painful to all of us who had to work with him. I conceived that the word would be a problem in the case, but I didn't want to be accused of having others change their words to describe Darryl's performance.

With a sneer on his face, the OSC investigator asked me if I knew what being a whistle-blower meant. I said of course. He then asked me the context of its use in our official communication on Darryl's proposed non-recertification as a senior executive. I told him that my image was of the Charlie Chaplin movie where all the cops are running around blowing their whistles and accomplishing nothing. I said that was what Darryl did. He sneered some more. I was beginning to get a sick feeling.

And so, it all seemed to come down on the use of the word *whistle-blower*. I got an attorney through my management malpractice insurance. Darryl skated, becoming an untouchable due to his anointed whistle-blower status. The Office of Special Counsel got some kind of acknowledgment from the VA that they had erred in approving my proposal, and they got the VA to agree to give me appropriate disciplinary action. My attorney consulted with a senior federal attorney experienced in these cases. He promptly said I would be terminated. I was advised to retire at the earliest possible date. I decided to wait it out. After I was detailed from the network to run the VA's Capital Asset Realignment for Enhanced Services (CARES), I left the day-to-day management of Network 2, never to return.

After I left the network, Darryl reportedly didn't get any better and seemed to resist implementing in his own management any of the advice and guidance that he had received. Maybe he was simply incapable of being a responsible manager and leader. He retired as soon as he became eligible. Two years later, I accepted a reprimand to close the file and to get the dark threat removed from over the top of my head.

Chapter 12.3: The West Point Punishment

During my time as network director, a sentinel event occurred with our youngest son. Since it bears on leadership, I have included this story here because it tells of a different approach to leadership training. It certainly affected my thinking about promises and punishment.

We had made arrangements to go to West Point and pick up our youngest son, Jamie, one Friday evening. We were taking him to Duke to visit with one of his former high school classmates. Since our older son, Jason, was enrolled at North Carolina State University, it also gave us a chance to visit with him as well. As we drove down from Albany, the snow began to fall. At West Point, there was a significant accumulation. The roads were icy. We had made arrangements to pick him up on top of the Thayer Building, which has a rooftop parking lot. He was right where he said he would be, standing at attention in his great coat with snow all over him. We picked him up and immediately headed for North Carolina.

He told us that the campus had been closed a few minutes before we got there. He had anticipated that and so had signed out about thirty minutes before so that his leave would not get canceled on account of the snow. We drove carefully but successfully navigated the hilly roads around West Point. We stopped in Delaware for the evening with the snow finally looking as if it would stop.

The next day we drove on to Durham, dropped him off, and then visited with Jason. On Sunday, we picked our cadet up and drove back to New York and dropped him back off at West Point.

A few weeks passed, and we were due to go back down to West Point for a visit. When our son called, I could hear rising disappointment and anger in my wife's voice. It seemed that our son had violated the honor code and therefore was getting a quite severe punishment of marching the area. To work off the required marching would take Jamie several weekends. This is a severe punishment given all the academic, military, and physical work that the cadets routinely have to accomplish. He asked his mother not to complain to the commandant or congressman. She reluctantly agreed.

The honor code violation came about because of an incident that happened at the dormitory where our son had stayed with his friend at Duke. During that Saturday evening, some of the students had been drinking, and some kind of a minor ruckus ensued. Our son, Jamie, intervened in the ruckus and calmed the situation. The Duke police arrived and wrote up the incident, praising our son for his role in resolving the incident without anyone getting hurt or having to go to jail. Then the vice president for student affairs, who apparently reviews all police reports involving students, read the report and was impressed. So impressed, that he wrote a letter to the commandant of the United States Military Academy at West Point. He attached a copy of the police report, which in addition to praising our son noted that he said he had one beer. Since our son had signed an agreement with the army upon his enrollment not to drink alcohol until he was twenty-one, here was a documented honor code violation. The matter was delegated downhill until it reached Jamie.

Our son was a fine person when he enrolled at West Point. Getting this punishment was almost certainly not going to make him a better cadet. I believe that the punishment was to support the West Point legend as much as to uphold the honor code. Here was a cadet in good standing with a fine academic record who received a punishment for doing a good deed! But in the process he admitted an honor code violation. I support their logic.

Chapter 12.4: New England Is Lovely

Network 2 continued to far exceed its performance measures and its fiscal performance. It was increasingly being hailed as the best example of the networks in terms of its overall performance. Having led the achievement of all of this, despite the difficulties previously outlined above, I began to feel that I needed a greater challenge, a chance to do something else for a while. Without communicating this to anyone, I received a phone call from Ken Clark, the chief network officer. Ken asked me to accept a detail to New England, Network 1. I immediately accepted, knowing that my wife would support the detail since we both love Boston and much of her extended family lives in the Boston area. I also told Ken that I would not be a candidate for the job. I didn't want to move to Boston, nor did I want to stay in the Northeast. If I moved, I wanted to move south. He laughed.

The next day, I flew to Boston, rented a car, and drove to the network office in Bedford, Massachusetts. I found that the office was functioning but timid about my arrival and what would happen next. I deduced that no major changes would be necessary in the office staff. They were willing and eager to get on with the work of the office. There was not much teamwork or togetherness as I had experienced in Network 2. The spacious offices in Bedford may have contributed to that; the group of network employees was far more spread out and not as conveniently located. Part of that lack of togetherness had to do with their organization, which stove piped people into functional activities without any meetings or communication that would have let them express an opinion on other matters before the office.

My detail to New England allowed me direct experience with Boston's big dig project. On two occasions, I was so stuck in traffic that I missed my flights. One time I was stuck for over an hour behind a school bus loaded with children. I hoped that the driver had a radio and earmuffs. I once complained to a gate attendant, and all he said was, "You're lucky you don't have to come here every day." There were no large planes on the short hop from Albany, New York, to Boston, but fortunately the flight was less than an hour and most of the time quite scenic, flying over the Berkshires and over Boston Harbor. I quickly got into a routine.

Network 1 had budget problems and intense rivalries that complicated matters enormously. The network hadn't done the budget cutting that Network 2 had done. They hadn't done the analysis that would have convinced most of them where to cut, and they had done some things that complicated effective management change. The medical center directors felt that they were autonomous, and they had long-standing reasons why their medical center was being picked upon by others. Everyone, other than Boston, resented the VA medical system in Boston as being inefficient, arrogant, and bloated. With six states in Network 1, the politics were more complicated as well.

The previous network director, who had come from the private sector, had resigned. Whether this was a result of his own frustration with the system, pressure from VACO, or the disillusionment of others, I will never know. He lived in Worchester, about an hour away from the network office. He got into the habit of reporting to the clinic in Worchester and calling into the office for meetings. Later in the day, when the traffic was better, he would report to the main office. Apparently, there were other charges, from what I was told by folks in the network office, possibly misuse of government vehicles and alienating the unions. I could see from personal observation that he hadn't done much better with the Veterans Service Organizations. In any event, he elected to resign. I was told by several in the office that he was a yeller and always berated the VA in his verbal communications, disparaging the pay, the rules, and the inefficiencies that he speculated the VA had.

One of the first things that I had to do was to get responses out to several audit reports. The former network director had several staff members gathering data to support memoranda in progress that would refute most if not all of the critical recommendations in the audit reports. As I read the audit reports and the proposed responses, I realized that he was simply trying to defend the actions that he had taken and maintain the status quo. So I told the staff to prepare letters accepting all the recommendations that these various organizations had made and to thank them for their efforts. I also directed the performance improvement activity to track these recommendations carefully. I think that the staff breathed a large sigh of relief.

The director at the VA medical center and regional office in Togus had been put on a performance plan. Togus was one of the oldest veteran-related facilities in the country and had been built shortly after the Civil War. Togus was located about ten miles outside of the capital of Maine—Augusta. As I was to find out later, Maine was the only state to ever lose population in a decade between censuses. While I don't think that this is true any longer, it was certainly true for many decades. The reason was the number of deaths that the state suffered in the Civil War. It is also a large state, quite rural, with only one VA medical center, making travel to and from it a time-consuming and problematic matter. Because of Togus's workload, many special procedures were only available in the VA in Boston.

The veterans bitterly resented their six-hour van trips to obtain services in Boston. The staff bitterly resented the customer service that they received from Boston and the fact that a disproportionate share of the network's funding appeared to be going to Boston. I determined that the Togus Medical Center was doing better, going in the right direction in performance measures and improving primary care, so I took the director off the performance plan. He was most relieved and deservedly so.

Because Togus needed to change and downsize somewhat, I felt the need to do a town hall meeting there. Two TV stations were in attendance. A large number of patients and staff were there in the large auditorium. There were members of the community and representatives of the various politicians. It was a difficult and challenging town hall meeting, the most contentious that I have ever participated in. The patients, concerned about the proposed staffing reductions, argued loudly and sometimes incoherently against cutting staff. Many of them were from the post-traumatic stress disorder program, which was over-staffed. This program, however, had not been targeted by me or anyone else in VA Central Office. The PTSD staff knew they were overstaffed and underworked and so did many other of the staff in Togus. One patient got up and yelled, "You are killing patients!" The PTSD staff had apparently decided on a preemptive strike. I calmly plodded my way through the town hall meeting and then met with representatives of all the veterans' groups.

The veterans' service groups were calm and apologetic. I think that they were embarrassed by the scene that had occurred in the town hall meeting. I told them that the changes were to make Togus better, provide more services, and open more clinics. With its tough winters and nearly complete lack of public transportation, conveniently located clinics were needed. They pledged to help me and Togus.

The media that appeared after this town hall meeting was largely negative. Fortunately, many Togus employees told me later how embarrassed they were by the questions and the acting out. Fortunately, the folks in VA Central Office supported me, and I didn't hear anything negative from them.

After the town hall meeting and before I could get to the veteran service officer meeting, I talked to several veterans who came to the front of the auditorium to speak with me. A small, wiry man of about seventy complained of the six-hour van trip to Boston for surgery on his carotid artery. He showed me the scar that ran down the side of his neck for about two and half inches. I asked the man what really bothered him about that trip, since obviously his life-saving surgery was a success. He said simply, "It's the loneliest that I have ever been." I was stunned at his response. Maine is a big, rural state without a lot of industry. And this man was complaining about being lonely in a large urban medical center in Boston! I quickly asked why.

He said that no one spoke to him. He said that the long corridors were cold and unfriendly. He said that no one seemed to care about him as a person. I quickly told him that I did. I told him that I would personally check out the Jamaica Plain VA Medical Center, one of the medical centers that make up the VA Health System Boston, and see what I could do to change that coldness. I thanked him profusely for sharing his concern. I will never forget him.

I was surprised one day by a visit from a cardiologist from Portland, Maine. He had come down to my office expressly for the purpose of offering his practice for veteran patients. He wanted to be paid, of course. The problem was that if we contracted with his practice, clinical workload would be diverted from the Boston health system. Resources would have to be shifted as well. The VA would have slightly more contented veterans in Maine. They would not have to leave the state and would have an hour shaved off their trip. Of course, if there were complications, the care would have to be provided in private sector hospitals at a much greater cost. He said that he wanted to work for veterans. He had gotten all of his training at the VA medical center in Washington DC. His preceptor there had been Dr. Ross Fletcher, now the chief of staff. Dr. Fletcher is also an innovator and primary contributor to the VA's computerized patient record. I never took the cardiologist up on his offer.

This transportation from rural VA medical centers to tertiary VA medical centers was a problem. We haven't adequately explained the reasons for it. Certainly, our nation has not been as determined to solve rural health-care issues as we should be. Maine is thinly populated, and certainly the VA doesn't have enough workload to warrant hiring a vascular surgeon. Our fragmented health-care system doesn't allow us to work together sufficiently to solve this problem for the VA or for anyone else in the rural areas of our country. The Togus VA physicians are largely devoted Mainers who prefer living there. Boston is overpopulated with physicians who choose to live there for different reasons. I believe that permitting the VA to use Medicare funds for these patients in Portland, Maine, for example, would improve quality and customer service. There are other federal beneficiaries who could utilize the VA's rural health centers like Togus, including the military and federal employees.

During my involvement with Togus, the negative media coverage and apparent pressure from the Maine congressional delegation, I was fortunate enough to be summoned to brief the VA secretary, Togo West, on two different occasions. I met Dr. Garthewaite, who by then had become the undersecretary for health, in his office. Dr. Garthewaite then would accompany me to the secretary's waiting room via the keyed executive elevator.

Once ushered into the secretary's office, the same thing happened both times. First, a photographer would appear as if he had been hiding under the desk. Then the secretary and I would pose in front of the window with the White House view. Two or three photos would be taken. The photographer would be excused. Second, we would sit at the secretary's conference table, and I would brief the secretary. Dr. Garthwaite would add a few points. Third, Mr. West would then repeat back to me almost verbatim what I had said to him. Fourth, he would ask if he had it right. I would say he did. Fifth, he would excuse himself graciously and on the way out, he would give me his personal commemorative coin, about the size of a silver dollar.

I would then go brief my supervisor, Ken Clark, the chief network officer. Ken would say after each briefing that he had never been given such a coin by the secretary. I would tell Ken that he better get his act together because I didn't think Secretary West would be with us much longer. He would laugh. From the time that Secretary West came over from his previous job as secretary of the army, rumors floated that he was leaving. So much so, that many VA employees referred to him as To Go West.

The VA is accomplished at finding ways to deliver care that are cheaper. I believe that the VA monitors its care as well as anyone; one of the problems in Boston is that the Jamaica Plain VA Medical Center is poorly designed, and too little customer service training and emphasis has been given to its employees. Its employees, especially those with the most patient contact, are continuously turning over.

Although it's been renovated, the designs left long, lonely corridors in too many places. Many hospitals have open atriums where patients and families can congregate and communicate. Not Jamaica Plain. Jamaica Plain makes the problem worse by providing too little parking, again discouraging visitors and volunteers. The volunteers could brighten the waiting areas by talking to patients and escorting them to their various treatment sites. Merely serving coffee would be an improvement. My intervention arrived too late to prevent yet another long, cold walk for patients. The Metro area transportation system had worked with the VA's local leaders to build a waiting area for people taking the bus or tram. It was about a 200-foot uncovered walk to get into the medical center. The construction was well underway and too late to change. We need to do better.

The great management difficulty in New England was that not nearly enough time could be spent on any one medical center. There were eleven VA medical centers under eight different directors. There had been little attempt to standardize business practices, identify common services, and build on economies of scale, other than two areas: laboratories were in the process of being consolidated, and education had been centralized to Bedford. While the laboratory centralization was going smoothly, the centralization of education proved to be a source of friction throughout the network. Many believed that it was a sign of the former regime's arrogance, and it forced them to travel to Bedford far more than they would have otherwise. Of course, televideo health consults are emerging, and video would reduce some of that travel eventually, but the resentment remained high.

The network was attempting to convert to product lines as well. Its effort was cautious and tentative. I met with the product line manager for primary care and was amazed at what she reported. She had to travel to each director and get them to sign a memorandum of understanding. This meant that each site would have slightly different variations on a theme. I gave her much more authority. I directed that the same authority be given to the product line managers of long-term care and behavioral health. I talked to all the directors repeatedly, trying to refine their approach to management and emphasizing standardization, economies of scale, and cooperation rather than competition. It did little good.

A network-wide hiring process was implemented, whereby each

medical center had to come to the network for approval for hiring anyone other than primary care physicians and nurses. Because some of the directors were opposed to this level of review, the congressional letters started flying into the network office. Many of our leaders had interpreted this process to mean a freeze on employment, and so careful explanations to our congressional delegation and other stakeholders were necessary. I know that some of these directors and a few chiefs of staff lobbied our own network leaders into approving some positions without a full accounting in the network office.

Making any change proved difficult in Network 1, particularly any change involving the Boston health-care system. Boston has a history of politics being a blood sport. It seemed that everyone joined in the fray, creating a crazy quilt of incentives and agreements that frequently resulted in a stalemate. The unions were opposed to any staff reductions. The medical schools were fearful of product lines and losing power from their affiliated medical center to the network; the Veterans Service Organizations were put squarely in the middle, resulting in their confused support for their local medical center, even though it often resulted in less-than-stellar service and services.

My argument of adopting best practices within the network fell on deaf ears. "We are the Boston health-care system. We are the best. We need what we have and more," went the refrain. Using data didn't seem to motivate them. They really believed that Boston was so superior that data showing their relative inefficiencies had to be flawed. Their own internal rationalizations about how bad they had it consistently dominated their thinking. I decided to expose their rationalizations and bad practices to all in the network. I talked about these differences in practice in the network's board meeting. I aired them in every possible venue. But the Boston management was not shamed enough to change.

The VA has Geriatric Research, Education, and Clinical Centers (GRECCs). In the bad old days, influence and the aura of some of the medical school affiliates in the Boston area led to their being three GRECCs in the Boston area. One was at Bedford, one was at West Roxbury, and one was at Jamaica Plain. These last two were under the same medical center leadership team but had different affiliations.

I should also point out that Network 2 did not have a GRECC at all. The director at the GRECC in West Roxbury had been vacant for about two years. Every month, I was getting calls from the long-term care leadership in VA Central Office about the status of getting this position filled. Local management blamed the network's hiring freeze. In reality, the medical school couldn't find a candidate worthy of the position. The VA ended up spending a lot of money bringing in candidates, but the position stayed vacant. The local medical center managers preferred to use the centralized, allocated funding for the GRECC for other purposes. When GRECC staff positions were filled, they often were allotted a full range of workload in the medical center and not enough time for research. These GRECC staff also had to scrounge for supplies and office space, even though VA Central Office was fully funding their program. So the GRECC employees called their counterparts in VA Central Office to complain, and their counterparts would call me. I would then call the respective director and order them to straighten the matter out.

Another way this round-robin worked in New England involved not filling positions in the homeless programs. The VA had started centralized funding for homeless programs some years before based on credible data that about one-third of all the homeless were veterans. We had to account for the use of these funds to VA Central Office. In Network 2, none of this was a problem. I was to find out that this was a huge problem in Network 1.

One day, I was invited to a meeting in the office of Senator John Kerry. I went to his office, not knowing the subject of the meeting, but reasonably prepared for anything that might come up. In his office in downtown Boston, I was ushered into a spacious office-conference room combination with a large-screen television perched at one end of the room. There were two other people in the room and Senator Kerry with one of his staff. When I was introduced to the other people, I quickly learned that they were directors of nonprofit homeless programs in the greater suburban Boston area, including a homeless shelter director at a meeting in Washington who joined us via televideo. I also learned that they were VA contractors, expected to provide housing and services to homeless veterans. I got my notebook out, expecting to be given a laundry list of complaints about the VA, and I was not disappointed.

The first complaint was that the VA was not filling its own coordinator positions. These centrally funded positions were the liaisons between the VA medical centers and the homeless contractors. Without them, the homeless shelters and programs had to spend much more time tracking down their clients, arranging transportation, and so forth. I knew immediately that this was a situation just like the GRECCs (Geriatric Research and Education, Clinical Centers); local medical center management, in an effort to prevent or delay having to take actions to reduce their own staff because of budgets, preferred to delay filling any centralized positions. The second complaint was that because the various VA medical centers were so autonomous, it was hard to determine which of the VA medical centers had their clients. This meant that the client's meager possessions would often be lost in the shuffle as the client worked their way through the VA's clinical programs. Third, the transportation network operated by the VA was cutting the shelters and programs off. This meant that the programs would have to go to great expense in hiring transportation and/or spending additional time trying to arrange transportation. I took copious notes.

We had a summit conference of the senior executives the next day and began to address the VA's service problems, at least until the directors began to feel that they were off the radar screen, at which time they reverted to pattern. I was thrilled that Senator Kerry had handled the problem in this way. I understand the concerns, and I understand that the homeless program managers could be shrill in voicing their desires to acquire assets and protect their clients. The homeless programs were often fragile, and certainly these difficult and often contentious clients provide their own challenges without having the VA make matters more difficult for them. Senator Kerry could have toasted and roasted me by simply calling VA Central Office, but he gave me a chance to correct things. I really appreciated that approach.

The transportation issue is worthy of further comment. Since the network hadn't been competitive under the VA's resource allocation model, it had been forced to use allocated equipment funding and other nonrecurring sources to put into operating accounts. Because the replacement of clinical equipment is always a higher priority, any remaining equipment funds were insufficient to meet transportation and other administrative demands. The VA's vans simply got into worse shape. The Disabled American Veterans (DAV), which runs a volunteer transportation network and donates most of the vans, simply couldn't keep up. Therefore, patients were riding a long time in vans that were well beyond their useful lives.

I used the network's executive leadership council to attempt to transform the network. The idea of reviewing all positions was to create alternatives to the long-established business as usual. Some directors seemed to understand, but those with the biggest budgets (and probably the worst set of management skills) did not. Although I knew that I was being stymied many times a day, I kept on trying.

The situation involving VA Health System Center Boston's prosthetic clerks was a classic case in point. All networks had been directed to centralize all prosthetic activities under one chief of prosthetics service in the network. In the case of Network 1, this meant doing business as usual, promoting the selected chief and having the others report to him only for program reviews and rolling up of the network's numbers. There was, in other words, no attempt to reengineer the delivery of prosthetics in the network. Boston was hiring prosthetic clerks who were leaving as fast as they came on board. Boston was paying moving expenses for GS5 prosthetic clerks who transferred or quit almost as soon as they came on board.

Network 2 reengineered its prosthetic service, consolidating the clerks in a medical center where recruitment could be easily facilitated and where there was low turnover among staff. Boston could not do this, because it didn't want to do this. In the hottest job market in the country, a few congressional staff still complained about attempts to reduce or realign staff, particularly in the Boston health-care system. I don't think that Senator Kennedy or the various congressmen representing Boston really knew about it or cared, but protecting jobs was a time-honored tradition, so the congressional staff continued to protect the employees, abetted by the unions, of course.

The comparison between Network 2 and Boston could not have been bolder. Network 2 lost thousands of federal jobs during the reinventing government era; Boston didn't. Boston was in a growth-driven, incredibly hot real estate and jobs market. Network 2 and many parts of Network 1 weren't. States like Maine, New Hampshire, and Vermont, as well as western Massachusetts, would have been ideal places to consolidate office staff who could do all of their work via the computer. Computer systems of the VA would have facilitated it. But the VA directors and their political contacts weren't going to let that happen.

When I discovered that Jamaica Plain and West Roxbury medical centers in the Boston health system were enticing pharmacists from other VAs in the immediate area, I had to intervene. They were solving their problem maybe, but by exacerbating recruitment problems elsewhere in the immediate area. It seems like the executive branch, at least the VA part, had to work together in New England, but very little else functioned that way—to the detriment of its taxpayers and citizens.

After touring the Manchester, New Hampshire VA Medical Center, I had a meeting with the dean of Harvard Medical School to discuss the product line organizations that the New England network was also trying to implement. Much of the rest of the VA was doing the same thing; most were further along. I was anxious and somewhat proud that I was going to be in a meeting with the dean of Harvard Medical School. Frankly, I was thrilled that the VA was giving me the chance to set foot on that hallowed campus.

On one occasion, I visited the VA medical center in Manchester, New Hampshire. This was one of those facilities doing everything right. They were increasing outpatient care, they had improved emergency services, and they had greatly reduced inpatient beds. The problem was that they received none of the supposed benefits for having done all the right things. They had good leadership and were a tight team, focused and ready to meet any challenges. I told the director that high performance was always the best thing. He smiled and said, "Adequate resources would sure make us feel a lot better about the high performance." I silently agreed.

After departing Manchester, I had been driving on the interstate for about five or six miles when the traffic came to a complete halt. It was one of those beautiful New England days: the sun was shining, the snow was melting, and the pine trees were shiny and green. The traffic, however, was backed up for miles. I got out and walked around. I called the office and asked them to call the dean's office to reschedule. One of the more enterprising drivers ran down to the cause of the stoppage and jogged back by me. I asked him what the problem was. He said, "A tractor trailer jackknifed across all three lanes of traffic. The emergency vehicles just got there. We'll be here for another hour at least." I thanked him. I sat in the government vehicle and got caught up on my inbox reading.

The day finally arrived for my rescheduled meeting with the dean of Harvard Medical School. My staff carefully went over the directions with me, since I had gotten lost several times already and driving in Boston traffic is challenging to say the least. I found the building without a problem. The directions were perfect. As I was driving to the dean's building, I was wondering where the parking garage was. As I turned into the building, I realized that the parking garage was under the old, elegant medical school administration building. I drove the car down several floors and was instructed by attendants at the very bottom to leave the car where it was with the keys in it. I jokingly told the attendant that it was a government car, not to lose it or it would be an FBI case. He told me, "Happens all the time." On my way to see the dean, I wondered what happened all the time—visits from the FBI or losing cars.

The dean was charming. His office was old and entirely in keeping with my limited expectations of what the Harvard Medical School dean's office should look like. For sure, it had more space than most dean's offices have. The room was antique in appearance with dark wood paneling and furniture. The associate chief of staff for research for the VA Boston Health System was already there. He was a distinguished, highly regarded, and respected researcher and VA research administrator. I don't know why he was there, but I certainly enjoyed meeting him and didn't mind. Maybe the dean thought that the product lines were in some kind of research phase. I did my presentation. The dean asked all the right questions and created the kind of dialogue that results in true learning. He seemed to understand product lines and was not concerned about them. I was pleased and somewhat shocked. The associate chief of staff for research also made contributions to the discussion. We adjourned. I went back to the sub-, sub-, subbasement, where they actually found my car. I heard later that they couldn't find the associate chief of staff's car until after he had taken a cab back to work.

Some months after the visit to Harvard, all the network directors were summoned to the annual meeting of the American Association of Medical Colleges (AAMC). Due to many complaints, the AAMC and the VA were meeting jointly so that the network directors could explain to the deans what exactly was happening in each network in regard to product lines. The chief network officer and the chief academic affairs officer from the VA were both there. I waited patiently to hear from my deans. I was representing both Network 1 and 2 at this meeting. All of my colleagues seemed to be very busy, except for me. I took this as a sign that we had adequately explained product line organization to the deans. More likely, it was that product lines were not sufficiently high on their list.

Circumstances forced me visit the White River Junction VA Medical Center on several occasions. The medical center is in a beautiful location, right across the river from its affiliate, the Dartmouth Medical School. For a little medical center, it is prominent in research and education. Yet the workload really doesn't support the level of academic training programs. The state of Vermont and its politicians certainly support it, however.

I believe that its mission should be broadened to serve all veterans and to serve all active duty and reserve service personnel, retirees, and dependents. This would save some of the taxpayer's funds and rightfully preserve this jewel of a health-care system by making it more productive and able to serve society in a lower-cost, higher-quality way.

In the same way, other rural VA medical centers could have their value maximized. As the veteran population changes and more eligible veterans move to Arizona, Florida, and other parts of the country, the role of these medical centers could be expanded; perhaps they could even serve as an affiliate of the National Institutes of Health. Having high patient volumes means so much to health-care quality (repetition is the art of learning and improving). This rule of quality in health care means that more of the federal beneficiary workload and financing should be congregated, especially for the rural VA medical centers such as White River Junction and Togus.

The VA health system of Connecticut also required me to make multiple visits. This health system consists of two medical centers, Newington and West Haven, and several outpatient clinics. The health system is affiliated with Yale and the University of Connecticut, but the affiliation is most visible with Yale and West Haven. Like Boston, Connecticut management really didn't believe that they could be more efficient, even though they had the national best practice in behavioral health care in the VA. Innovative, cost effective, and highly productive, I used behavioral health as an example to not only VA Connecticut's leadership but around New England as well. I learned that there is some truth to Mark Twain's old saying, "There is nothing Americans hate worse than a good example."

The leaders of behavioral health tracked their costs and relative costs, their quality, their customer service, and their productivity in delivery of health care and research. Incredibly innovative, they reduced their reliance on VA funding through community support and grants, all the while improving on their performance measures and quality. To my knowledge, none of the other care lines in the network adopted this best practice. All it would take for anyone in or out of the VA to duplicate this is to adopt the fundamental belief that everything can be continually improved. Attitude may not be everything, but it certainly helps in continuous quality improvement.

The Connecticut VA Health System lost one of its patients in West Haven. In the VA, we must report these matters urgently to VA Central Office. This is followed by multiple white papers until the patient issue is closed. We have learned a lot about how to find missing patients and how to prevent their becoming lost in the first place. In a huge medical center with a booming patient workload like West Haven, we are fortunate that we don't lose more to the urban environment with the crowds of patients and visitors, the vans and cabs coming and going, and the complex arrangement of clinics and labs. Sometimes the patient just wonders off in search of a bar. Furthermore, the frail, the mentally confused, the drug-addled patients, and the elderly add to the mix. Since we live in an aging society and increasingly urban environments, we need better systems for identifying and monitoring patients at risk. Of course, families that stick their loved one on a van without an attendant or a note need to be educated too. Fortunately, this missing patient was found, somewhat dehydrated, in a closed-off construction zone within the hospital. This was a close call.

The highly esteemed, greatly respected chief of medicine from the VA's Boston Health System came to visit one day along with his director. This legend of the VA and Boston medicine came to complain about safety on the acute medical wards in Jamaica Plain. He felt that the staffing levels were so low that mistakes were occurring. I said that might be so, but, if it was, without any data, all I could suggest to him was to shut the units down one by one and review the safety practices. I said that Boston's comparative staffing analysis showed that additional staff wasn't necessary, but each and every process needed to be performed safely.

He didn't like my answer and retired shortly thereafter. He probably needed to retire, but I didn't like being the reason. The patient safety issue was just emerging, and I am proud to say that the VA was a leader in the patient safety movement. While staffing is certainly an issue, the safety issue is one of the complex variables that need to be studied and analyzed. The VA is still a leader in this regard. While much needs to be done, hospitals are safer today than ever.

My main self-assigned task was finding the person who would replace me in Network 1. I found her in Dr. Jeannette Chirico-Post. She was detailed to the network office to be the clinical manager. The clinical manager who was there when I arrived in Network 1 had decided to transfer to West Palm Beach. Dr. Chirico-Post had an extensive background in quality and had been the chief of staff at the VA medical center in Providence, Rhode Island. She was willing, intelligent, and tough, with enough attitude to take on the significant challenges that the network faced. Fortunately, VA Central Office agreed, and she serves in this capacity as of this writing.

Chapter 12.5: The Curious National Media

Shortly after beginning the network director job, I received a call from Dr. Larry Flesh, then the director at the Albany VA Medical Center. He was on the line with Dr. Kizer, who was inquiring about the medical center's recent request for donations. I quickly ran over to his office and explained to Dr. Kizer what had happened.

The employees' association, with Dr. Flesh's blessing, had decided to have a bake sale to raise money to buy something for the medical center. The leaders of the employees' association had put together a list of items that they might buy. The list reflected the diversity of employment of those leaders and had been arranged in alphabetic order. The day before, one of the columnists for the *Albany Times-Union* had reported on this. I think he intended it as a jab at management for not funding these worthwhile endeavors. In his write-up, he mentioned that the employees were buying necessary clinical equipment.

For some strange reason, this little column spread across the country the next day, coming to the attention of the secretary of Veterans Affairs and then to Dr. Kizer. The gist of the discussion was that we should not solicit donations, and, secondarily, we should have advised the public affairs staff and VA Central Office as soon as the little column had appeared. I assured Dr. Kizer that many VA medical centers collaborated with employee associations, veteran organizations, and community groups to raise funds for certain projects or activities. The list of items that had been provided to the columnist had only a few clinical items on it, and the dental equipment was still in research and development. He was mollified.

I then got a call from my regional public affairs person, who told me in his most angry voice how wrong I was about this and that the entire VA was embarrassed. I told him that I was embarrassed for him, repeating the briefing that I had provided Dr. Kizer.

In the next few days, we received numerous cards and letters from people, mostly retired ladies offering to bake us cookies and cakes for our bake sale. We had messages from Florida, Texas, and California among others. The employees association had raised a fair amount of funds. I was then driving a 1983 Pontiac LeSabre wagon that my children called the Malph mobile. I had offered to take the winning bidders to a coffee break at the then-new Starbuck's in town. In addition to the bake sale, the organizers had arranged for others who couldn't bake, such as me, to provide other services and products that could be bid on.

Much to my surprise, six winning bidders—all women—were chosen! At the appointed time they showed up and jumped into the Malph Mobile. They had conspired to submit the winning bids so that they could get a coffee break courtesy of the network director. Once there, I got my final surprise of this fundraising effort. I ordered my usual: black coffee. They ordered various drinks. My bill was over $32. For this "coffee" break, I was surprised that I was the only one drinking regular coffee. The ladies paid or donated $130 in total. For that, I also received an education in the wonders of the media.

Another unrelated curious thing happened when one of the medical centers in the network appeared on the "Fleecing of America" segment of the NBC *Nightly News*. My excellent PR person, Linda Blumenstock, reported that she had been advised by her Central Office counterpart that the Albany VA would be appearing on the NBC *Nightly News*. I found this disturbing, knowing that the network was leading the VA in productivity and cost effectiveness. Linda told me that apparently the Albany laundry was to be featured. This was curious to me because I knew that the laundry had been cited by the general accounting office as a best practice. I determined to get to the bottom of this as rapidly as possible.

The very next week, I watched the Fleecing of America segment. The reporter, Mike Taibbi, was shown just outside the property line of the VA, but in the background, clearly shown, was the VA Medical Center Albany. From the time of Linda's informing me of the segment to the showing of the segment, I had heard from no one in VA Central Office. Nor did anyone call me afterward. This is very curious, because usually some senior bureaucrat feels offended enough to call and blast away over my obvious lack of foresight or some such. I think it makes them feel better about themselves.

My own investigation had started the very moment after Linda's initial briefing. Having a contact on the House VA Oversight Committee was helpful. I initially called a dear friend in the congressional affairs office of VA Central Office. At that moment, he was buried so far down that he actually thought he would never get a higher level job in the VA. This proved untrue. I called him because he made it his business to know what was going on with congressional interactions and the media. He told me that Arthur Wu, the staff executive director of one of the subcommittees, had given a follow-up GAO report on the laundry at VA Medical Center Albany to NBC.

Supposedly, Arthur had informed his VA Central Office contact of this, but the news failed to trickle down to me. Nor did I know anything about the follow-up GAO study. The director at VA Medical Center Albany knew about it when I asked him, but thought that it was much ado about nothing and therefore failed to inform the network and VA Central Office of all external audits. Of course, VA Central Office knew already, but I did not.

After learning this, I called my contact on the House Oversight Committee. He confirmed Arthur Wu's involvement. He added that NBC had called the committee searching for dirt on the VA. Art Wu was happy to oblige. Having just read the GAO's follow-up report, he knew that the GAO had made a finding of fraud, waste, and abuse in the laundry at the VA medical center in Albany. I was not aware of this report at the time.

The NBC report that aired had correctly mentioned a loss of thousands of dollars. What was also correct is that the issue involved the contractor who was using the VA's equipment and space to do the laundry. The contract called for weighing each load of laundry. The VA employed a laundry supervisor to manage the contract. The commercial laundry's owner and the VA supervisor had apparently grown up and gone to school together in Rome, New York. They had agreed to estimate the poundage. This resulted in higher payments to the contractor. If memory serves, this amounted to about $15,000. As soon as the practice was discovered, it ended. The VA's supervisor was so embarrassed that he resigned.

This taught me that the media is curious, but not nearly curious enough about the actual facts. This loss of $15,000, or however much it was, is inexcusable, of course. The curious part is why NBC would do such a story when the fraud, waste, and abuse at all levels of government and corporations is far more than that. On any given day, would a loss of $15,000 be in the top thousand of losses? I don't think so. I doubt if it would be in the top ten thousand of losses. But it was easy pickins.

Chapter 12.6: My Brother Update

During my detail to New England, I encountered news of my brother. I should explain that my brother was a source of much pain and continuing concern on my part. Some of the things he did and said, the way he acted at times, just seemed abnormal. In fact, at times, he seemed to be threatening my own family.

Between adolescence and the time of my detail, I had been in his presence three times. Twice, I visited his home. Once, he and his family came to visit us. His wife and two daughters seemed OK. My wife and I were both uncomfortable with his demeanor and felt like he tried to manipulate us. Some of the things he said I took to be veiled threats to the health and welfare of my children. When I told him about the birth of our first son, he said that I had one-upped him once again. His rare inquiries about the kids seemed centered on where they were rather than how they were doing. He would try to manipulate my wife and I into saying or doing things that neither of us was comfortable in saying or doing. Because I knew he had been violent in the past, I adopted a cautious stance that prevented any further direct contact between him and my family. During most of the intervening years, he and our mother had lived in the same place: Waco, Texas. This essentially meant that I wouldn't visit her either.

My brother became a captain in the army. He had first been an armored officer, but switched to intelligence. After he got back from Vietnam, he rapidly sank into manic depression—what's known today as bipolar disorder. He left the army. His family had moved to Phoenix, Arizona. From there, his family left him to go back to Maine. He roamed the country, avoiding me, but occasionally showing up at some relative's house. I don't think he knew all the places that he visited. He told me one time that when he regained consciousness, his plane was on the ground in Madrid, Spain.

In the meantime, he was rated 100 percent service connected and given a pension. This meant that he would show up or be taken to the nearest VA facility when he was found wandering or got into trouble. Typically, prior to today's patient confidentiality laws, I would get a call from some psychologist or director about him. They would want to know if I wanted to speak to him. I would always say yes. But my brother never wanted to speak to me. He would finagle out before any serious treatment could occur. Or he would con someone to get him into a setting where he could elope, which in the health-care context means fleeing the hospital.

Because of our unusual last name, the VA officials would immediately think that they should contact me just in case. A wonderful and now retired director, Jose Coronado, talked to me several times during these years. Once he said he regretted the beating my brother gave one of San Antonio's best nursing assistants. And so did I. Later, I was to learn that over this period of fifteen or twenty years, he had married three more times, divorced four times, and had joined at least one religious cult.

The telephone call came in one Sunday afternoon from the director of the VA medical center in Togus, Maine. Jack Sims kindly and tactfully explained that one of my brother's daughters, who lived in Maine, had heard that my brother was heading to Maine. She was afraid that he would do harm to her and her children. All she knew was that he had left Texas, where he had been living, and was heading north. She demanded that the VA stop him.

I told Jack that I appreciated the call, but I doubted my brother was in any condition to successfully drive from Texas to Maine. At the time of this call, I was acting director of Network 1. Jack was concerned that I would be upset by this situation being reported to VA Central Office. I told him that this was just the latest in a long, sad trip and that I expected that he would report the matter since it involved a VA patient. I also told him to disclose the relationship. I knew that my brother had begun to break down physically. I also knew that the last place he wanted to come on his mystery tours was to see me. My brother had remarried, and I called his wife. She was upset, but thought my brother was still in another part of Texas visiting with friends. After several weeks, he came back to his wife in Waco and resumed getting mental health services from the VA.

I was back in Network 2 when I received a call about my brother that did devastate me. The call was from Paul Schultz, who identified himself as a U.S. Secret Service agent. He told me that I was to call him immediately when my brother showed up. They had heard he was heading to New York. I explained to the agent that I would be the last person that my brother would contact. He asked why. I told him that my brother knew I would have him hospitalized in the VA as soon as I could find him. I asked him why he was looking for my brother. Agent Schultz explained that my brother had threatened the life of the first lady. I told the agent that I thought that was just his usual braggadocio or delusional state when not taking his meds. This time, however, I was devastated. When I got home, I drank plenty of scotch while contemplating the sad, strange journey of my brother's life. Eventually, I discovered that my brother had not gotten out of the state of Texas. His continuing downward spiral got him admitted to a locked ward in a state hospital where he remained for over a year.

Chapter 13
2002: The Really Big Detail

After a few months back in Network 2, I was contacted via cell phone while I was on the train to Montreal with my wife. After our three children had left home, we had started spending Thanksgiving in Montreal. The train ride up there is lovely. Of course, it isn't Thanksgiving in Canada, so we enjoyed the city without the trappings of Thanksgiving in the United States.

The phone call was from the VA's chief of staff. The chiefs of staff in medical centers are physicians. This chief of staff, as are all the others in Washington to my knowledge, is administrative. The secretary of Veterans Affairs wanted to talk to me. I hastily agreed. I was to travel to Washington to meet with the secretary of Veterans Affairs in early January. I was concerned to some extent. I didn't want to transfer back to VA Central Office. I was practicing turning the secretary down with the truth; my wife had a job that she loved, and, since she had moved a lot, I didn't want to move her again. I really didn't want another tour of duty in Washington either.

I dutifully reported to his office suite at the appointed time. The secretaries were gracious, offering coffee and expressing concern over the weather in Albany. I reassured them that Albany and the rest of upstate was prepared for whatever Mother Nature threw at them. They laughed.

When the appointed time arrived, the secretary's personal secretary came over and ushered me into his office. The secretary, Anthony Prinicipi, came over, shook my hand, and seemed pleased to meet me. We sat down.

He explained, "You are running a great network up there. You've really done a fine job."

I thanked him profusely.

"I need someone to run the CARES office here in Washington, Fred." He smiled and added, "I think you are the only person for the job."

I kept on smiling, but I knew (or thought I knew) what the CARES job entailed, and it would be a tough and demanding assignment for anyone. CARES was an acronym that stood for Capital Asset Realignment for Enhanced Services. This was the name the VA had given it to meet the congressional mandate to totally justify the capital assets (land and buildings, almost all hospitals and related clinics, nursing homes and domiciliaries) that it had. This was the VA's equivalent to the Department of Defense's Base Realignment Commission, or BRAC. Except that the DOD had a law that said that an independent commission would determine which facilities would close, and Congress had to accept that recommendation in whole or reject it in whole. DOD, I was to find out later, would model their health-care facility realignment after the lessons that it was to learn from the VA's CARES effort.

"What will it take for you to take this job on?" he asked.

After giving the matter some thought, I said, "First, it would have to be a detail, I don't want to move. Second, I think that I could only do the job for six months. My heart is in the field, and I don't want to be absent from that work for more than six months."

"Fine, fine," he said. He quickly followed up with, "I'm going to get you help. You'll have advisors and a staff of twenty-five here in Central Office."

I said, "I really would need fifteen in the field. Ten here would be fine."

"I think that could be worked out." He went on to explain, "The pilot program was in its final stages of completion. It had been done on Network 10, which is based in Chicago and covers most of Illinois, Michigan, and Wisconsin." The secretary didn't hold back from expressing his displeasure with the results there. "We spent far too much money on that contract. We don't want to repeat that. The staff running that contract just can't do the job that we need to be done."

I said, "Mr. Secretary, before I tell you yes, there are some things that you need to know. First, I have been absent too much from Network 2. I'd hate to leave them for another six months. It wouldn't be fair. Second, I am in receipt of a proposed admonishment and have a possible disciplinary action coming from the Office of Special Counsel."

He quickly said, "Don't worry about that, Fred."

I was surprised and somewhat taken aback; I was hoping that disclosure would be my ticket back to Albany.

Mr. Principi leaned back in the beautiful overstuffed chair in which he was sitting and asked, "Would you be interested in Network 8?" I immediately said yes with great enthusiasm. The truth was that I was ready to leave Network 2, but only if I could get to Florida, my home state. Network 8 encompassed Florida, part of Georgia, and Puerto Rico.

"But Dr. Rosewater is in that job," I quickly added.

"Rob is going to be nominated to be the undersecretary for health," the secretary said, adding, "That's confidential until his paperwork is cleared by the White House." He said, "Rob's in an office on the fifth floor. When you leave here go talk to him about it."

I was getting excited: a chance to return to my home state, and I was getting all the inside information.

"Fred, this is the most important thing that I'm going to do. CARES will be the hallmark of my administration." He smiled and quickly added that there someone that he wanted me to meet. He got up quickly and walked out of the back door of his office. After two minutes, he returned with a big grin on his face. A distinguished-looking black man of about forty was with him. "Fred, this is Dr. Leo McKay, the deputy secretary. You'll be working directly for him."

I gave them both a big grin and warmly shook Dr. McKay's hand.

"Leo, Fred has agreed to come on board and run CARES for us. He'll meet with you weekly, and you get him anything he needs." I sensed my time with the secretary was coming to an end. I thanked them both and was on my way to the fifth floor to meet with the probable nominee for undersecretary for health of the VA, Rob Rosewater. My understanding was that the CARES job was a detail for six months, not a real reassignment. I would be reassigned to the Network 8 job on paper so that I could relocate but wouldn't actually do the job until my six-month CARES detail was over.

Dr. Rosewater stood and gave me a little smile. We shook hands, and I sat down. He was immersed in reading material, preparing himself for the huge job that lay ahead of him and for the hearings that would propel him to confirmation. I explained where I had been and what I had been asked to do. Bob seemed concerned.

"Fred, I want someone else in that job as network director," he stated with an air of some finality. Fortunately for me, I handle rejection well. "Elwood Headley is already acting, and we really need somebody who's going to be there."

I readily agreed. I loved being a network director except for all the air travel.

He asked, "Would you be interested in going to Gainesville as director and taking his place?" I said I would be thrilled. I had begun my career some thirty-three years earlier as an accountant trainee in Gainesville. We shook hands, and I was on my way back to see the secretary.

The secretary frowned and looked quizzically at me. He asked me, "Why do you want the job in Gainesville? The network director job is a better fit for you."

I smiled and looked out his window to the White House. "Because Network 8 is the largest and most complex network, I will be gone for six months, and it's too important to be left to a caretaker. Plus, I'm a Gator!"

He looked at me, clearly not comprehending my decision-making process. But after a few seconds, he smiled and said OK. I went back as quickly as I could and sealed the deal with Dr. Rosewater.

The detail meant flying to Washington every Monday morning or Sunday evening and flying back to New York every Friday afternoon or evening. I learned all that I could as fast as I could. I quickly discovered that there was an enormous amount of ill will and fear about CARES. Every stakeholder seemed to have a divergent view about it. Reconciling these views would be difficult, but I was resolved to get the best possible product completed.

I enjoyed my meetings with Dr. McKay. I knew access to the secretary was limited, and frankly I enjoyed meeting with Dr. McKay. I quickly put together a planning guide and left a copy with Dr. McKay. The next week, he informed me that it was not satisfactory. He implied that it needed more volume.

As the staff that I was to eventually assemble was not on board yet, I depended on bringing excellent people from the field. For ten to twelve hours a day for eight or nine days over a two-week period, we put the planning guidance together. Jay Halprin, who was a vastly experienced VA health-care planner, assisted me tremendously. In fact, the document would never have been done without his help. Dave Wood, who is now the director at the VA medical center in Oklahoma City was also a tremendous asset to the process. I was to learn that CARES was and would probably always be a work in process. Many adjustments would be made, but the secretary blessed the product about four weeks after the version that he had rejected. That version was about two inches thick. My previous submission had been a twelve pager.

My two consultants came on board. They were excellent folks who had labored diligently and effectively on behalf of the VA for many years. They were both close to Secretary Principi. Over time, they would meet with Secretary Principi and relay his decisions and comments back to me. Sometimes, I did not like the secretary's comments, and this was dissatisfying given the sacrifices I was making and the progress the CARES team as a whole had accomplished.

Because I had to use these consultants who were both retired from the VA, they had a steep learning curve to get up-to-date, and I would have the time-consuming additional responsibility of supervising their work. I was to become for the first time in my career a contracting officer technical representative.

In other words, I was to supervise the consulting contracts directly, account for their work, and certify their invoices for payment. Because of this, a contracting officer was assigned to me whose expectations of me were far more than I had the time for. She tried valiantly to educate me, but being a contracting officer was never one of my aspirations. There were too many rules involved and not enough common sense. In other words, the maximum effort was given to pass legal review and get the contract signed off and not enough time or effort to meet the real needs of the government. In this case, however, the real need for these two outstanding individuals was that of the secretary, not the needs of the CARES program. They contributed as best they could, and I used them to the best advantage of CARES. The two of them were advisors, not contributors to the overall work required of the CARES effort.

Among the myriad difficulties was the already appointed CARES director who was assigned to me. She and the deputy undersecretary for health had been responsible for the expensive and botched effort in Network 12. The deputy was demanding and argumentative about the new approach with me. Both were undermining about this new approach to CARES.

Despite his displeasure with the results and the costs of the pilot program, Secretary Principi left the staff that had led the contract effort in place. They were constant critics of everything about the new approach to CARES. Everything that I did was second-guessed and criticized. The secretary's chief of staff told me that they constantly came to her to voice their doubts, concerns, and allegations of mistakes on my part. If I often heard about it from the secretary's chief of staff, then that meant that the secretary and others were hearing it as well. Although unprofessional and unethical, they continued their sniping and backstabbing throughout my time with the program.

At every weekly meeting that I had with Dr. McKay, the deputy secretary of the VA, he would ask me to identify problems and people who were not cooperating. I hesitated for many weeks to take him up on this offer. The difficulties were myriad, and the lack of cooperation was widespread. The deputy undersecretary for health often gave me orders that contradicted those from the secretary or others. She frequently gave me direction that I knew that I was not going to accept, and so I ignored them. When not sniping at me directly, she took her criticisms of CARES to the various committees that she chaired. I would do my best to rebut them with facts, knowledge, or logic whenever and wherever the opportunity presented itself. Fortunately, I was a known quantity in VA Central Office, having previously worked there for a total of eight years.

Another difficulty was that all the various planning organizations in the VA, who should have been given this CARES assignment in the first place, only wanted to liaison with my office. They wanted the opportunity to criticize and debate the issues, but they didn't want to do any of the real work. As a group, they proved unable or unwilling to provide documents, assistance, or data analysis beyond the most superficial level. This was true, even though we in CARES were doing their work and trying to catch the VA up from years of neglect in capital asset planning and management. I know why they avoided it. CARES was a highly sensitive political topic, and they did not want to get tarnished by what nearly everyone saw as its inevitable failure. Some of their other projects, such as bed-planning models, were so flawed they blew up at the first exposure to real data and analysis. The list of those failing to cooperate would go on and on. The person that the planning group did finally assign as a liaison provided helpful assistance and served the CARES team well. He was the sole exception to the otherwise complete lack of effort on the part of the official VHA planners.

One day in a meeting with Dr. McKay in response to his question about who was not cooperating with me, I replied that the deputy undersecretary for health was not cooperating. I gave him several examples. He said he would take care of it. He told her to never talk to me again. This did not make her happy, and it probably made me an enemy for life. Because of his approach, I bit my tongue on numerous occasions to prevent more overkill. I tried to improve cooperation on my own. Still, my appreciation for Dr. McKay's many kindnesses, understanding, and guidance is a bright spot in my overall experience with CARES.

Another interesting fact is that I was assigned an office in the primary VA building at 810 Vermont. The staff that I accumulated was situated across the street in an older building without the environmental qualities that would have been desirable. Early in the CARES effort, one of the supervisors in the older building advised me not to drink the water. The air quality also left something to be desired. Finding people and the right offices in the building was also a challenge. The previous occupant of my office had died. He was a highly respected human resource specialist who had a great sense of humor and a practical, pragmatic approach to solving human resource problems. Since I was assigned that office and had the same phone, on several occasions I had the privilege of telling Jimmy's friends and acquaintances that he was dead.

In my CARES work life, I often met with potential contractors who regularly prospected for business in VA Central Office. They would be sent my way if their work products and proposed services had anything to do with capital assets, planning, analyzing, or designing buildings. Meeting with these people took a significant amount of my time, but I did it. I thought if I declined they would end up meeting with Dr. Rosewater, who didn't have the time and might make some kind of commitment to them. My budget was limited, and, as we invented the CARES process, I learned that we would not need most of these vendors or contractors.

The gripe many people in the VA had over the pilot project is that they spent a huge amount of time and effort getting the contractor data, educating the contractor, and revising various drafts of the contractor's reports, and so forth. They claimed that they did not get any credit. As far as I could tell, this was a genuine anger that fed into some of the difficulties that we were experiencing in CARES. Fortunately, we hired people in the field, across the United States, who were knowledgeable and dedicated to the task of getting us the data and analysis that we needed. These folks brought a lot to the table in terms of knowledge, skills, and attitude that was frequently lacking in the staff offices of the VA Central Office.

After approval of our planning guide, the briefings started. I briefed several policy or planning committees in the VA, the Veterans Service Organizations, the White House domestic policy council staff representatives, the staff of the congressional committees on appropriations and veterans affairs, and the VHA national executive board. There were many other individual briefings and media interviews. Fortunately, Jay Halprin kept the slides up-to-date and modified them as policy changes were approved from the latest round of meetings. Our own research and recommendations were frequently modified as we developed better understanding of the data and the actuarial interpretations. E-mail copies of these slides went to numerous internal stakeholders. I also briefed the surgeons general or their deputies in the Pentagon on our progress.

Our research reviewed the literature. We were disappointed to find that there were no standards that we could apply to our analysis. In fact, we invented our own standards and reinvented them as we got data analysis or feedback from stakeholders. When we were finally able to run our data against the VA's approved bed models, the models were proven to be completely useless, even though they had been part of the VA's planning process for years. These models—long-term care and behavioral health essential—had to be created by the CARES office.

Thanks to the efforts of Jay Halprin and the field-based CARES staff and after much effort on my part, our three CARES contracts finally got approved. The contract approval process was difficult under the best of circumstances. Added to the multiple layers of review, Dr. McKay had to sign off on each of them. These contracts were for actuarial services, including education, consulting, and analysis. We had one actuary on the VA's payroll and he helped us tremendously, but he had many other projects to do as well. When I got to the secretary, he questioned several of the consulting items in one of the contracts. I agreed to take them out, largely to get the contracts finalized. It was clear that he had read the contracts and understood what was included. Therefore, I conclude that he had a personal hand in and knowledge of every major contract that the VA awarded during his tenure.

Growing increasingly frustrated, I pushed the limits of our CARES model. At meetings with planners and other network representatives, I mentioned possible changes and gave examples. Changes like closures and expanding outpatient capacity were not well received by most network representatives because they knew they would get into extensive, serious debate with their own stakeholders. Only a few of those facilities actually would be closed. The credit for this limited success belongs to the courageous VA health systems directors who accepted the challenge.

As I passed the six-month mark of my detail, I had to consider the time limits on my patience and the wear and tear from the constant travel and briefings. My consultants told me that Principi was now talking in terms of a year or more for my detail. This was of concern, obviously, because neither he nor Dr. McKay nor anyone else had mentioned it to me. Since I hadn't been transferred on paper to the north Florida/south Georgia health system, I simply reiterated that the detail was for six months, but I would continue until my transfer went through. If that didn't happen in two or three weeks, I would simply go back to Albany. The transfer happened in two or three weeks.

Dr. Rosewater never could find the time to be briefed by me. The deputy undersecretary was no longer allowed to speak to me, and the chief network officer simply didn't have the time. The deputy undersecretary did find time in numerous meetings to trash the CARES effort. All three of them must have been among the numerous people that the secretary never told that CARES would be the hallmark of his administration. We tried to keep them fully engaged, however, by inviting them to our meetings, sending copies of slides, and providing a weekly executive summary of our work and progress. All of these materials, as well as invitations to conferences on CARES, were delivered to the network directors as well. Only a handful of them seemed genuinely engaged in the process.

In November, after ten months of the detail and fresh from the latest briefing at the Office of Management and Budget, I was to brief the National Leadership Board once more. As I walked into the hotel conference room, I was stopped by a network director, who told me that at yesterday's meeting with the undersecretary for health, two network directors said that CARES wasn't sending out briefing materials, that the VHA wasn't ready to proceed with CARES, and that the program was set for failure. Needless to say, I was furious, but I put on my game face and told her that I was sorry to hear that. I was on the way to the men's room when I was stopped by another network director, who basically told me the same thing. I was steaming by then but took the time to collect my thoughts.

I quickly went through the slides and my accompanying spiel. I had numerous questions, primarily from the two network directors who had complained so mightily to the undersecretary for health the day before. I answered every question. It was clear that they had not availed themselves of the materials that had been sent out. I told them so. They questioned whether the materials had been sent out. Thanks to Jay Halprin, who had joined the meeting as support, we had the dates, times, and the specific materials that had been sent out. After the briefing was over, another network director caught up to me and said that the two network directors were not prepared and told me that the briefing went well. I told him that I appreciated the feedback.

I also caught the chief network officer and told her what I thought about the performance by the two network directors. Sadly, no one at that meeting spoke up on my behalf. As is often the case in group settings, people are more influenced to get along than to confront their colleagues. She expressed her regret and was sympathetic about the matter, but passed it off quickly as she said, "That's just they way they are." In one sense, it was the way these two very influential network directors were, but it was me getting skewered over preparations that they had not bothered to review. I said that I had provided all the materials to Dr. Rosewater and expected him to talk to me if he had questions or doubts. I expected his support and should have received it. I had to leave the meeting as quickly as I could because I had to go to the next briefing on the Hill.

Taking the subway back to VA Central Office, I got in the assigned car to take us to the Capitol Hill meeting. Most of the time, I was assigned congressional liaison staff and/or staff from the deputy secretary's office. This day I got both. About a third of the time, I was allowed to brief by myself, and, when that happened, I took the subway or walked to the briefing. On the ride over, I let my anger get the better of me, and I regaled the two of them with how really angry I was over the National Leadership Conference meeting. The meeting on the Hill went well, and I was pleased that there were no policy conflicts to take back to VA Central Office and work out.

Back in the office, however, I was still steaming. I should have gone for a steak and some single-malt scotch, but I did not. I should have called Dr. McKay and cried on his shoulder, but I did not. I had my assignment in Gainesville already, and my heart and allegiance lay with the Veterans Health Administration, not to VA Central Office. I had logged over ten months against a promise to do six.

I was frustrated by the lack of response from the management support office, which was assigned all executive human resource issues. I had such an issue and had been trying to get it resolved for about six weeks. All I had succeeded in doing was getting its director hostile with me. On my third attempt to resolve the issue, I had asked via e-mail in a quite sarcastic, but I thought somewhat humorous way, what the status of my issue was. He had not responded. Later, I caught him in the hallway, and his anger had been quite apparent. I was frustrated by this, since the matter was definitely not inconsequential to me. A representative of the general counsel's office had told me that federal employees on continuous details of over one year would have to pay taxes on all of their per diem and air travel. This was not good, and I did not want to run the risk of having to pay taxes for the privilege of being on this long-term detail.

Based on this anger and frustration, I decided to resign from the CARES detail. I prepared my e-mail that evening and sent it out. The next day was Friday, so I sat in the office and collected all of my personal items and briefed Jay Halprin on what I was going to do. I told him that I would continue to help in anyway, but I was through with the detail. I half expected someone to come see me or to be summoned to the secretary's office but was not. I was on leave the next week and had made arrangements to go to Las Vegas. As I left the office shortly after noon, I was elated to be done with CARES, proud of our efforts, and saddened that the detail was coming to a close in this matter.

The weather in Las Vegas was cold. My wife and I settled into the hotel, and I realized that I was coming down with a sinus infection. My physician readily called in a prescription, since sinus infections were a chronic problem for me. I was sick and tired. I logged on to the Internet and saw the first of two responses from among the many people that I had sent my resignation e-mail to. They were both critical of my actions. I tried to explain. They seemed to be more concerned about the embarrassment to the secretary and perhaps to themselves. The deputy secretary and secretary both wanted me to call them. I exchanged e-mails with Dr. Rosewater, the VA's chief of staff and the chief network officer. The first call I made was to Dr. McKay and was one that I dreaded most of all.

Dr. McKay was concerned and disappointed. I apologized to him repeatedly, because he deserved better. He had been unfailingly supportive and helpful. I knew beyond any doubt that I had let him down. Although his reputation in VA Central Office was that he could be brutally candid and ruthless in his actions, I can honestly say that I never saw that side of the man, if it truly existed. He asked me who he could talk to that would support my view of the events in the National

Leadership Conference. I told him any of the network directors or others who had been there.

I knew that I had to resign and needed to get away from CARES. As he pointed out, leave could have been approved. I could have been taken off the detail for two or three weeks. There were options, but I didn't exercise them, and I know that the secretary probably blamed Dr. McKay for my abrupt departure. I can say that for most of the weeks that I was detailed to CARES, Dr. McKay was the bright spot. I will always treasure his friendship and support.

My final conversation with the secretary occurred later that same day after I had talked to Dr. McKay. He was critical of course. To a certain extent, I had some sympathy for him, because I was sure that he would have to act quickly to restrain the possible political embarrassment. He told me that he had called the two network directors involved in the undersecretary's meeting and they had both denied my description of events. I simply said, "What else could they do?" He implied that it was not too late for me to change my mind, but that the e-mail had been sent to too many people and probably forwarded to others. I told him that I was done with CARES. He hung up.

In many ways, I disappointed myself. I realized that there were situations where no one could transcend the adversity of the situation. CARES may have been one of those. I do think that there are lessons learned.

In VA Central Office and in Washington, there are far too many coaches, general managers, and critics and not nearly enough linemen blocking down field, or those highly skilled operatives in positions of authority. These key positions should be motivated by solving problems, not creating them. Drucker's knowledge workers are in serious shortage too. Too many of them are isolated in the organization and not given enough credit or acknowledgment.

Human Resources needs to better identify the knowledge workers, pay them commensurately, and reduce the number of supervisors, most of who can't supervise effectively anyway. I think that this is true in many fields, not only health care. We need subject matter experts who can turn data into information. Often this is not appreciated by political appointees and others who, in the words of my late friend and colleague David Worthen, preferred to be "quick, sure, and wrong." Wrong is OK all too often because they won't be around to be held accountable. Wrong doesn't matter because decisions fall along a continuum of good to bad, and often intervening circumstances so muddy the water that reality is easily avoided. If they are ever caught, blame can simply be ascribed to others or rationalized away because of circumstances that are never perfect.

And then there is political correctness, which in the case of CARES means that the political scientists in the administration probably determined that the presidential election was going to be close and therefore the administration could not afford to be closing any VA facilities. And neither the Veterans Health Administration nor I could afford to be put into the position of not doing CARES either; hence the probability that the sacrifices and efforts of me and others were a good cover for those who really didn't want to do it in the first place.

Failure does have some rewards. It's a great learning experience if you survive it, and I survived it. Fortunately, I achieved optional retirement eligibility during my waning weeks in CARES, so I had a parachute of sorts, albeit, a tin parachute. I didn't want to retire but knew that being at the top of the secretary's bad list would result in some negative consequences. I was resolved to them. I was not disappointed.

I returned to the north Florida/south Georgia health system (NF/SG HS) based in Gainesville, Florida, full-time the first week in December. Appraisals had been completed for the preceding year, during which I had not been actually managing (NF/SG HS), even though I had been the director on paper since late August. My supervisor, the Network 8 director, gave me a highly satisfactory award, for which I received a bonus of $6,000. I had expected nothing but had been in charge of the committee that recommended the merger of two networks that were merged successfully, and for that I received nothing in the prior year.

For all my hard work with CARES and ten and half months of constant travel and briefings, I received nothing. Network 2 had again finished at the top of the performance measures; for that, I received nothing. I had been nominated for the Presidential Rank Award of Distinguished, which would have resulted in $40,000, and that nomination was pulled because of my departure from CARES. The next year I received an Outstanding evaluation that was approved, but the approximately $20,000 award was not given. In fact, no bonus was given at all. So I figure that my resignation from CARES cost me about $75,000.

Chapter 14
2002–2006: Home at Last

As soon as I could after reaching Gainesville, I got out of the rental car and kissed the ground. I had never thought that I would be the director of the North Florida/South Georgia VA Health System. My wife and I had always wanted to return to Florida, preferably near the coast, but Gainesville, where we both had gone to school, would be perfect. Her family was in Orlando, two hours away, and we had a daughter who was working in Miami. This was the closest that we had been to family in many years.

On our house-hunting trip, the newspaper reported two graphic incidents, both which received national coverage. The first was a pathologist affiliated loosely with the university and author of an acclaimed pathology textbook whose girlfriend had reported to the police that he was keeping body parts in his house. This proved to be true, and, since he had arranged for photographs of them posing with the body parts, it was a juicy media event. The next situation was that the director of the Gainesville botanical garden had his arm taken off by a twelve-foot alligator. The director was pulling weeds out of a pond, and, soon enough, his arm was gone. These two events resulted in numerous phone calls and e-mails from my friends elsewhere, questioning my sanity at wanting to live in Gainesville. We found a beautiful home. It was the kind of home that would hopefully be our last, and I had the kind of job that would or could last for as long as I wanted it.

To my knowledge, there were only two original employees who had been at Gainesville when I started thirty-three years before and who were still there. One was a finance employee who had taught me how to keypunch, a skill of limited historical interest now. The hospital had grown extremely busy over the years, and the facility showed it. Employees were crammed into office spaces that were far too small for either comfort or productivity. This employee who taught me how to keypunch transferred with the business office function when it moved into leased space. She happily retired a couple of years later.

Thinking of the possible repercussions against me every single day, I nevertheless immersed myself in the job. I read everything that I could get my hands on: old files and committee reports, and I talked to every single service chief. I walked the halls and cheerfully greeted the employees. I learned that the hospital organization was a traditional one. The secretary of Veterans Affairs and my immediate boss had banned the further proliferation of product line organizations. The secretary had ruled that the product line organizations in those networks, like Network 2, that had service lines would have to eliminate them. Although discouraging, it was nearly as bad for me as it would have been had I still been the director of Network 2. The days of innovation and of taking risks were over. The command structure ruled from the top-down. I was pleased to be where I was but concerned over what still might happen to me.

My immediate supervisor, Dr. Elwood Headley, was kind and essentially left me alone to lead and manage this large VA health system. He definitely resented not being able to select his own person and said so on two different occasions. He would soon be overcome by too many dragons to be concerned about me, so I smiled and tried to make NF/SG VA Health System the best in the network. Elwood had some top-down tendencies of his own and left me with some issues that I set about correcting. In the VA, many of its medical centers and health systems were driven, for good or bad, by the service chiefs. No matter what happened in the director's suite, the service chiefs ran their operations, did what had to be done, and in many cases created pockets of genuine excellence. From a systems perspective, the lack of consistent high performance was an issue. Once truly high performers in all performance measures, under Elwood, performance had drifted down, and there was a widespread attitude that, given inadequate resources for the demands being placed upon them, performance was quite all right. Change was resisted. Acrimony between the medical centers in Gainesville and Lake City was high and heated. The clinics felt like forgotten orphans left to their own volition to solve problems and deal with the ever-increasing workload.

For many years, from its inception in the mid-1960s, the Gainesville medical center had been directed and led by a Navy veteran, Malcom Randall. Mr. Randall left a wonderful legacy when he finally retired in 1998. The Gainesville VA Medical Center had a strong affiliation with the University of Florida Medical School; it was low cost and highly productive, and it had long-standing and positive relationships with the Veterans Service Organizations and the community. Mr. Randall retired in his early eighties. He had fifty-five years of government service and retired only when forced to do so. I thought that he had stayed on too long, but he was devoted to the VA and it was his life. In any event, I faced some of the situations that had grown problematic over the past few years and needed to get them resolved.

As I arrived to be the full-time director, the problems were not obvious, but the organization was in some disarray. Dr. Headley, my supervisor in the network, arranged to promote his former Gainesville VA executive assistant, Nancy Reissener, to the network office in Bay Pines, Florida. This lady had been in nursing for years and was a resource to all and an activist for positive change in the medical center. Within a few months, the chiefs of medicine, surgery, and human resources had departed. The job of chief of psychiatry service had just been filled, and the new incumbent began to be a problem. The chief of nursing service retired, as had three of her associate chief nurses. The recruitments allowed for my input not only into the selection but into the type of person that I was most desirous of bringing on board.

After completing my self-imposed orientation, I listed the problems as the following:

1. Inadequate resources.

2. Too many leaders too comfortable with what they had been doing for years.

3. Customer service was deficient in every aspect.

4. Space was incredibly deficient.

5. Many of our leaders had negative reactions toward the network and VA Central Office in ways that were not helpful in solving our problems.

6. Our internal processes were flawed or dated, particularly the internal processing and dissemination of information from our collected data.

As I made my rounds through meetings and the health system, I told everyone that I intended to manage through the principles of Baldrige, or the criteria-based awards programs started by the U.S. government to award and recognize those corporations and institutions doing the best process improvement and meeting or exceeding the other criteria. This caused some negative feedback but was largely positively received. I began to see books on the Baldrige process around the health system. We also began to do training and buy more books and other resources.

The criteria for the Baldrige Award in health care are: leadership; strategic planning; focus on patients, other customers, and markets; measurement analysis and knowledge management; workforce focus; process management; and results. The award is not really the objective. The real objective should be the improvement journey. If your organization is not moving progressively in all seven categories, then there is a problem.

All this Baldrige rhetoric is theoretical until the organization accomplishes all the hard work that it requires to make it part of the everyday business. Among other things, that will take some cultural change. To illustrate my point, one particular distraction comes to mind. An AIDS inpatient had been in crisis over the week. Those of us at the morning meeting learned of this one Monday morning. The patient was believed to have eloped, or fled the hospital. The police couldn't find him, and none of our neighboring health-care organizations had seen him, nor had the Gainesville police, who had been notified and were also looking for him. A missing patient required notification to the network office. When the patient was found later that morning, we learned that he had barricaded himself in a social worker's office, trashed her office, and smeared feces all over the room. The health-care organization had to maintain momentum despite the daily occurrences of events such as these.

The first crisis that arose was that the pharmacy bar code computer system had not been implemented. The NF/SG health system was the last in the VA to begin implementation. I told everyone that I didn't understand this, because the kind of health system that we ought to be would be among the first to adopt proven new technology. The key staff was ready for me, and they outlined all the reasons: they had visited the so-called best practices, and these places were doing work-arounds, Pharmacy didn't have enough staff, nursing hadn't been trained, and the system caused medical errors.

After listening to these concerns, I simply reiterated that we would be the last to implement, that we didn't make major policy decisions, we were part of a health-care system that did, and that overall patient safety would be improved because of the reduction in medication errors. The executive resources board decided that they had to give it a go, and the chief of staff worked incredibly hard after his initial resistance to make it so.

The next crisis came when I decided to make nursing service report directly to me. I had been contacted by Dr. Headley, the network director, who asked me to implement this. The chief of staff had been hostile to this. As I explained my reasons to the chief of staff, this was a reasonable request, I had done the same thing in my last assignment, it would not change clinical practice, rather it would elevate nursing in the eyes of the staff and those nurses being recruited. After receiving a considerable amount of aggravation, tense meetings, and papers produced designed to show how dumb the idea was, I implemented it. The nurses seemed to be pleased, and nothing much else changed.

About this time, CARES reinserted itself into my work life. I was visited by a veteran who was going to be appointed to the National CARES Committee. This committee would make recommendations directly to the secretary of Veterans Affairs. This veteran was a bilateral amputee from Vietnam, and he had Hepatitis C. His lab results were going in the wrong direction, and, if something didn't change, he would end up needing a liver transplant. He lost both legs above the knee in Vietnam, receiving over eighty units of blood. He was one of our patients. I immediately asked the chief of staff to review the case and get him to a transplant center for further evaluation. As the CARES committee would be traveling around the country, the veteran was understandably concerned about the possible impact on his health. Fortunately, the transplant center at Nashville carefully retested and monitored this American hero. Not only was he able to serve capably on the CARES Commission, his health improved and having a transplant stopped being a consideration.

Dr. Rosewater, in a misguided attempt to be fair, decided to add medical centers to the list of possible reduced in size or closed facilities provided by the CARES office. This is the office that I had once headed. Despite not meeting any of the carefully reviewed and vetted criteria, Dr. Rosewater apparently thought that the list was not geographically balanced enough. Of course, geographic imbalances in the number of facilities and the disparity in the number of veterans being served were the central issue in the first place. Therefore, he added, among others, the medical center at Lake City.

I knew that we would go through an enormous amount of work and ultimately prevail but disliked the fact that his warped idea of being politically correct was intruding upon what was intended to be a carefully analytical approach reflecting actual utilization of veterans and the growth of the veteran population. He must have thought that there was not enough geopolitical balance, so he added a facility in Florida, where the fastest growth in the nation had been occurring and where the number of major construction projects had not kept pace with the clinical demands to any significant degree.

The addition of Lake City to the CARES list of facilities to be reviewed unfortunately fell into the collective bias held by many in Lake City that they were being picked on. The ongoing distrust by many in Lake City of the Gainesville Medical Center definitely complicated the issue. Even though I was the director over both and tried to spend as much time as I possibly could up there, the feelings of hurt, distrust, and hostility were real and layered just under the surface.

The consolidation of the Lake City and Gainesville facilities had begun in 1999. Each had a complete set of front office staff and service chiefs. By the time that the dust settled, only two service chiefs had been chosen from Lake City: human resources and engineering. Because most of the front office staff, including the director, retired, a vacuum of top management leadership was created there. Labor relations were among the many aspects of management to suffer. Adding the medical center to the CARES list just added fuel to an already glowing fire. Being allowed to provide input to Dr. Rosewater prior to his autocratic decision would have been nice.

Two women from Lake City, the former director, Genie Norman, and the executive director for the county commission, Mary Kay Hollingsworth, mobilized the community under the banner "Save Our VA." The retired director, who I had once had a hand in promoting in VA Central Office, proved to be the wild card in Dr. Rosewater's addition of Lake City to the CARES list. Genie was energetic, knowledgeable, and a great communicator. Mary Kay was also energetic and a great communicator. Together, they were a dynamic and tireless duo who dedicated themselves to "saving their VA." They organized the political constituency in both Florida and Georgia. They developed information to constantly keep media outlets up-to-date as well as the Veterans Service Organizations. From the moment that they started their effort, I knew that closing the Lake City VA Medical Center was doomed to failure. The Lake City VA Medical Center continues to provide services to this day. Although we received a CARES commission visit, our documentation and analysis, together with this dynamic duo, had made their work a forgone conclusion. Of course, Dr. Rosewater couldn't have anticipated that this small town would be so driven to "save their VA."

At the same time, we were forced to manage our recently appointed leader in mental health. This appointment resulted in nurses and others in my office sobbing. I attempted to provide them with assurances that things would get better. My attempts at mediation, conciliation, and education failed. I approved unusual organization arrangements to protect employees. I directed the mental health leader to spend all of his time doing research. When these arrangements failed, I found myself forced to call for investigations on the allegations of sexual harassment. I had to make sure that the complainants would be protected while the investigations were ongoing. I was threatened directly by this individual. The VA police were alerted to protect various members of the staff.

Somehow, newspaper articles from Albany, New York, involving my previous interactions with Dr. Leach were circulated. Dr. Leach apparently made numerous allegations about me directly to this leader, including that I was a member of the KKK. Unfortunately, this leader put all of these allegations in an e-mail to all the other employees whom he believed were involved in their own disciplinary procedures. And then one of them sent this package to their attorney, who wrote a nice letter to his fellow Naval Academy graduate, the secretary of Veterans Affairs, bringing these allegations to his attention. Of course, no one ever called me to verify or even for comment.

Ultimately, the VA prevailed. In this case, the Office of Special Counsel, despite the mental health leader's numerous appeals, declined to take his case. All directors can do in these situations is keep a positive attitude and keep people informed of the actual truth.

North Florida/South Georgia VA Health System was approved for a bed tower, a critically needed addition of space and beds. This necessitated additional work with the architect in developing the actual plans for construction. At six floors, we knew that all of our space needs would not be addressed, but it would bring single-patient bedrooms, standardized wards, and, most importantly, additional space.

We worked carefully to justify our most compelling needs in space deficiencies and to meet additional patient demands. For many years, right up to the present, we had four- and five-patient bedrooms for acutely ill patients. All of this was something that CARES was designed to fix, but political concerns over fitting it into a predetermined budget level have so far failed to materialize this desperately needed project.

The leadership of social work service was a nagging concern. I had confronted this leader in a budget meeting over his lack of preparation and knowledge in certain key areas of social work responsibility. Specifically, the community nursing home program was vital in getting our patients out of acute beds and nearer their homes. Because he had finally brought the program in-line with national requirements, he felt that he should get a sizeable award. Because this was about five years after the fact of the revised national requirements, I felt his egotism and mismanagement should be rewarded but not with any award. In one particular budget meeting, he threw a Baldrige booklet onto the table as he was sitting down. I asked him several Baldrige-related questions and suggested that he actually read the booklet that he brought.

About three weeks later, I learned that he had filed an EEO

complaint against me for age discrimination. Although we are both approximately the same age, white, and male, the EEO claim was investigated. He alleged that he felt humiliated and embarrassed by me in front of his staff. I felt that he should have been embarrassed. We went to arbitration but failed to satisfy his concerns. I offered to get him a mentor. He declined. Ultimately, he retired.

I believe that this was a talented person who hadn't been challenged in any way about his job, his performance, or the performance of his service in a long time. Top management was undoubtedly partially at fault in not keeping this talented and bright administrator better educated and challenged.

One of the most overworked functions with too little room in the medical center was the emergency room. Often, the physicians and nurses who worked there had to call for help from other areas of the hospital. Because of the constantly increasing workload, getting a handle on the workload in the ER was a contentious process. Getting the VA to enlarge the ER by adding space also proved to be a contentious process.

One of the highlights of the ER was the night that John Travolta brought a friend to the ER. This was an exciting change of pace. It was an incredible morale boost and a real treat for all those hardworking professionals. Come back anytime, John, and bring your friends!

14.1: Listen and Improve, Please

Two activities of the NF/SG health system were in sad disarray when I arrived and continued to be for too long. Of course, it took me awhile to realize how bad they were. It also took some time to work through the existing supervisors, trying to get improvement. I acknowledge that I had lost some of the will to get it done that I had learned from Dr. Kizer. Being aware of the counter allegation with which I would have to contend, I was a little too comfortable in the job and in a place where I would like to stay, and that took the edge off management actions. This was my excuse in any event. The two activities were central to the organization and to patient care and deserve special attention here and in real health-care administration.

These two activities illustrate the case for determined, consistent, unrelenting managerial demand for process improvement. Usually, as in the case of sterilized processing and distribution (SPD) and medical administration service (MAS), the problem to be solved is complex.

The problem contained elements of human resources, customer service, attitude, and the actual requirements of the job. Medical administration service in the VHA is often called health administration, but in essence it admits patients, collects patient data, determines eligibility, and obtains financial information from enrollees. I have taken the two activities in tandem because they paralleled each other in development and because they illustrated that problems in one area can become huge issues in all the key focal points in the health-care system. The two also illustrate the problems of concentration and focus in health care while also trying to maintain a constant effort of improvement in all areas.

MAS first came to my attention when employees of the admissions area came by to see me. First individually and then in groups, they came to complain about a difficult, arbitrary, and somewhat whimsical supervisor and her methods. I have always maintained an open-door policy. This was a marked change from the two previous administrations. I might add that this also applied equally to patients or visitors. At first, I relayed my concerns, the concerns I heard from these MAS employees, to the associate director. When feedback was slow in coming, I asked him about what MAS had said. He said, "These employees are troublemakers." I said I doubted that. I told him that the employees seemed sincere, and they were sincerely angry about their treatment. The associate director then explained that the employees who were coming to see me were simply trying to avoid serious consistent supervision. I said OK, we'll wait and see.

With SPD, I knew that the function had been troubled in the past, simply because I had read previous audit reports, special purpose external visits, and past internal efforts to create process improvement. The SPD problem crystallized for me when complaints came in meetings and directly from nursing supervisory personnel.

In the far distant past, but in some places still, SPD is led by a nurse and/or is still in nursing service. Of course, institutions that have organized into product lines very often no longer have a huge, unified nursing service, but the relationship is a direct interface with SPD providing sterile supplies and instruments to the operating rooms, cardiac catheterization labs, and many other places where special surgical or invasive procedures are done. Infections, scheduled surgery cancellations, and unhappy nurses and surgeons are frequently the outcomes when SPD is disorganized or dysfunctional.

At the beginning of my administration in NF/SG, I had asked the administrative services to prepare IOIs, or items of interest. In Network 2, we had borrowed this practice from GE. After a rocky start and some critical feedback, most services began to comply with a reasonable version of the week's most important events, problems, issues, and, most importantly, providing data and graphs to illustrate the trends or to highlight an intervention.

I attacked the problems of both SPD and MAS by adding a charge that they much more succinctly report on their issues with data. I gave them both constant feedback, often through the associate director, sometimes through my able executive assistant, Nick Ross, and sometimes directly. For me, it was a slow and tedious process without enough learning on their part, as well as frequent cheap shots from the managers in these areas about their having less time to do the important stuff.

The performance didn't improve, despite instituting a process improvement team and appointing a facilitator to conduct weekly meetings between the warring parties of SPD, surgery, and nursing. It was clear that the basic message to the frontline staff was being garbled with other messages: the front office doesn't care about you, they don't understand the problems, and the like. After another year of more external visits and reports, it also became clear that the facilitator was managing the relationship process, but that the goals were process-oriented and not performance-oriented. So the goals were met, but performance didn't improve. I was ready to reorganize and get some managers who would attack the performance issues in both SPD and MAS.

I abruptly reorganized MAS, taking ward administration and all the clinic clerks and assigning them to their respective clinical service, for example, behavioral health. Nursing service took over ward administration. My executive assistant worked assiduously with human resources and the unions to make the changes effectively and not violate labor management agreements. Then we reorganized MAS, creating a data quality section with responsibility for all MAS data collection, reporting, and analysis. This became a nationally recognized best practice. We also reassigned MAS to a different associate director and stepped up the performance requirements for the service. The increasing expectations led to numerous changes in MAS supervision. Finally, MAS began to improve.

SPD also continued its rocky road with increasing frustration among surgeons and nurses. The bickering back and forth had long since ceased to be productive. Allegations reached the level of SPD accusing the others of fraud and abuse. Accusations of nurses deliberately sabotaging the instruments packages and being verbally abusive to SPD staff became weekly occurrences.

The associate director supported the chief of acquisition and material management who had responsibility for SPD. Neither saw the need for a change in SPD's organizational status. Negative attitudes toward performance improvement and poor communications were part of the problem. Indulging in the blame game was also a large part of the problem. The SPD supervisors lacked some of the skills readily acquired through training. This lack of training was not their fault. The skills included systems analysis, performance management, and data management.

The addition of a masters-prepared nurse to the assistant chief position helped. Since her appointment, the necessary gains had not been forthcoming. There was some improvement but not enough. Therefore, I reassigned SPD to report directly to me. SPD's performance, attitude, and accountability almost immediately improved.

All through this arduous and contentious process, I had proffered the example of our nutrition and food production service and its able chief, Marion Korzec. Marion had come into a mess. The prior chief had not been able to manage the service, and EEO complaints and grievances abounded. Marion was selected and arrived shortly after I did. Her attitude and professionalism made an immediately positive impact. Moreover, she faced the same kind of problems that both MAS and SPD faced, in that there were external reviews with long-standing recommendations that hadn't been corrected.

She improved services, contributed intelligent often humorous IOIs, and succinctly showed us her process improvements with results almost on a weekly basis. She made contributions widely across the health system by heading up investigations and serving on important committees and special assignments. She ultimately was rewarded with national recognition as the most outstanding chief of nutrition and food production in the VA. She received no more resources, no external assistance, and yet produced outstanding results simply by being a professional manager with a clear focus on internal process improvement. The best facet of Marion's management effort was that she recognized that continuing to improve every aspect of her program was essential.

Referring to the leadership guide that we developed while I was at Network 2, here are the steps for managing performance and quality. As a sidenote, Network 2 improved its performance and quality quickly, going from worst to first in two years and achieving a number of individual best practices.

1. Reengineer that which is not working optimally.

2. Take the initiative to improve all processes to improve services.

3. Quality is everyone's job.

4. Individuals on the team and the team should always be flexible and responsive to opportunities to improve processes.

5. Be a fixer, not a finger pointer.

6. The team and the individuals on the team must hold themselves accountable for meeting all outcomes at the highest level.

7. Focus and push on all objectives and performance measures. If necessary appoint an owner, a junkyard dog, to communicate, facilitate, badger, incentivize, and motivate everyone involved with a mediocre performance on a measure.

8. The team must know that they are required to ask for help and encourage involvement when the performance demands it.

9. Provide support without removing responsibility.

10. The person doing the job knows it the best but needs education and perspective to do it better.

11. Seek best practices inside and outside the industry. Abolish rationalisms from the organization including the following: We are different. We are unique. It won't work here. We tried that. We don't have time (or some other resource).

14.2: Discipline, You Want Discipline?

One of my most difficult tasks as a health system director was being the decision maker on the final internal VA appeals of disciplinary actions. It was often an emotionally charged event. The VA's system of due process takes too long and requires an adversarial nature. Often the accused charges the supervisor and others of ill will, less than desirable interpersonal treatment, adverse favoritism, and the like.

I believe that part of the problem is that the human resource experts and leaders in VA Central Office have not seen their responsibilities for designing and implementing streamlined processes that are quicker, more defensible, and more balanced. This continuation of imperfect process ends up quite often with a face-to-face discussion in the director's office with the accused and their union representative, if the employee chooses to bring one.

From my many year's experience with this process, I have come to believe that not only does it need much reform, but the process also fails to account for that most important of organizational imperatives—that of improving someone or something.

The VA has a table of proposed disciplinary penalties ranging from counseling (oral and written), admonishments, reprimands, suspensions from one day to two weeks, and, finally, termination. Having suspended someone for ninety days once, it is true that we managers are verbally accorded with some flexibility, but, once the process gets started, we get attacked for not sticking to the proposed table of penalties. My one disciplinary action of a long suspension actually worked; the employee returned and has to my knowledge done a good job and now is retirement eligible if not retired.

Most of us have been counseled, usually orally. Our supervisors have usually couched that criticism in the form of work improvement, and we, almost all, respond admirably and don't take offense. However, the elongated process is seldom balanced or timely. As soon as the poor performance, outrageous act, or inappropriate communication is documented, the human interactions intensify greatly. Too many executives who deserve discipline don't get it. The executives vigorously protest the proposed discipline until they exhaust all possible remedies. One of the issues here is that for the federal executive, discipline often becomes part of the public record. This is akin to pillorying in public. Another part of the problem is that everyone is unique and personalities can cover the spectrum from completely compliant to ego-maniac narcissist who is firmly convinced that he has never made a mistake. Thus, finding the precisely right discipline to provide the right incentive to improve is tough. Thankfully, most employees accept their discipline and go about continuing to do a good job.

Situations involving disciplinary actions impact the organizational culture. Often there is internal pressure for managers who fears personal embarrassment if they don't act or who feel pressured by their own direct reports to rush to judgment. And most of the time, the manager's thinking is clouded with the desire to get the work done and to eliminate the distractions that seem to prevent it. The VA's disciplinary system also does not account for the principles of process improvement, in that some of the time the system is at fault. According to Deming's published theory, 80 percent of the time, it's the system that's at fault.

In the early years of being a VA director, I signed off on terminations of registered nurses for medication errors that today we realize almost certainly were the fault of the system and not the nurse. In many professions, we will probably see such an evolution as well, but our human resources processes are slowing that evolution down.

In some cases, where employees decided to call each other bad names, get into physical altercations, or simply walk off the job, the decision-making process is clear. These kinds of cases are few and far between, however. If a patient doesn't get fed, no one wants to admit it, and therefore employees offer numerous excuses, including blaming the patient for not eating! We need to improve our internal feeding processes to make sure that employees are motivated to always do the right thing in all matters, but most especially for those concerning the patient.

My own indoctrination in supervision was provided in part by those old fiscal officers over thirty years ago who said that if anyone didn't have a write-up in their jacket, they probably weren't trying hard enough. A jacket is an official personnel file, and a write up is an admonishment or reprimand. Our society has changed since then, and those who willingly accept responsibility are rare.

In the latter stages of my career, it seemed that there were more crack-addicted employees. I have become a believer in not cutting them a break, because in every case where I did, they failed to recover. Many, if not all of them, have been through rehabilitation, presumed recovery, and had all kinds of assistance. I believe that at the first suspicion of drug involvement the supervisor should generate weekly drug testing, with positive results causing an indefinite suspension without pay or benefits until the person can pass two drug tests successfully. The current disciplinary process is not an effective venue to use because it just gives the drug-using employee false hope. The current process focuses on the observed quality and quantity of work being produced, not the underlying cause. It also gives drug-using employees more chances to disrupt patient care.

Since it seems like double jeopardy, a reinstatement with a last chance agreement and drug testing would be an improvement. This kind of requirement is the best protection for employees and employers. The last chance agreement is signed by the employee, agreeing that any proposed disciplinary action including further absences without leave will result in the employee's immediate termination.

One of the manager's most important but least effectively used tools is the giving of positive, proactive feedback to a direct report about their performance. In my own career, Al Washko, one of my former supervisors, was masterful at providing such feedback to me without hurting my feelings or becoming negative. This ability to critique usefully without angering employees is a rare skill. All too often, the manager provides little feedback about performance specifics until the day arrives when he or she can no longer tolerate the performance. Too often, an employee hasn't established a level of trust with their supervisor. The acuity of the work assignments dwindle until one day that employee is significantly underutilized and a chasm of doubt and mistrust exist. Continuous process improvement is a way to provide feedback on an ongoing basis that is necessary for improvement and greatly lessens the probabilities of injuring the employee's feelings or confidence. Ultimately, however, the responsibility for improving must be the employee's.

A cardiac surgeon came to visit with me in my office one afternoon. He had received a notice of the VA's intent to report him to the medical board for malpractice. In that letter it said that the practitioner could appeal the matter to the director. As we chatted, it became clear to me that he was mostly interested in getting more background on why the VA used this process of external review of reported cases in which an adverse event occurred. This report had come back stating that the surgeon had committed malpractice. I asked him if the report was true. He said it was.

An elderly patient was being operated on to repair a valve, and, as the surgeons were about to close, they couldn't account for one of the sponges. They looked for the sponge extensively and couldn't find it. Because of the length of time that the elderly veteran had been under general anesthesia and his poor overall health, this cardiac surgeon decided to close the surgical opening. He had been faced with a difficult decision, and he had made that decision knowing what the probable consequences were. He accepted the findings. He added that shortly thereafter they had switched to towels for soaking up blood in the cavity instead of sponges for the very reason that towels were much easier to account for. So here was a situation in which there was a system solution, and, in part, the OR system had enabled the lost sponge to happen. There was no question of the facts. In my opinion, such cases should not result in determinations of malpractice or no disciplinary action. This surgeon said that if he were to seek a job elsewhere, he would have to appeal, because he wouldn't want to have to explain the situation to a prospective employer. He also said, and I have since seen data to support this, that the VA is a much more rigorous reporter of malpractice than other health-care institutions, thus creating a potential reason why physicians wouldn't want to be employed by the VA. The lesson learned is that the VA and all of health care should relentlessly pursue best practices and that the leveling of the playing field for recruitment and comparison purposes must also be accomplished constructively.

14.3: A Lark

During the course of my government career, I applied for two non-VA jobs. The first was while I was in VA Central Office for the first time. During a particularly idle time, I perused the openings in the Washington area and discovered that one of the Smithsonian museums had an opening for a supervisory budget analyst, which is what I was at the time. I went out at lunch and dropped my application in a mailbox. I never heard back. I was satisfied not to hear because I felt guilty about applying for the job. Why should I feel guilty? I have no idea. It's the second application that I really want to explain.

In my daily reading of the local paper, in this case the *Gainesville Sun,* a *New York Times* affiliate, I read of a nasty scandal that had been discovered at the University of Florida Foundation. The UF Foundation is the primary fund-raising arm of the university. The foundation's CFO had been embezzling money for some time. He resigned, was eventually tried in court, and found guilty. Interestingly, the judge also forbade him to attend any University of Florida events, such as football games. I thought, since I was retirement eligible, that that was a job I could do. I would bank my retirement pay and step into a lesser but still well-paying job with prestige. I would also be working for my beloved alma mater. On a lark, I sent my application to the foundation.

I received some e-mails from their human resources person assigned to this job. I replied to those e-mails and waited. Nothing happened.

I watched their job announcement board, and one day a different job appeared. This job was called a controller, but its duties were clearly those of the former CFO position. Those duties had been rearranged some, but it was essentially the same job.

I must have been the most qualified candidate. Perhaps whoever they really wanted in the job could not get his/her application rated highly enough to compete with mine. After all, I had once been in charge of $17 billion. I did think that being an alumnus, having a fairly decent track record in finance and budget, being local, and being employed in a fairly responsible position that I should have at least rated an interview. I decided that with that kind of leadership, it was an organization for which I would almost definitely be unhappy working.

14.4: Do Not Lose Your Government Laptop

You may be asking yourself why there is a subchapter on lost laptops. Losing a laptop is a bad thing, of course, but the management actions that are taken in this situation are the real reason I find this subject worthy of illumination. It all began when an analyst in the VA Central Office had his laptop burglarized at home. He was a senior level analyst in the VA's Office of Policy and Planning. Many VA employees work at home using a VA computer or their own laptop, most of them on their own time. I doubt if any of them carry around 26 million names on it. Having downloaded huge files that were not encoded, including veterans' names, addresses, and other demographic information, onto his laptop, he had been carrying around an information bomb.

Executives at the highest level of the VA first delayed telling the secretary and the deputy secretary for several days. When the delay didn't produce the laptop, the matter became public. A key executive accelerated his retirement. The employee was proposed for termination. The politicians availed themselves of quality air time in which they castigated the VA. Other federal agencies found themselves in the media for having lost laptops as well. From newspaper accounts, it seemed like the FBI lost a lot of laptops.

Somewhere in the bureaucracy, I am sure that someone has the total number of laptops issued to employees, the identification number, type, and model. Most of the VA managerial and clinical staff who have been issued laptops have serious work that they have to perform on them at home, while traveling, or even on vacation. Many VA clinicians use laptops to review patient information and to make needed changes when they would otherwise be unavailable. This is exactly what happened prior to the installation of the Decentralized Hospital Computing Program, known as DHCP.

VA Central Office, in response to its lost laptop, issued directives requiring mandatory training for every employee in the VA. The loss of any laptop anywhere must be reported. At NF/SG, we had had a laptop stolen out of inadequate storage space. VA Central Office was not concerned with that because it had never been issued to anyone. It was new, never used, and had no VA data on it when purloined. So it was really the information on the laptop that was to be protected at all costs, despite the fact that no reengineering has been done that would seriously deter laptop theft. Although all laptops lost were reported to VA Central Office, each was examined on its own merits. Punishment was assigned or not, the directors received a tongue-lashing, and no lessons were learned. Recently, I learned that the latest VA Central Office requirement is to report missing laptops to them within the first hour that the local VA person realizes the computer is missing.

When I took my oldest son, Jason, to his freshman year at North Carolina State University, we went to the bookstore on campus. While there, I talked with the computer customer assistance person. He advised strongly against buying my son a laptop or even a personal computer! Laptops were easily lost and frequently stolen on campus. Personal computers took up a lot of space in the dorm rooms, and computers were widely available on campus. I took his advice, and it worked out fine.

Laptops were designed to be portable, and certain design or systems flaws existed that could reduce or eliminate the loss of laptops. Although there is a growing movement with Microsoft and others in developing much more secure software, I don't think that this will solve the problem. Installing a tracking device, a remotely activated alarm, a destructive device, or an imprinted bar code inside that would be impossible to remove without destroying the device would all simplify the management issues involved. And each agency, especially the VA, could consolidate its reports of loss and see what common factors are involved in the losses and work to correct those. Make the assignment of a laptop contingent upon a home security system or a lock-down device, physically attaching it to something relatively unmovable. Requiring more training and white papers isn't going to make laptops more secure. Better design and physical security systems will accomplish far more.

Continuous learning and process redesign will make laptops and thus all security better. Collect the data, analyze it, and do drill downs to create better laptop systems and designs. With physical security in mind, feedback on every lost laptop and near miss is a gap that needs closing. I fail to see how this has been done in numerous situations. Collecting data on lost laptops in a database would facilitate data mining. This process would quickly result in better information for decisions and the elimination of recriminations and blame that have characterized the federal response so far.

To better prevent terrorism and improve federal productivity, we need a solution that protects our data as perfectly as Fort Knox is supposed to protect gold. It seems we do trial and error, dictate, but never sufficiently follow up, never or hardly ever listen to user's informed opinions, and so are destined to be embarrassed again and again.

According to the leadership guide I helped to develop while at Network 2, here are the steps for managing knowledge.

1. Capture, nurture, share, and deploy knowledge proactively.

2. If it's a problem, collect data, analyze it, and report it.

3. Manage information accurately to create intelligence.

4. Actively use a constant flow of information concerning priority issues and problems. Implement my tennis ball theory of management communications. Always return a communication (a tennis ball) even if it is only to say, "Nice idea. Let me think about it."

5. Furnish information to all interested and concerned parties as soon as it's available.

6. Practice open-book management; keep all available information, except for confidential information, open and accessible to all.

7. Continuous learning and reflection are critical to management improvement and the true knowledge of complex systems.

14.5: Protecting Information

Several years ago, the Health Information Protection and Portability Act (HIPPA) was passed into law. The egregious blunders that caused HIPPA to be enacted were caused by a few, but, as in many, many cases where the federal government gets into the act, the innocent were punished along with the guilty. HIPPA caused an incredible change in the way information is handled in health-care organizations. In an environment rich with data, the efforts to comply have been enormous. Given the tremendous amount of information being transacted, reported, and saved, HIPPA requires some adjustment. I won't make another plea to base law and its administration more on data, but HIPPA has caused some unintended consequences that I believe should be corrected, and not just for the VA.

For an executive at close range of the impact of HIPPA, the overall change has been for the better. Certainly, everyone in health care has been trained to accommodate the law. However, information unintentionally swamps the day-to-day resources of those folks actively engaged in the release of information. Computers don't offer much help and add to the rapidity of possible unauthorized releases. Writing e-mails in code to protect patients' information from all without a need to know can also be a challenge. Congress has passed laws that require health-care organizations to balance revenues against the costs of higher expenditures, but it seems to me that they err consistently on the side of adding to the higher costs of health care. HIPPA is just such a budget buster. Unlike much in management that has been tested and derived from experience if not actual case law, we still dwell in the fuzzy arena where legal opinions are at their tackiest and those with real experience and confidence in the administration of legally required information security are few and far between.

The threat that this law poses has been drummed into our heads. My own physician, upon seeing my wife in public, begins to ask her how I am but realizes that she might be violating HIPPA and so swallows the thought.

Research has been impeded. Those great academic health centers, including the VA, have an increasing amount of problems with getting potential research subjects to the point where an informed consent can be had. We need to develop some form of systemic approval up front with patients, so that research can be facilitated by specific agreements.

The past bad habits of some health-care employees did need to be changed. Let's say that a nurse develops an illness and is admitted to the medical center. She is a qualified enrolled veteran. Her numerous friends and acquaintances, in an attempt to wish her well, quickly look up the room she is in via the computer. The nurse has not authorized the release of her patient locator information. They go directly into the patient record. Out of the twelve employees who looked up her patient information, only three had a patient care reason for doing so. Although discipline was issued, despite many conversations, letters, and formal proceedings, no amount of reassurances are ever going to convince this employee that she wasn't much more severely wronged. Human factors analysis and research seem to apply in this case as well. This would result in better systems in which human nature and past practice wouldn't result in a major distraction for the organization.

14.6: Preparing for Terrorism

Terrorism is a particularly serious concern for health care. By their very nature, hospitals have to be accessible. The VHA, including each of its medical centers and outpatient clinics, plans and drills to be prepared for the unthinkable. The concern really began prior to 9/11. It began for the VA with the Oklahoma City Federal Building bombing. Much has been done. Much more needs to be done. Even so, the VHA has a considerable national resource in the response to terrorism and its prevention.

Responding to the aftermath of a terrorism incident is widely understandable. Prevention, as in many health-care issues, is another matter entirely. My belief that the VA is a force in prevention is related to the large number of people who routinely deal with epidemiology and local outbreaks of common illness. In addition, the VA works extensively on its own safety and security. Its affiliation with most of the major universities in the nation combines its own expertise with the dynamics of an engaging environment where multiple disciplines are amassing expertise and research.

Our war on terrorism may be a repeat of the cold war, with a real solution decades away. Responding to localized disturbances and then analyzing them as they relate to patient safety adds to the understanding of the VA health-care system. Solving these problems and minimizing the impacts is part of the customary operations of VHA field facilities.

Some problems need to be addressed that impact the VA as well as every other institution of health care. Hurricane Katrina is a classic example of inadequate transportation and planning for evacuation. The recent hurricanes in Florida and elsewhere illustrate the clogging of interstates, whereby moving patients via ground ambulances becomes problematic. Mass movement of patients places real limitations to those health-care organizations relying on ambulances. The required amount of time for ambulances to get to where they need to go and back is an inherent limitation.

Finding or creating adequate housing for large numbers of disabled patients, as illustrated by the unsatisfactory response at Walter Reed Army Medical Center, is yet another example. Centralizing the care of all these patients is another strategy that should be rethought.

. So, more effective transportation is a critical need. Moving large numbers of chronically sick and disabled patients needs to be rethought. Centralization of large numbers of disabled and wounded patients needs to be rethought. Having centers that could be compared for effectiveness and efficiency, combined with real research potential, would improve matters.

Patients, visitors, and sometimes employees can do unexpected things. This keeps the VHA perceptive and aware of its responsibilities in preventing accidents and resolving them as rapidly as possible. Its staff is constantly reminded of the potential dangers that lurk in today's environment. The nation should build on this expertise. We should expand the research efforts to apply hard science to prevent terrorism.

HIPPA has perhaps helped to foil potential terrorist efforts by making the acquisition of information somewhat harder, but I doubt it. To an extent, it makes people with a need to know work harder to acquire that information. Running correlations on data often produces intelligence in both research and clinical information. *Data mining* is the term that I use to describe what is suffering because of these restrictions.

If a terror event or disaster happens, will medical information be readily available? For VA health care, the answer is yes. The ability to access huge amounts of patient information in the case of an epidemic or terrorist event should be a critical success factor in our planning.

Preparation for a possible terrorist act has changed health care in other ways. Walking into the VA medical center, directions to clinics are hopefully still clear. Finding the boiler plant or the director's office is another matter. In times past, the standard was for the director's office to be clearly marked by signage so that a visitor or patient would have no trouble finding it. Now, that is not the case. Employees and volunteers have become the first line of defense to detect and deflect terrorism. Finding the computer center or the main pharmacy would be even tougher. Necessary adjustments to better counter terror all come at a price. Openness and accessibility have decreased to improve safety and security at too great a cost of intelligence.

In addition, a national 911 system needs to be implemented. If not for the general public, then certify its use for federal employees, firemen, mail handlers, and police. Perhaps make it available also to the delivery personnel for UPS, FedEx, and others who are out on the roads every day and are bound to notice suspicious people or changes before the rest of us.

Preventing terrorism and predicting flaws in security is a predominant strategy for the nation. Referring again to the leadership guide developed in Network 2, here are the leadership requirements for strategy.

1. Predict risk and return with high accuracy and confidence. Practice this on a continuous basis.

2. Adapt, survive, and prosper. Do not let the bastards get you down, but rather plan for the best possible outcomes.

3. Regularly scan and assess the environment.

4. Get the ability and commitment to act.

5. Plan, do, check, act.

6. Understand trends and continuously maintain a dialogue to further the development of valuable intelligence.

7. Change direction before you have to, even if it's embarrassing.

14.7: The Sunshine Network

Network 8 is commonly referred to as the Sunshine Network. The Sunshine Network was in a state of transition when I first arrived. The former network director, Dr. Rosewater, was now the undersecretary of health. He left quite a few decisions in place that would come to haunt the incoming network director, Dr. Elwood Headley. How much latitude he gave Dr. Headley is a question that I do not know the answer to; however, I suspect that the job came with certain limitations.

When I arrived in the Sunshine Network, it was a network in name only. Only rudimentary efforts had been made to centralize and control anything, and those were apparently the pet interests of Dr. Rosewater.

Another very compelling factor was that the network for the preceding years had been allocated significant increases in funding. So many veterans had been moving to Florida that, without any effort, the VA's resource allocation model actually moved additional funding to Florida. However, capital expenditures didn't keep pace. San Juan, Tampa, NF/SG, and Miami VA medical centers all had significant shortages of space, adequate structures, or both. The analysis being done by the network on costs and finances was rudimentary, and wrong in most cases. The network staff was specialized to only a limited degree, and all of them had to respond to the crisis of the moment and to provide constituent services for VA Central Office, the large number of congressional offices as well as numerous others demanding attention.

In addition, a number of initiatives were late in arriving to Network 8. Each of these initiatives was, for the most part, left to the individual director to fund and implement. I have previously mentioned the bar coding of medications, with NF/SG being the last in the nation to complete this initiative. Patient safety in general lagged behind the other networks, particularly the efforts in Network 2. Training for patient safety, case management, utilization review, and other critical areas were not being funded by VA Central Office, so the Sunshine Network wasn't emphasizing them. The Sunshine Network was interested in telemedicine and so had funded a number of initiatives, primarily for NF/SG, which had the most rural territory to cover. The network was interested in primary care and so had training and a number of funded initiatives to try to close the gap in accessibility to primary care.

Among the areas that did not have a network focus were oncology, radiation therapy, traumatic brain injury, PTSD, cardiac care, emergency services, fee basis (that which we paid out to eliminate backlogs or because the VA didn't provide a particular clinical service), and mental health.

Shortly after I came into the network, it began to appear that, because of trouble and bad press at Bay Pines, where the network office is located, the new network director and staff would have no time to strategize and start initiatives because their every moment was consumed with trying to manage the situations coming out of Bay Pines VA Medical Center. Among these situations were numerous patient incidents, medical staff management issues, poor customer service, and the numerous vicissitudes of the financial management system being implemented there with largely off-the-shelf software called Core FLS.

Because of these incidents and the financial management system not being implemented, Dr. Headley had to resign, Congress established an office of the VA's inspector general at Bay Pines, and congressional hearings were held in Bay Pines along with numerous investigations. The investigative reporter of the *St. Petersburg Times* kept the pot boiling with numerous articles critical of top management at Bay Pines, as well as leadership in general.

Of course, the financial management system, Core FLS, contributed to the problems. It simply didn't work. The top management didn't know where or what their expenditures were. Vendors weren't getting paid. Eventually, surgery had to be shut down. The chief of staff resigned. The director's job was finally filled by a seasoned VA administrator, but, after a year or so, he simply retired to avoid further abuse. As I mentioned, Dr. Rosewater had to resign, apparently because his on-the-record testimony conflicted with other highly placed VACO opinions. The confusion was whether he did or did not volunteer Bay Pines for Core FLS.

Because of these events, not much progress was made during my first two years in the network. But we did lay the ground work by implementing continuous quality improvement and better data management. Because of this, NF/SG greatly improved its actual performance in each assigned measure and set about improving mental health, primary care, oncology, surgery, and information analysis. It seemed that the network was pleased, but it wasn't directly involved. The network began to harangue us all over deficiencies in the network's performance, not focusing on the facilities with the worst performance. They didn't systematically implement best practices. This was probably because of major physical plant deficiencies that consumed so much of the network staff's time. And those facilities with the worst physical plant issues were also those with the worst performance on assigned measures.

But, because of Dr. Headley's allegedly forced retirement, improvement efforts were further delayed while a new network director was chosen. New directors at Miami, Tampa, and Bay Pines were in place, as well as the new director in Orlando, which the secretary had approved to be a stand-alone facility and to get a new hospital.

The new network director arrived, followed shortly over the next three weeks by four hurricanes that caused significant damage in Florida, especially at the West Palm Beach VA Medical Center. The hurricanes obviously required our complete focus, especially the new network director, Buzz Gray.

The West Palm Beach VA Medical Center lost power and water for several days. Most of its patients were transferred to other VA medical centers, and its employees were hard hit as well. This event caused VA Central Office to reprioritize funds into repair construction projects to get West Palm Beach operating as soon as possible. VA employees were selected from all over the nation to assist in getting the medical center back into operation.

Many lessons were learned from this event and the impact of Katrina to New Orleans and Biloxi. The VA facilities will be much more able to withstand hurricane force winds for longer periods of time. All VA facilities will be provided complete backup power throughout the facility. This is critically important for better service to patients and employees, but also as a potential refuge for the community. For the Sunshine Network overall, it meant that time and efforts to strategize and tackle the preexisting problems continued to lag.

The Sunshine Network worked hard. Its leader stayed in a conservative, bureaucratic mode. Not having worked with him directly before, I can't say for sure if that style is the only style he has, but that's my guess. The two facilities in the network that wanted to do the Baldrige system of management were given the OK to do so, but the network director made it clear that the performance measures were more important.

By this act alone, he signaled to all of us that once again we were a network in name only. We tried to share ideas and talent, but some leaders in the network worked against us for doing so. Therefore, doing the right thing became more and more time-consuming and potentially argumentative with whatever official in the network happened to be responsible.

The budget was done for the fiscal year 2005 in the traditional manner. Since NF/SG was growing so fast, we were, or should have been, the biggest gainer, since several of our sister hospitals had become losers under the Veterans Equitable Resource Allocation (VERA) model. The financial managers met and argued about it. The network's executive resources board met and argued about it.

My financial manager told me that NF/SG was $50 million short. He showed me the analysis. I accepted it. I told our network director, Buzz Gray, that we were $50 million short. By short, I mean we couldn't maintain employment or do any more than we were doing in workload. This would mean having to curtail employment and not open any new clinics or supplement staff to meet the increasing demand for specialty services. Mr. Gray said that we would have to manage within our available funds. I told him what the consequences would be. We started the fiscal year $50 million short.

The NF/SG health system was already managed in a fiscally conservative manner. All of the services individually and collectively were among the most productive and cost effective in the nation. Our number of physicians and nurses were also among the lowest per patient. We were simply on the razor's edge continuously. Any unanticipated event, such as physicians resigning, caused an increase in someone else's workload beyond the standardized 1,200 patients per primary care physician, for example. We were exceeding other standards as well, and except for access and the ability to meet patient demand, we led the network in nearly every category. These facts and more were sent to Mr. Gray, but to no avail.

At the end of the first quarter in FY 2005, our projected deficit was confirmed, and we requested a budget survey. Few, if any, budget surveys in the past had confirmed that there was a deficit. The reports done by skilled financial managers and executives always found more than enough areas where "savings" could be reapplied to areas needing additional funds.

When the team visited NF/SG, they were amazed and appalled at the financial circumstances. They were in awe of the volume of really sick patients arriving in our emergency room. Two or three months went by after their report was written and accepted before we got the word that we would receive additional funding. We received it early in the fourth quarter of FY 2005. This was a clear indication that our network leadership would not be easily swayed by the facts. Neither would they reward those who were really achieving low costs, high quality, and high performance.

Of course, no one in VA Central Office delivered anything except promises that the future would be brighter and that we should continue to do the right thing. The unwritten rule was to make no political waves and certainly not to give an honest assessment to the media.

The only direct impact that the financial near miss of NF/SG had was on the network's scorecard. For the following fiscal year, the values on the balanced scorecard were changed. Access was given much more weight. This put NF/SG near the bottom of the network because it was not able to meet demand because of four satellite outpatient clinics that had been promised but never opened because of fiscal constraints.

The severe space shortage affecting all clinical services in the Gainesville medical center also continued to be ignored. The Jacksonville and Daytona Beach outpatient clinics were severely undersized, and Jacksonville existed as best it could in a dated and poorly designed building. The Gainesville VA Medical Center was several hundred thousand square feet of space short.

The network's approach was to ignore all the positives and accentuate the negatives by forcing more pressure to accomplish even greater miracles. The staff was certainly capable of greater miracles and delivered them, but without more space, the options were limited, for example, to try to open fully staffed second-shift operations in diagnostic and procedure services. Based on our analysis, these already difficult to recruit professionals could not be hired for steady second-shift work. Many of these services were already working until 6:30 pm and on Saturdays. The coverage for the rest of the time was provided only to inpatients. At the network level, their thinking was not focused on this system as a whole.

The network leadership seemed either incapable of convincing VA Central Office of the real need for more construction funds or were told directly and forcibly not to do so. The network seemed uninterested in accelerating any of the approved construction projects. The network leadership was apparently incapable of reallocating funds within the network to those facilities, in part because they had to self fund the increasing management staff at the new—but hospital free until 2011—Orlando VA Medical Center.

At the end of FY 2006, NF/SG was awarded the best in the network award for its high percentage responsiveness to the network's action item assignments. These assignments were often generated by VA Central Office, patient or family, congressional offices, or specific offices such as the VA's Office of Inspector General. We were quite pleased.

This responsiveness is part of my overall management thinking, specifically, managing the horizon. By horizon, I mean meeting the requirements of those external customers who need our information, data, and intelligence put together in a response more quickly than should be expected. By doing the external customer tasks well, external customers will think more highly of us. A more favorable attitude then exists that usually serves to create more opportunities for the staff and the organization.

The need to change processes in health care is constant. The need for better ideas is constant. A role for the VA's network is to identify those best practices and get them into place at other sites, unless those sites can prove by the data that they are even better. This internal competition among health-care organizations does not seem to drive positive change. Instead, the focus is on the financials and the installation of new buildings or scarce medical equipment. The desire is to be the biggest and best in the community, according to those metrics that health-care executives think the community will best understand and be impressed by. How long the waits are for individual clinics or the customer satisfaction with a visit, including all its possible elements: radiology, laboratory, administration, and so forth, is not a visible concern. I once called the chairman of a department at a major university hospital directly after I couldn't get his receptionist to take a message, only to find that his telephone message box was filled and would accept no more. The need for reengineering improvement is vast, and the VA and its Sunshine Network can do better as well.

The most prepared knowledge workers should be in the VA's networks and Central Office, but they are not. Individual physicians and others have amazed me at times with their incredible understanding of their specialty and its clinical and administrative metrics. These high performers are not paid to analyze workload within the network at a high level.

Tumor registry is an example of data-driven accounting and reporting. This database provides information on individual cancers and the related operative surgery and is an educational and clinical source of information for strategic planning. Not all tumors have been recorded because it has gotten lost in higher order priorities. Neither has it gotten automated within the VA.

The VA had a champion, Dr. Kizer, who managed all facets of the value equation. He made faster, cheaper, and better not only a viable real management strategy, but operating reality. He managed the political interface that required politicians to practice their skill set, managing the politics to get the right work accomplished.

The political realities appear to make us less willing to deal with the truth. CARES is but one example of how we could get more value out of the equation, but there is no will or no one with the ability to deal with the political pain. One congressman in the Tampa Bay area coerced VA Central Office to force the Bay Pines VA Medical Center to open the Fisher House for his family's use. This is contrary to the wishes of the Fisher Foundation, which provides the homes. I wonder how much funding this individual has bothered to get for the VA or for veterans?

In part because of such congressional members and other pressures, the Sunshine Network stays in a reactionary mode. They pass the criticism down, but responding to the criticism and concerns is too much of a distraction from more important work. Somewhere along the way, VA Central Office and the network quit listening. Is this because no one listens to the Central Office leaders?

Drucker says listen to your customers. In the book *The Definitive Drucker*, Elizabeth Haas Edersheim writes about connecting with your customer. This is a fundamental tenet of Drucker's management philosophy. She writes that customer results are determined by four questions:

1. How are you measuring your outside results?

2. How are outsiders measuring and sharing results about your products and services?

3. Are you fully leveraging the information that your results provide?

4. Are you honest and socially responsible in presenting your results?

VHA is striving to do better. Much of health care is not. As to Question 2, the outsiders as defined by the Veterans Service Organizations and certain health-care organizations are recognizing and participating with the VA in developing better solutions. Question 3 poses an unknown. For the VHA, the answer is partially, but the VA and all of health care need to do much better. For Question 4, the answer for the VHA is that it has the best report card available, but much more needs to be done in health care. In a sense, the customers are also those providers and administrations who do the work and the patients who receive it. The Sunshine Network and VHA in general need to get better with the art of managing improvements and innovation within the framework of the real velocity of change.

Dr. Edershein reports that Drucker said, "There are no longer competitors, just better solutions and more choices that can be put together in more ways." In other words, she says, "Companies focused on competition are focused on the past, not a future full of technological and demographic opportunities." This same principle is true in health care. In the Sunshine Network and in most of Florida, the demographic imperatives require the shift of resources to meet the demands of customers, our patients, and our mission. Managing through Baldrige and the process of constant improvement and reinvention, we can develop the technologies and systems that better serve our citizens.

Referring to the leadership guide we developed in Network 2, here the steps for meetings challenges and mastering change:

1. Recommit quickly to changes and challenges.

2. Maintain the burning platform. In other words, be passionate

individually and as a team to raise the level of performance and responsiveness to change to the next highest level.

3. Accelerate responsiveness to maintaining innovation and mastery to stay up with the velocity of change.

4. Build commitment consistently among the team.

5. Be passionate in your individual commitment.

6. Lead by example.

7. Accept that ambiguity and uncertainty will be part of the solutions. There are no perfect, or for that matter, lasting, solutions.

8. Hold onto the gains.

9. Alter your expectations quickly to fit the new reality.

10. Be painfully honest with yourself, your team, and supervising leaders.

11. Ignore distraction and extracurricular commentary. It's almost always negative, nonconstructive, and detrimental to the cause.

Chapter 14.8: Bats in the Lobby

I mentioned hurricanes and their resulting problems in an earlier chapter, but there's more to tell. Plan carefully and in detail, but expect the unexpected. Hurricanes are not unique, and damage can also be the result of tornadoes, earthquakes, tsunamis, blizzards, and ice storms. Emergencies could also be the result of a terrorist act or bird flu or other epidemic.

One example of expecting the unexpected was the mini-invasion of bats that slightly preceded the arrival of the first hurricane to pass over Gainesville in many, many years. It was mid-August 2004 when Hurricane Charlie arrived to pummel the city. The bats were residents of the bat house at the University of Florida. The bat home is about a mile or so from the VA medical center in Gainesville. A group of bats, about twenty or so, came into the medical center through the primary outpatient door. We suspect that the hurricane caused changes in barometric pressure and perhaps other phenomena that caused the bats to seek shelter at the VA. Patients were calmly enjoying the bat show, but some of the clinicians were worried because bats do carry rabies and might cause an environmental issue within the hospital. Our environmental management service was on it in a flash. Several housekeeping aides and two supervisors tried valiantly to capture the bats. They learned quickly that enthusiasm alone will not help one to catch a bat. Enthusiasm alone, however, will make the bat gathers look like fools. A tennis racquet is the perfect instrument. Anything with more solidity will be instantly perceived by the bats, and they can turn on a dime. Nets were secured, and the bat invasion quickly came to an end.

Communications are critical. Some cell phones were not working because of the damage in New Orleans. We were able to get cable hookups into the outpatient clinics that were impacted and thus able to resume almost normal clinical service. Constantly telling employees about all the services at the medical center, including showers, food, and milk that can be purchased in the VA canteen and arranging transportation for stranded employees is equally critical. Most important is the need to maintain power and water. Employees need to know where to find bottled water, day care, and other services that may be closed temporarily because of the emergency.

At the command center, it's important for those running the center to have up-to-date information about the gas stations that are open, roads that are closed, motels with room availability, and so forth. Keeping the Web site up-to-date and having an 800-number for employees is also critical. Some hospitals contract with gas stations with emergency generators to provide gas to their employees. Hospitals without their own laundry services need to make certain that they will receive uninterrupted services.

As I was inspecting the area that had the bat fly-in, I ran into a patient who had just climbed out of a taxi. It was Friday afternoon, we were sending patients home, securing staff, and going over the preparations made for the storm that we expected to arrive in full force in about nine hours. This veteran was clearly unhappy. We had sent him to a community hospital to obtain cardiac surgery. At the time, we had a significant backlog in cardiac surgeries, so some had to be contracted out. All the arrangements had been made. He had gone over in the morning, waited nearly all day, only to be told that the surgery had been canceled. No further information was given him. This man's despair was painful to see. We got him rescheduled on Monday and put him up for the weekend. This patient taught me that the healthcare leader must be responsive to the consequences caused by other organizations not doing the right thing.

At the VA medical center, we canceled outpatient visits that afternoon, but the rest of the schedule was business as usual. Knowing what the patients are hearing on their media outlets is critical to good decision making if there is a need to consider canceling outpatient visits or even moving those patients who can go home out of the hospital. One town in the northcentral Florida area made an announcement that only emergency vehicles were permitted on the streets. This was probably an overreaction on their part. We had told all our clinical workers that they qualified to be an exception and to come on into work. The patients who heard this message stayed home. This led to a lot of no-show visits. We were much assisted by the Florida State Division of Veteran Affairs, whose daily meetings in the state command center greatly facilitated our own efforts and certainly reduced the overall level of anxiety.

Getting an assessment of the personal costs and issues to employees is also necessary. The VA, through its canteen and employee associations, donated funds to assist employees to recover. Recognizing their sacrifices is also a good idea. The ability of the organization to respond to crisis should never be taken for granted. During one of the near storm misses, the University of Florida canceled the outdoor activities for its summer campers. After about two hours of having hundreds of adolescents in the dorm without structured activities, they changed their mind. Unforeseen consequences result from day care cancellations, spouses who have to work elsewhere, such as in law enforcement, and so forth all contribute to the unique circumstances of a true emergency.

After Hurricane Charlie, we were visited by Hurricane Francis in early September. We were ready. After Charlie, most of the things that were going to be blown down or off were already down.

Chapter 14.9: Affiliations/Partnerships

The Veterans Health Administration began its affiliations with medical schools in 1947. Since then, the affiliations have expanded to include virtually all medicals schools and schools of osteopathy. In addition, schools of nursing and allied health professions also affiliate with local VA medical centers and health systems. Without a doubt, this is excellent public policy and probably ranks only behind the GI Bill as one of the greatest government societal benefits ever enacted.

Over time, however, the local affiliations have become routine and expected. The medical schools, some of which years ago owed their very existence to the VA affiliation, have changed. All too often because of administration pressures or the desire or mandate to compete for the best and the brightest and/or the bottom line, the VA affiliation has been taken for granted and in some cases questioned and manipulated for the medical school's benefit. The parent universities are even further removed from the accurate understanding of the VA's contribution. The university presidents and other top-ranking officials often don't bother to educate themselves either. Because of the value that the VA offers, some observers have suggested that the VA put its educational and research affiliations out for bid periodically. In today's global economy and worldwide Web, university affiliates do not have to be located across the street from the VA.

In the case of the University of Florida, the affiliation with the medical school has been one of mutual, long-standing appreciation. Society gets huge benefits from the clinical care provided, the increased potential for research and collaboration, the benefits to the local and regional economies, and the educational benefits rendered.

Where the problems lie are in the structure of the universities, which for the most part have research oversight and control close to the university presidents. In the quest for higher rankings in the media, the

VA's research is often managed and controlled in a way that stifles the development of the local VHA facility's own programs and accountability. So, despite bringing the funding and the residency slots for hundreds of residents and providing the funding for hundreds of physicians, the career noose is tightened around the physicians, who clearly see the disadvantages in having the VA administer and gain credit for their research work, even though the VA is cheaper and better managed on almost all accounts.

Edersheim, in her book *The Definitive Drucker*, discusses collaboration and orchestration. The scorecard for major universities is research dollars funded and grants. By opening themselves to collaboration with others, such as the VA, the VA's university affiliates would stand to benefit and be able to explore one of the world's best and largest health data repositories and its unique and successful automated patient records. Without orchestration from the VA and others throughout the organization, the VA loses credit for its vast contributions to the increase in health-care knowledge.

Probably because VA top leadership is a political animal, it's goals lie somewhere else: get their party reelected and avoid major embarrassment. For the nation to gain a huge benefit in its investment in universities and the VA, the highly desirable requirement to play together better in the sandbox probably lies in legislation. Certainly, an executive order giving the VA some clout in this relationship and negotiation would help.

There has been no fundamental reshaping of the nation's health-care research and development in decades. Disease-specific research thrusts and funding seem to rule the day, as they have for decades. Redirecting funding into systems approaches to categories of disease or basic research targets would facilitate improvements in both areas. Orchestrating that funding to seek better designs in patient databases and, as importantly, the design of quality and performance management systems could vastly expand the reach of systematic health-care delivery.

Conceivably, discoveries could be made on a daily basis with the power and size of these dynamic academic giants working together.

More importantly, while we are shooting for the stars in genetic research, we would not be missing as many heart attacks in the ER.

Chapter 14.10: Bad Grief!

For a long time in my career, I saw examples of patients, families, and employees who couldn't let go of an issue. After considerable experience in trying to manage and assist these individuals, the idea dawned on me that the real impetus to their striving to get something corrected or an apology was grief. Their grief generated by a bad outcome drove their behavior to such an extent that their actions quickly left the realm of someone pointing out an error, clinically or administratively, in order to improve the VA's performance or operations. From my own careful observations, I have concluded that this fixation, while it certainly consumes a lot of the VA's time and effort, makes for a sad and angry existence.

Shortly after arriving back in NF/SG, I encountered four classic examples of grief driving an individual's behavior to such an extreme that I feel compelled to include them in the book, so that others may comment or research this phenomenon.

The first example involves a family member of a deceased former patient. At my second Memorial Day celebration in Gainesville, I was approached by a woman in her sixties, normal build, average height, nice smile, and dressed appropriately. I thanked her for coming to the VA medical center for this ceremony. The nice lady then told me that she was sorry for me. She said that I apparently believed that the VA was an excellent caregiver. I told her that I did believe that. She went into a long ramble about a neurologist on our staff and that of the University of Florida who had killed her sister and insulted her. I was by this time taking notes, getting her name, the neurologist's name, and the sister's name. I apologized for the actions that she was complaining about. That wasn't good enough; she wanted the neurologist fired. I told her I would look into the matter and get back to her.

On Monday morning, I asked my secretary to get me the file, using this lady's name. My secretary grimaced, her jaw tightened, and she said that the chief of staff kept the file. About an hour later, she brought the file into my office. The file was thirteen inches thick. I grimaced. My secretary simply said, "She's well-known in the chief of staff's office." I sat about reading the file. For fifteen or twenty minutes a day for two weeks, I delved into the file. I read about three inches of it, at which point the material became totally repetitious. While I was reading the file, a letter from this woman appeared in the *Gainesville Sun*. The letter castigated the VA. It alleged that VA employees only pretended to care at public ceremonies; the reality was that the care was terrible and that we kept employees on the payroll who should be fired. I was tempted to write but never did. Her letters to the editor of the *Gainesville Sun* appeared about every three months, always critical of the VA.

The summary of the reason for the woman's grief was clear from the voluminous file. Her sister was a retired army officer who had been treated by the VA for a considerable number of years. As she aged, the sister was more and more infirm and fragile, until finally she was admitted to the VA nursing home in Lake City. The sister had received a number of specialist consults, mostly geriatricians and neurologists. During one of these neurology consults, the woman heard what she interpreted as a callous comment from a neurologist who was in the vicinity but had never actually consulted on her sister. During the woman's visits, the medical record included documentation to prove that the patient had wanted no heroic measures taken to extend her life. The patient was determined to be competent, and so her wishes were followed. The woman went on vacation for about a week early one summer, and the sister died in due course as a result of her condition. That's when the trouble began.

The chief of staff met with the woman twice and carefully documented the meeting and his own findings upon looking into the case. He took the case to the ethics committee. They concurred that there was no wrongdoing, and, in fact, the patient's own wishes were paramount and they were followed. He eventually brought in an external consultant to review the case. The consultant's determination was the same. After scores of letters to and from the woman, the VA medical center notified her that they would no longer respond to her letters and the reasons why. So she wrote other parts of the VA and the file grew.

One day, the communications director from the state Veterans' Affairs office came to see me. He told me that he had to write a response to the woman. Somewhat gleefully, I asked my secretary to get the file, knowing that it was slightly in excess of thirteen inches in height. This retired Marine Corps colonel nearly lost his composure when he saw the file. I had a meeting, so I left him alone with the file. He was gone when I got back, and I never heard from him again. Whatever the state did, it didn't help; she continued to write letters to the editor and come to the ceremonies, but she no longer attempted to talk to me. I did get dirty looks, however.

Employee grief arises in situations usually where he or she has applied for a job and doesn't get it. The next example involves such an employee. Sometimes, employees do get the job, but their performance is so bad, they lose the job, or they are so unhappy that they leave the job. Most hardly ever blame themselves. They keep the notion that the VA has done them wrong. They grieve and file complaints, but they never prevail. They hold their pain close to them and talk about it with their friends, who must support their notion that they have been wronged. The emotional grief carries them for the rest of their lives; they are depressed, rejected, and seemingly unwilling to let go.

An attractive woman in her early forties once came to my office. She wanted to discuss with me why she never got selected for a promotion. I told her that I had no idea and asked her what she thought. She said that supervisors were biased against her education. I asked her what her education was. She said she had a bachelors and masters degree in health-care administration. I said I had seen some supervisors who were biased against people who had a better education than they did, but, almost always, supervisors are really alert to finding the people with the skills to make them look good. I told her that I would follow up with her and that we would have another meeting where I would give her some suggestions on how to interview and improve her chances at moving up.

I checked into her background and with the chief of the service where she was assigned. Some years before, she had been identified as a high potential person and given enhanced training and project assignments. She was tapped for a higher level position, but whatever her personal circumstances were at the time led her to fail in this position. Not only did she fail, but she antagonized and angered others in that office. The story that had developed around this woman was that she was found sleeping on the job, wouldn't complete assignments, and failed to be a considerate communicator in basic areas, such as phone messages and work coordination. She was able to go back to her old position. Years passed, and she applied for many jobs but never got any of them. I checked some more. Supervisors were afraid that she wasn't what her evaluations and immediate past performance indicated. Where the truth really lay was difficult to establish. Apparently, the smoke from the initial foray for a promotion still lingered.

When I talked to her again, it was apparent that her attitude was infected with remorse from the job situation in which she had failed. But her focus was on her master's degree. She couldn't understand why she was never chosen when those who were had less formal education. I think that she stayed in a perpetual state of low-grade depression. She wasn't as excited about another job as she was about being nonselected when, in her mind, she was clearly the superior person.

I suggested that she get a mentor. I suggested some names. I told her that it would be an opportunity to have someone else go to bat for her, give her another good reference, and that she should work on being more positive about herself, especially given the intense competition for the jobs that she was applying for. I don't think that she wanted to address the original job issues; she found solace in more grief. I suspect that she heard much commentary from her friends about what she should do. She didn't get other jobs and she waited, frustrated and unhappy, for something to be created for her.

The next example concerns a volunteer. The volunteer had retired from his long career as a boiler plant inspector. His volunteer assignment was in the engineering service where, given his technical background, he was quite useful in helping with inspections throughout the facility and developing checklists that reflected the most up-to-date national policies and directives. He had relocated to southwestern Florida to be closer to family. While he was at the VA medical center, he had been respected and had a certain camaraderie with the engineering workers and managers. Once he was gone, he apparently began to grieve the loss of his volunteer assignment and his association with the workers that he considered his friends and peers. That's when the letters started arriving at the director's office.

The former volunteer wrote that the VA medical center's boiler plant was dangerously flawed in design and maintenance. His letters were full of technical jargon and were well written. Our engineering leadership staff took the letters seriously and hired a nationally known non-VA boiler plant expert to come in and review our designs and our operation. The consultant issued us a clean bill of health report for our boiler plant. Engineering drafted a response for my signature and included a copy of the report. A couple of months later, the former volunteer wrote again, pointing out perceived flaws in the consultant's report and reiterating his complaints about our boilers. Engineering again carefully reviewed all the particulars of the complaints and developed a responsive letter back to him.

This went on for about three years. Finally, engineering asked to put him on the no-response list, to which I agreed. The former volunteer continued writing, and, when we didn't respond, he went to VA Central Office. They found nothing correctable in our design or operations. The circle of grief was complete, with a depressing low orbit around a false idea wrapped up in a fixation of beliefs formed when something treasured was taken away from him.

The fourth example arose when a seventy-year-old veteran arrived in my office with a complaint. The complaint was about the Ocala Police Force. He had been driving his Ford Expedition and had been given a speeding ticket. During the writing of the ticket, the police officer felt compelled to arrest him for obstructing justice. He was taken to jail, where he filed numerous complaints, and, when he was released after his thirty-day sentence, he hired a lawyer to sue the Ocala Police Department. Since this gentleman was currently our patient and receiving mental health counseling among other care, I listened very carefully to his complaint. He wanted the VA to clear his record in Ocala and get enough funds to purchase another Ford Expedition. He had to sell the Ford Expedition to pay his attorney's fees. He felt that the lawyer had led him on until he ran out of money.

Interestingly, the man had been a military policeman in the army assigned to Fort Leavenworth. Among his other duties was to accompany prisoners from around the country to Fort Leavenworth to begin their sentence. He had been married and divorced three times but had been fully employed until he retired and moved to Florida in his mid-sixties. He acknowledged that he was overeating and had gained fifty pounds since the incident. He also said that he was no longer seeing his friends and had come to think of his condo on a golf course about forty miles away from Gainesville as a prison cell.

In a soft, encouraging way, I explained that I had no authority to do what he had requested. I also told him that I didn't know of a single VA avenue that would lead him to success in this endeavor. I suggested that he have his psychiatrist write a letter to the city. He replied that his psychiatrist had already done that. I told him that I was at a loss and felt that he should keep all of his appointments with the VA. He told me that the VA had the responsibility to clear his record. I said I was sorry.

The veteran came to see me several more times. I always listened patiently. His story never changed. He did seem positive about the psychiatric care he was receiving, but he wasn't having any luck in losing weight. At our last meeting, he told me that he had nothing to live for. I told him that he certainly did and that he had a lot of support at the VA medical center. After he left, I called his psychiatrist and relayed the veteran's comment. He said he would see him. For many months thereafter, I would occasionally observe him in the waiting rooms or elsewhere, sitting quietly by himself, as overweight as ever and always appearing very, very sad.

I was trained to respond to all correspondence. Certainly, the policy of the VA is to diligently respond to all letters that are received. After many responses to no effect and when there is nothing else that can be said on the subject, the director may sign a memo that no further responses should be sent to a particular individual. Almost always, the individual then goes to the next layer of supervision or VA Central Office or to their congressman or to the entire congressional delegation or to the media. When they run out of federal officials, they write the governor, the state health department, the Joint Commission on the Accreditation of Healthcare Organizations, the Office of the Inspector

General, and so on. These are but four examples of people unwilling to let go of their grief. Often what should be said is please get some professional help, but that certainly oversteps necessary boundaries.

Chapter 14.11: Undying Gratitude

Whenever I could, I would visit in the waiting rooms of both VA medical centers and our nine community-based clinics and satellite clinics. I would talk to veterans in the waiting rooms, ask about the health care that they were receiving from us, do a follow-up on anything that was of concern to them, and give them my business card. I did the same thing at the Veterans Service Organization meetings and conferences, where I was often invited to speak. For the vast majority of these interactions, I was fortunate enough to hear that the care being delivered was great, the staff was caring, and, frequently, I would hear comments like, "If it wasn't for the VA or doctor so and so, I wouldn't be here." Throughout my career, I viewed these visits with veterans as an executive perquisite, a pause to stay in touch and to get motivated and energized on those occasions when I was angry or down about something going on with the VA.

Although we are definitely in an era of high-tech medicine and probably will increasingly be so, the caring and customer service that health-care employees provide is still the basic building block of a true system of care. This was definitely true of the VA's NF/SG health system. I was privileged to be able to interact with these fine men and women who served our nation, as well as those who served those who served our nation. Having been in public service almost all of my adult life, the services rendered really comes down to the direct contact with individuals who need the care of VA medical centers. Many of these people are not the easiest to provide services for and create their own complexities, which fortunately the VA's skilled employees have learned to address. My special heroes are those patients who could get their care anywhere, including the Johns Hopkins, Mayo Clinic, the Cleveland Clinic, and so forth and who chose to come to the VA because it's the best care, it's a true system of care, it's where their buddies get their care, or simply because they believe that it's where they belong.

The VA is more than a health-care provider, and it's more than a payer for care across the entire spectrum of health care. It's more than the best automated medical record and its outstanding affiliations; the VA provides care, comfort, and social welfare services to all of its clients, most especially those who are at the fringe of our society. I am proud to say that we have helped veterans get their cars repaired so that they could go home, provided funds so that they could reimburse their families for the gas it took to get them to the VA, and provided hotel rooms and meals when they couldn't afford it.

In this section, I simply want to discuss some special veterans and others who came across my path. There are so many. I wish that I could share all of their stories with you, but time and space prevent it.

One evening at a veterans meeting, I got to sit beside a Korean War veteran. He was friendly, outgoing, and had a good sense of humor. I enjoyed chatting with him. He told me that he had the best doctor in the VA. I had heard this from many veterans before, so I asked him who it was. He said, "Dr. Allen." Dr. Mary Lynn Allen was the VA's associate chief of staff for ambulatory care. Then he added, "I'm a diabetic and always do what she tells me to do."

I laughed and said, "I wish I could say that."

As we concluded the evening, I asked this veteran leader to let me know whenever I could do something for his members. This was how I came to learn about the following three Korean War veterans.

The first veteran my Korean War friend, Timmy Thomas, told me about was named Paek, pronounced Peck. Paek was a native of what is now North Korea. During the Korean War, he escaped to South Korea and agreed to go back to North Korea as a spy. He served in this capacity until the war's end. When he was discharged, he resettled to Brooklyn. Because he was a farmer, he eventually bought a farm near Starke, Florida. When Paek reached his mid-seventies, his health declined, and he began about a two-year interaction with the VA medical center in Gainesville, which concluded with his death in the medical intensive care unit. He had many interactions with the VA's health-care system. His friend, Timmy Thomas, kept me informed about his membership, especially those who had been admitted to the hospital. If I had time, I would visit these patients. I always came away feeling better and hoped they would get better as well.

I wish there was way that I could have issued a press release with Paek's history of service to his adopted country. I would also have liked to rent a billboard along the interstate saying something like, "For a real tourist attraction, take the next exit and visit a real American hero. Today's featured attraction is Paek." These folks often do not want publicity, but I fear that, without some way to highlight their achievements, we lessen the fabric of our culture because there is a massive amount of advertising that brings our attention to new products or celebrities.

The next Korean War veteran was Doug Smith. He also died in the VA medical center's intensive care unit. Doug was a former prisoner of war. He had been captured by the Red Chinese Army and kept a prisoner in China for three years. He had received all of his health care from the VA. He was a distinguished gentleman who was extremely active in church, veteran, and civic affairs. Doug's visitors were many, including the chief operating officer of a local community hospital. He touched many lives and personified quiet heroism. I am honored to have been associated with him in a small way.

The third Korean War veteran is also a patient of the VA and as far as I know still receiving care from the VA medical center. Like many of the heroes in this book, I have lost track of him, and, because I can't contact him, I cannot reveal his name. He was not officially a former prisoner of war but had been recognized at one of the ex-POW ceremonies held annually in their honor. His story embodied the concepts of "the fog of war" and "all I want is to get out of here alive" found so often in veterans' stories of their military experiences. He had been a forward artillery and air bombing observer. In the course of performing this task, he was frequently in front of his unit, radioing back coordinates for artillery and air bombardment. A North Korean shell landed near him, blowing him up and over a large snow bank and knocking him unconscious.

He woke up in a peasant's hut alongside another soldier from a different unit. He thought he was there three or four days, being fed and given water infrequently, slipping in and out of consciousness. He was awoken one day by a U.S. soldier who was yelling back to someone in his unit that there were two more of them in his hut. He was evacuated, first to a MASH unit and then eventually to a U.S. hospital in Japan. His wounds healed, and he was sent back to his unit and the war. He resumed his duties. He was again blown up and rendered unconscious. He was again taken prisoner, and his unit recovered and evacuated him along with some other severely wounded soldiers. His war story essentially ended here.

This time his injuries were so severe that he was evacuated to the United States. He recovered, was restored to active duty, and completed a career as an army officer. He never bothered trying to get his POW status. He was simply delighted to be out of harm's way. No one else documented his story. No witnesses could be found to corroborate his story. No one, including him, could establish the exact dates and duration of his imprisonment. He would like his status as an ex-POW established for the benefit of his family. Old age and frailty are likely to defeat his quest.

Many others are memorable as well. One day, a woman and her significant other came to see me about their concerns for her care. They gave me their business card. It seems their business was playing golf and cards in The Villages, a community designed for retirees. The Villages was also designed for golf cart travel, so there were golf carts all over the place. They seemed to be a happy couple who took problems in stride. In our brief chat, I discovered that neither one of them were veterans. I immediately thought that this was going to be an interesting story.

She had raised two kids after her husband died in combat in Vietnam. She had never remarried, and her significant other and she had retired to The Villages about six years previously from north of Chicago. As a combat casualty's widow, she was entitled to care from the VA. She had cancer and simply wanted her follow-up appointment with the oncologist moved up. She was scared. I had our patient advocate's office arrange that. Over the next few months, they stopped in to see me several times. Her care seemed to be progressing, and they seemed very happy with the VA medical center. They were thinking about starting a catering business in The Villages. They are among the many clients of the VA that I think about and wonder if there is a way that we could all stay in touch.

Several months later, another couple came to see me. He had been referred for radiation therapy at the VA medical center in Tampa. Something had gone wrong, they lost track of him, they complained to somebody at the VA medical center in Gainesville, and he had been authorized to have local radiation therapy closer to their home. He was from Maine originally and worked in construction all of his life. In fact, he had built log homes in New York for many years. He was involved in building a small subdivision of homes in southern Marion County, not far from The Villages.

They had decided that since the radiation was making him very sick and unable to finish work developing the roads, lots, and other requirements of their little development, he was going to stop taking radiation. They understood that the outcome either way was fatal. I asked why they wanted to see me. They said that they just felt that they should tell someone in the VA that they appreciated everything that was offered to them, despite the original screw-up in Tampa. I told them that they seemed very comfortable with the decision. They said they were. We shook hands, and I walked them out of the office. I sent e-mails to the oncologist, the authorizing physicians, and the patient advocate's office.

Another veteran that I was privileged to meet was a man by the name of Arthur Corbett. I met Arthur at a state-wide meeting of blinded veterans. I knew him from ceremonies of the ex-POWs. Arthur was taken prisoner by the Germans during the Battle of the Bulge. He served out the rest of WWII as a prisoner of war. Although he was able to walk and had no visible injuries, Arthur was 100 percent service connected due to his combat experience. And he definitely wasn't blind. I was curious as to why he was attending the blinded veterans meeting. This quiet and friendly man introduced me to his wife. She was the blinded veteran. For some of us, the challenges of life are seen as unfair, but, of course, that isn't necessarily so. For that reason and many others, Arthur Corbett is truly a hero, just like many of his fellow veterans who have served so long and so well.

Shortly after I arrived at NF/SG, I was smart enough to hire Karen.

She was a retired army first sergeant who had accomplished much in the army and in the private sector. She was placed in the patient advocate's office. She was a dynamo and was an obvious choice when the time came to hire someone as coordinator of the returning Iraqi and Afghanistan veterans. She would visit with me periodically to request small official purchases and to update me on her outreach efforts. She worked countless hours of her own time. She frequently introduced me to the young men and women who were in her office. Sometimes I think that they realized that this retired army first sergeant would never let go of them until they had signed up. For her as for so many of our VA employees, it was a labor of love.

Of course, I encountered patients who seemed to be seeking drugs that they didn't need, wheelchairs or electric carts that they didn't need, and patients who didn't know what or why they were talking to me and many others angry about missing appointments, discourteous employees, and all the other snags that complicate the delivery of care. More often, they came to see me because they wanted to praise an employee. Sometimes, they'd leave a note or send a letter. In a few cases, they would send flowers to the ward or leave a big box of chocolates at the nurses' station or the clinic.

On some of my rounds, I have seen patients kiss the back of the doctor's hand and leave with tears of gratitude in their eyes from the care they had received, or because of the bad news that they expected and didn't get, or because of the bad news delivered in a quiet, humane, and sensitive way that helped to reassure them about their future. One day, in the oncology clinic, I asked an elderly African American if he liked his doctor. "No," he said, "I love him." I have been blessed and privileged to have been witness to all these occasions and interactions with these truly amazing folks.

14.12: My Brother, the Finale

I was visiting the VA's Jacksonville outpatient clinic when I received a call from my brother's fiduciary telling me that my brother had died. He had had a massive heart attack in his sleep. He was very overweight, smoked constantly, and had had congestive heart failure for the past fifteen years or so. Sometimes I was his best friend, and sometimes I was an outcast for reasons that were never apparent. I think that the VA not only kept him alive, but kept him from destroying the life of anyone else. At least, I don't know of any. He was sixty-one.

My brother had asked me the last time I saw him about the requirements of a fiduciary. I had sent that to him in a letter after researching the matter and consulting with the benefits experts. My brother thought having a fiduciary was too confining for his needs, but I think having one added years to his life. I told him that my brother had two daughters and that I thought the oldest one would be the one to contact. I got the fiduciary's name and number. I called my mother so that she could call the fiduciary to give him the number. My niece told the fiduciary that my brother didn't want either his mother or me notified of his death. She had him cremated and supposedly picked up his ashes and personal effects and took them back with her to Canada.

This changing of attitude toward Mother and I had happened many times over the years. This was the way he had been virtually all of his adult life. Sometimes I was his best friend, and sometimes I was an outcast. Once he asked for and I sent him $300. About six months later, he sent the check back without a word.

I flew to Texas to be with my mother. The loss had been expected for years due to his declining health. We drove out to Teague and visited the cemetery where our closest relatives, the Mulkeys and the Merriotts, were buried. Her mother, sisters, father, and many others were there. This was where she wanted to be buried when that time came. We decided to get a memorial stone for my brother. He loved that part of Texas, so I also believe that his spirit if anywhere will be hovering around that rural cemetery by the railroad tracks. While his ashes were elsewhere, Mother would always have that stone to sit by and bring flowers.

On the way back to Waco, I was telling mother about an old friend who lived in Belton, Texas, named Monk. Whenever I saw Monk, he would regale me with hilarious stories. I saw out of the corner of my eye her jaw drop. "Why did they call him Monk?" she asked.

"Because he jumped around like a monkey in high school, and

the kids called him monkey. Over time that got shortened to Monk," I replied.

Very slowly she said, "That's what they called me."

I turned toward her. "What did they call you?"

She said, "They called me monkey in high school."

I laughed, thinking that I probably knew two of the very few people in the country with Monkey as a nickname who would admit it as adults—and one of them was my mother!

14.13: OEF/OIF

OEF/OIF are the acronyms assigned to the wars in Afghanistan and Iraq. The first stands for Operation Enduring Freedom. The second is Operation Iraqi Freedom. The health care and treatment of these heroes is provided by the VA for two years upon their return home, regardless of their continuing in service or discharge.

The situation at Walter Reed emerged early in 2007, and somehow the Veterans Health Administration was drug into the ensuing studies, investigations, and so forth. Unequivocally, I support the NF/SG VA Health System's efforts in providing care to these valiant citizens. Of course, I recognize that improvements need to be made on a continuing basis. After all, that's the central part of my management philosophy.

The story that I have to relay about these returning veterans is at best partial. The real story of their care and the VA's caring for them is still being written. Like the lessons we should have learned about serving Vietnam veterans, Iraqi and Afghanistan veterans really should be followed for the rest of their lives. The first contact should be within two or three weeks after the soldier returns home or resettles elsewhere.

The VA has probably never adequately addressed the suicide issue to the satisfaction of many veterans. I understand the great difficulty of responding clinically to someone who is determined to take his or her life. But, on the other hand, the VA's marvelous clinical database could be used for ongoing studies and a suicide registry set up that would facilitate correlations and enhance learning about these dreadful events. This registry should include all veterans, not just those who use the VA to receive care. The VA does psychological autopsies on every patient suicide. I do believe that the VA's efforts in recognizing and treating those with suicide on their mind have not received enough credit, but more needs to be done.

We all have learned of returning OEF/OIF veterans who have chosen to kill themselves. Obviously, this is a huge concern for veterans and their caregivers, both families and VA staff. With the relatively small number of returnees so far, I have heard suicide stories that would break anyone's heart. Having a suicide occur inside the VA medical center, or any medical center, is grounds for a full investigation. It is completely devastating to everyone involved.

The VA should not leave the determination of adequate care, patient safety, or clinical improvement to the mental health folks. I do not believe that the VA is covering anything up, but we need to learn more and try new approaches, using patient safety experts on every investigation. There are other victims beside the person who has committed suicide: their family, friends, colleagues, and caregivers.

Suicide, however, springs from many apparent causes and issues. Having an elderly veteran get a pass from a VA nursing home, only to go to the backyard of the house where he and his wife lived for many years to shoot himself is equally devastating. Today, there is a gap between those returning veterans who use the VA and those who do not. The non–VA users are no longer in the service, but the VA knows nothing about them. We need a faster, better clinical intervention. In the last few years, my staff has found veterans in our parking lot that had given every last measure of their strength to get that far but couldn't negotiate the final steps. The VA can be an intimidating challenge to some, and to some not even a thought.

Continues design improvement is essential. From my own careful reading of the newspaper accounts of the war, I would apply the same criticism to the tactics that our soldiers were given to use. In Colby Buzzell's excellent book *My War: Killing Time in Iraq*, published by the Berkley Publishing Group, he tells us that the army has the technology to trace the arc of incoming mortar fire back to the enemy. But this technology isn't used because of fears that innocent citizens would be killed by our return fire. I find this frustrating and probably veterans do as well. If someone in their unit dies due to mortar fire, these veterans may well develop that frustration into post-traumatic stress disorder.

In his book and most of the others as well, Buzzell writes of his overuse of alcohol and drugs. These drugs include those given to the soldiers by the army, as well as the illegal drugs used before, during, and after their service.

Lately, there has been much discussion in the media about torture. I am disappointed that the Department of Defense, CIA, and the Department of Justice have apparently allowed this to happen. A few dollars in research could have led us to an easily administered drug that would get the truth out of the most hardened terrorist.

I think that there is adequate evidence that the military's approach to the next war needs to be reexamined. Given the huge costs of the war, the nation really needs a faster, cheaper, better approach to innovation and change in the face of the war we are actually fighting. Having spent billions on *Stars Wars,* I think that we should spend billions on research that leads directly to improved technologies on the battlefields as the combat unfolds. And remember the now overused truism, "The definition of insanity is doing the same thing over and over and expecting a different result." The VA is on the receiving end of the DOD's casualties. Mistakes should be the data fuel to quickly and adroitly adjust tactics, techniques, and technology.

The difficulty is for the veterans to see the drug or alcohol use as a problem and seek treatment. Compounding this is the individual's ability to function in all aspects of life. Difficulties in this arena may not show up until years later.

I once sat next to a two-star Air Force general at a banquet. He seemed to be under obvious emotional stress of some kind, so I asked him how he was doing personally. He smiled grimly. He opened up like fire hydrant. "I got into a fight with my girlfriend last night before I left. I know it's me. I get frustrated by something and look for someone to take it out on, unconsciously, usually her. I'm afraid she'll leave me. I have a feeling that she's already gone. I flew a spotter plane in Vietnam, and I am constantly reliving one situation. I flew to where an F-16 had gone down. I was in radio contact with the pilot. He was hurt but moving and evading. I called for a rescue. Command wouldn't authorize it because of the danger on the ground. I yelled and argued. Finally, I got an order to come back. I cry every night in my sleep. That guy was never recovered."

I begged the general to seek treatment at the nearest VA. I told him that I was positive that he was suffering from PTSD. He agreed, saying, "All my ex-wives would agree with you." He seemed somewhat relieved by our talk. Did he ever follow up on my advice? I'll never know.

My recommendation is for the VA to keep doing all that it is doing, but more of it. The VA or the army should have a health-care professional call two or three times in addition to the patient's clinic visits to get a better understanding or that veteran's situation. I also recommend a home visit. Maintain a dialogue with the returned veteran for two or three years, regardless of what the initial diagnosis and clinical opinions are.

I went into veterans' homes once in a while. Are they sitting in a trailer out in the woods drinking cases of beer and chain smoking? When you walk into the trailer are you overcome by the smell of pot? Is their daddy, the Vietnam vet, sitting there with them, providing them with a convincing role model of how to be antisocial and dysfunctional? We must get more data into a database and use data mining techniques to develop information to feed back to the clinical professionals in both the VA and the army.

Finally, I think that we need to do better with customer service. We in the VA were constantly reminded not to recruit patients. This is as much for budgetary reasons as anything. Now we all know that there is a need for outreach. We have social workers and others actively involved in identifying homeless veterans and getting them services. We need to do the same for all returning veterans from combat theaters. Many of them are living in a room in their parent's house or a trailer in the woods and working. This shouldn't diminish the need to find them and get them services as well. The VA customer services database on inquiries and issues needs to be integrated with the clinical and administrative databases, because we all have much to learn.

Again referring to the leadership guide that was developed in Network 2, here are steps for excellence in customer service:

1. If it is good for our customers (in this case, veterans and more specifically, OEF/OIF returnees), it is good for the individual employee and the team.

2. The perspective that matters most is that of the customer.

3. In the final analysis, meeting our customers' needs is critical for success.

4. Always listen and respond with empathy.

5. Act and speak in a way that our customers and stakeholders can understand.

6. Each individual team member should see himself or herself as a service center. This means be informed, responsive, and helpful to customers in their quest to get the right answers, to get to the right place, and to better understand their options.

7. Service recovery is a learnable art. Mistakes are going to occur; therefore, apologize, assist in getting the situation corrected, provide a cup of coffee or lunch, and even visit the customer in their own home to get a better understanding.

Chapter 15
A Damn Good Reason to Retire

I retired on November 30, 2006. I had been thinking about retiring for a couple of years, off and on. I was still challenged by the work. I was annoyed with what seemed to be an increasing bureaucratization of the Veterans' Health Administration. But work reasons didn't play any factor in my thinking. I had been managing successfully with the changes in the VA. I considered myself to be very proficient in responding to whatever came our way. I set a target that would have been about two and half more years from the date that I actually retired. Despite having multiple reasons to retire or go on, in the end it came down to a very personal decision. The decision was to retire to be able to spend the rest of my life with the wonderful woman with whom I had fallen in love.

At age fifty-nine, with thirty-seven years of service, there are always goals not completed, challenges where I could have contributed to the solution, and others in NF/SG who saw me as central to their success. But the twinges of regret and loss that I feel have been few and far between. Based on advice I received from other retirees, I decided to retire but not to work for a year. I would try my hand at writing.

Part of the retirement process is the recollection of others in the VA and elsewhere who retired and what those circumstances were. Malcom Randall, the first director of the Gainesville VA, served as director there for close to thirty years and had over fifty-five years as a federal employee. The VA created many careerists like Malcom, who had a combination of devotion to duty, devotion to the VA and probably a mind-set that they were somehow indispensable to the mission. I remembered quite a few who retired so late that they really didn't have a retirement, and others who hit the beaches, the slopes, or their recreational vehicle and never looked back.

One of the significant legacies that Mr. Randall left at the Gainesville VA Medical Center was an environment in which retirees would come back to visit or just to say hi. I enjoyed meeting them and chatting if I had the time. Not all work environments are this cordial to those who went before. I have stayed away because not enough time has passed since I was the director, but I will go back and visit, talk to staff, and offer my advice if it's sought on matters.

Others have retired who didn't want to retire, who were at the top of their game, but for whom continuing on wasn't an option. I have often thought of Laghretta Bell, the now retired EEO manager for NF/SG. Laghretta was highly respected, and her advice uniformly excellent. One Sunday morning, she was awakened by her dog licking her face. She immediately realized that something was seriously wrong. She would soon learn that she had had a stroke. She was barely able to get to the phone to call her sister, who called the neighbors to come over and take her to the hospital. She had a difficult recovery. Physicians found a hole in her heart. Even when that problem was fixed, her health worsened, and she had to use a cane to walk. After making her own agonizing decision, she retired.

One day she visited with me and told me that her dog had saved her life yet again. They had been walking in the neighborhood, Laghretta very slowly with her cane, when the dog jumped between her and a small ditch. There was copperhead snake hiding in the grass. The dog harassed the snake into disappearing along the ditch. I told her that she should have a bronze statue made of that dog.

Laghretta would still be doing her thing professionally were it not for the health problems. I, on the other hand, determined to strike out on an entirely different life path. My primary retirement goal is to enjoy a journey through my retirement years that will hopefully give me the time to read, think, write, and enjoy life. So far, retirement has enabled me to write, which I do every day. I walk a lot and enjoy the hiking trails of northcentral Florida.

I feel I served well as a husband, a father, and a government employee. In the government, the transfers do cost more than the allowable reimbursement. Starting over on new mortgages with some frequency isn't the way to build an estate. Of course, going to work for the government in nearly all cases isn't either. My dedication, love, and support for the Veterans Health Administration will never fade. There is plenty of room for improvement, I recognize. But I love the business of providing health care. I have a deep respect for those who labor in the field. I believe that the nation desperately needs to reform its health-care industry.

I believe that the VA operates the best health-care system in the world. All of us must come together to improve performance, to automate and digitize all processes and every aspect of our practice, to achieve the ultimate levels of quality, to minimize the costs, and to significantly improve patient satisfaction. A tall order, but we can do it.

In my case, I had been unhappy at home for a long time. After I retired, my wife and were divorced. I happily remarried. Robin and I have muddled through the inherent difficulties presented by the divorce and the attendant misunderstanding, suffering, and anger. We will continue to make the most out of our lives and do as much as we can for those we love. I have no regrets. As my heroes know, life isn't always fair.

Appendix A: Outside the Box Recommendations to Improve Health-Care Delivery and Financing

1. Tax the net profits, surpluses, or net income for all health-care facilities, systems, and group practices at 10 percent per year. Put this funding into a protected health-care reform trust fund.

2. Reform Medicare by requiring payment to the Veterans Health Administration facilities. Those who serve in this nation's uniformed services pay into it, but, if they use the VA, they are denied the earned right to use these funds.

3. Publish annually the top ten salaries of health-care executives by name and position. Require separate lists for physicians, dentists, and large group practices, such as physical therapists and opticians. These individuals should be considered to be in the public domain in the same way as federal officials.

4. Cancel health savings accounts. Give the people the opportunity to manage their health by buying health-care reform trust fund bonds. In this way, they get interest on their money. With health savings accounts, no interest is paid, and you have to petition the insurance company to get your own money back. The bonds would be tax free until used.

5. Ban for-profit and nonprofit health-care organizations and health-care insurers from making PAC and political contributions. They have too much influence because of their access to the public's funds.

6. All chief executive officers in health care must get their personal health care in the hospital that they lead.

7. All health-care organizations must make annual reports to the state government and the community that include the top ten accomplishments, their top ten problems, and what they are doing about them. Not enough funding cannot be on this last list. All of the state's schools of medicine, health-care admin-

istration, public health, and allied health professions will also get a copy.

8. All health-care organizations must make annual reports that include the top ten process improvements being worked and the top ten improvements that have been made in the past year. JCAHO and other accrediting organizations would have access to these reports as well as the other organizations listed above.

9. Publish the mortality rates of all health-care facilities by service lines, including nursing homes and hospices by community, region, and state, as well as the entire health-care system in the case of organizations like the VA, DOD, and Humana.

10. Publish the top ten by dollar volume contractors, vendors, and payers.

11. Publish the cost of the top ten DRGs and the top ten out-patient procedures contrasted to the prices charged and the negotiated prices of the major contracts.

12. Make illegal the closing/sealing of files in malpractice cases.

13. Provide for mandatory arbitration by community-based facili-tators before a malpractice case can be filed.

14. Everyone into the pool. Assign television and newspaper reporters to spend an evening a month in emergency rooms where they will pick a patient, get releases signed, and go through the complete process with the patient. Repeat until real health-care reform is enacted.

15. Require nonprofits to account for all reserve adjustment trans-actions for the last two months preceding the end of the fiscal year. Require profits to report their charity care via detailed listings. Both would require annual auditing and reports to the board.

16. For health-care organizations that have medical staff on their payroll as opposed to independent practitioners billing sepa-rately from the institution, malpractice suits would have to

be filed against the organization, not the practitioner. Only in cases where it appears that the practitioner was outside the scope of practice (i.e., doing something illegal) could the practitioner be sued. Most medical errors have a significant component of systems errors as a part of the malpractice issue. This would make organizations more vested in improving and policing their own medical staff.

17. Require the GAO to assess the readiness, scope, and cost effectiveness of electronic medical records in all health-care systems and academic health centers.

18. Fund the National Science Foundation to do a study of the costs and benefits of changing the classification and nomenclature of drugs. My feeling is that there has to be a simpler way. Many folks, including most senior citizens, can't remember all of the names of the medications that they are on. Many of the current names are similar and are the source of medication errors. Reengineering the taxonomy of drugs could lead to a better understanding and fewer medication errors.

19. Make all World War II veterans eligible for care in the veterans health system now and presumed service connected for any injuries or illnesses that they claim. In five years, do the same for all Korean War veterans.

Appendix B: Outside the Box Recommendations for Better Government

1. Government in the sunshine. Model it on Florida's law.

2. Set up a nonprofit funded through donations to which Congress and staff would have to apply for grants to travel. Agreed-upon reasons for the travel would be established up front. If a corporation wanted some congressman to see their new idea, store, whatever, they would donate the funds for that purpose to the nonprofit fund, which would track and report expenditures. This would provide an upfront screening process and protect and resource congressional travel. Annual reports would enumerate all aspects of the travel.

3. Have real campaign financing reform. In the interim, tax at a 20 percent rate all campaign expenditures paid by the political party of the individual running for any national office. These funds would go as a direct supplement to the Veterans Health Administration's clinical operations.

4. Ban lobbyists from being on Capitol Hill or other government offices or calling on Tuesdays and Wednesdays so that plain folks have a time to get on the schedule and Congress has more time to get their work done.

5. Lobbyist proposals provided to any congressman, congressional committee, or party of congressional representatives will be posted on a congressional Web site ten days before the presentation so that the public might comment.

6. A constitutional amendment that Congress pass no law that does not apply equally to them.

7. Each enacted law or appropriation bill would have the timeline of every significant action, including OMB and the congressional committee's review, modification, and approval.

8. Line item veto on all legislation.

9. Require universal service. Everyone does something for the

federal government for two years. I would make enrollment in medical school, nursing school, pharmacy school, and a few undergraduate majors, like teaching and social work, count. Working for the VA would count. Service in the Peace Corps would count.

10. Federal white-collar criminals would be assigned to VA health-care facilities for work assignments while on parole or in lieu of actual prison time.

11. Create an absolute ban that elected officials and cabinet officials cannot come from corporations to the federal government. Too much winking and blinking is going on to truly prevent contractual fraud from occurring.

12. Assign a dollar limitation per member for all pork barrel, home district line items. I would suggest $1 million per annum per member.

13. Require the president and each other elected official to post the top ten problems on which they are working. This would enhance focus. This would maintain focus on the larger, more complex, controversial issues like health-care reform and campaign financing reform.

14. Create a national lottery whose purpose would be to provide additional funds for veterans' health care.

15. Merge the Office of Special Counsel into the EEO program. The Office of Special Counsel acts as investigator, judge, and jury for federal managers accused of illegal management activities. The small, pathetic OSC has a fundamental bias toward finding for the whistle-blower. Every employee knows the value of establishing a whistle-blower claim prior to any anticipated adverse action.

16. Require the Equal Employment Opportunity Office to publish annually in newspapers and Web sites the actual statistics of completely adjudicated EEO complaints by summary statistics (i.e., the number of complaints by white folks against others by age discrimination, religion, or other).

17. There is not enough focused research and innovation in defense, transportation, environment, health-care systems, or the war against terror. Miniaturization like that which has occurred in computers and cell phones would have great benefits in these other areas. Create a national awards program for ideas and prototypes.

18. Require vote alignment in Congress. Those voting against increases in taxes do not get earmarks or special items.

19. Ban contractor visits and presentations to political appointees and those officials who will after the contract have a role or direct responsibility for managing that contract.

Appendix C: Outside the Box Indicators That Someone in Government Doesn't Want to Do the Right Thing

The administrator, secretary, or other political appointee:

1. Assigns blame to someone much lower in the organization whose name cannot be revealed because of privacy laws.

2. Seeks a legal opinion.

3. Pretends that he or she is working assiduously toward the goal, but at the same time is keeping benchmarks and controls so tight that progress, if any, is minimal.

4. Asks for a study, preferably by a contractor.

5. Contends that timing, politics, workload, priorities, or the budget isn't right.

6. Finds a victim, preferably one who can retire, and tells/asks them to resign.

7. Pontificates and rationalizes extensively, in the hope that the stalling will become boring or some other issue with some other official will get the attention.

8. Blames Congress.

9. Changes the venue by stating firm support repeatedly for the principle of the thing (for example, accountability in government) while expressing concern for something intangible, like finding the best and the brightest to work in government.

10. Maximizes the face time at the problem site, has hearings, shows concern, fires contractors or federal employees, creates a lot of dust and confusion, but never really solves the problem.

11. During any media coverage, shows real pain and feelings.

12. Cannot be reached for comment due to important business travel requirements.

13. Maximizes photo ops with real American heroes (e.g., veterans).

14. Reveals very energetically that the troublemaker within the organization has been reassigned. Off the record: The troublemaker will find himself or herself in one of two places: the internal gulag where a supervisor will carefully monitor all calls and any work effort. Or the elephant burial ground where no phone, no computer, and no e-mail will mean quality recreational reading time.

Appendix D: A Leadership Constitution and Guide from the Veterans Health Administration

We, as leaders, in order to better serve America's veterans, commit to shared leadership and accountability. We recognize all employees as leaders. Together we embrace VHA being the nation's premier health-care organization.

I. Principles:

Leadership is a responsibility of every person in VHA. Leadership is more than formal roles and titles; every role is important. Those who set direction must serve those whom they ask to follow. Those asked to follow must do so with the enthusiasm they would seek from others were they leading. Leaders in the VHA support each other's success in the common purpose of serving veterans.

Leaders embrace honest and inclusive communication and decision making. Leaders value diversity of both people and ideas. Leaders are curious about the work of the VHA, and their curiosity drives innovation. Leaders foster collaboration and recognize and celebrate achievement.

Shared accountability means that leaders are accountable not only to themselves, but to others with whom they work. Successes and failures are shared because we acknowledge that we work through each other. We agree to be direct in communicating the help we need and the help we can provide. We will constantly assess the effectiveness of contributions to shared responsibility.

Balancing multiple interests and difficult choices in serving veterans requires courage. We place the common good of organizational goals above local or programmatic concerns. We acknowledge that we will face challenges that can divide our leadership community. Leaders understand the need and effort required to balance paradoxes, such as competition v. cooperation; status quo vs. innovation; and decentralization vs. centralization.

Conflict resolution will be addressed through communication by the individuals directly involved in the issue. Only when issues cannot be resolved by the individuals involved will they jointly seek assistance in resolving the issue.

II.   Roles and Responsibilities:

The undersecretary for health defines direction of VHA in service to America's veterans and communicates that vision to the nation. In order to fulfill VHA's mission, the undersecretary for health is committed to shared leadership and accountability. The undersecretary for health is responsible and accountable for the health of veterans.

Senior executives in the field and headquarters are delegated specific responsibilities and authorities but share accountability. Program leaders have a responsibility for guiding policy development in collaboration with field leadership. Field leadership has responsibility for operationalizing policy in collaboration with program leadership.

A council of headquarters and field senior executives deliberates and advises the undersecretary for health on significant national policy. The council exemplifies the principles of this constitution, sharing leadership and accountability.

We recognize all employees as leaders. All employees have specific roles and responsibilities. We share accountability for the successful accomplishment of the VHA's mission. All employees share a common bond as leaders in service to America's veterans.

III.   Ratification

The benefit of this constitution is in the hearts and minds of all VHA and will be openly and continuously ratified.

CPSIA information can be obtained at www.ICGtesting.com

233932LV00002B/49/P

9 780595 525126